The Making of a Bestseller

The Making of
a Bestseller

From Author to Reader

by
ARTHUR T. VANDERBILT II

McFarland & Company, Inc., Publishers
Jefferson, North Carolina, and London

Cover photograph by Marty McGee.

British Library Cataloguing-in-Publication data are available

Library of Congress Cataloguing-in-Publication Data

Vanderbilt, Arthur T., 1950–
    The making of a bestseller : from author to reader / by Arthur T.
Vanderbilt II.
        p.   cm.
    Includes bibliographical references and index.
    ISBN 0-7864-0663-1 (sewn softcover : 50# alkaline paper) ∞
    1. Publishers and publishing — United States.   2. Authorship.
3. Literature publishing — United States.   4. Best sellers — United
States.   5. American literature — Publishing.   I. Title.
Z471.V35   1999
070.5 — dc21   99-12074
                                                                              CIP

Manufactured in the United States of America

McFarland & Company, Inc., Publishers
    Box 611, Jefferson, North Carolina 28640

Contents

Preface

*H*ow a book makes its way from an author's head to a reader's hand is sometimes a miraculous journey, often an improbable journey, always an incredible journey.
Like the expedition of Lewis and Clark, a journey into that uncharted territory where art and commerce clash and mesh is filled with the unknown, the frightening, the unexpected, the wondrous. The twenty-six billion dollar a year publishing industry rests on those authors who survive the journey, who have endured the battles of fighting thoughts into words, the struggles of lashing those words onto paper, the manhandling of those pieces of paper into a manuscript. The existence of this twenty-six billion dollar industry depends on those authors who, weary and bruised, have pressed on, who have encountered the blows, the numbness, the self-doubts of rejection, who have hiked through the mountain passes of elation and exhilaration of acceptance, who have forded the rivers and navigated the rapids of working with the nations of publishers and editors, who have experienced the pleasures of prepublication dreams, the joys of holding a book, the terror and humiliation of a publicity tour, the ineptness of promotion and advertising, the silliness of reviews, the anticipation of awaiting sales figures, the nightmare of watching a book fall "dead-born from the press," the wonder of seeing it in a store, the amazement of watching a stranger reading it.
While editor-at-large at Macmillan, Edward Chase once commented that it was his experience that if writers are really determined to get published, "if they really stick at it, eventually — like salmon swimming upstream — they're going to make it. But it takes determination and endurance."[1] Maybe; though the sagas of such

Chapter notes begin on page 201.

1

upstream journeys are often a downright scary testament to the vagaries of chance, to the arbitrariness of rejection, to the luck of acceptance and strong sales. What would your advice be to people who want a career in writing? Harper Lee once was asked. "Well, the first advice I would give is this: hope for the best and expect nothing. Then you won't be disappointed."[2]

Sometimes authors, agents, editors, publishers, send back reports about their journeys, about the incredible things they've seen and heard along the way. Yet for all we know of the territory they have traveled, the journey never becomes easier for the next author, and in fact, seems to be getting even more arduous as the limited resources of publishing houses are devoted more and more to sure hits. Stephen King, one of the best-selling authors of all times, has recognized this problem:

> I actually feel a little bit sick to my stomach, if I'm to be honest. I've read some really excellent novels lately that were a long run from the best-seller list, and nobody in the publishing business seems to give a damn. The best novel I read last year was "Journal of the Gun Years," by Richard Matheson, but I didn't pick up my copy in the local B. Dalton, because they never got a single copy. I ended up special-ordering it.
> The point is: There are good writers out there telling good stories — stories no one has ever read before! — and a lot of these writers and stories are not finding their audiences. Some could be 'broken out' by dedicated publishers and publicity departments, but the money isn't there, nor is the commitment. What the publishers want is blockbusters. They want Stephen King, Tom Clancy, Danielle Steel...[3]

True enough. It's no secret that regardless of the merits of their books, Stephen King's or Tom Clancy's or Danielle Steel's latest will pop right to the top of the best-seller lists and stay there, week after week. Today, anything they write will be an instant hit. But King once wrote a book called *Carrie*, and Clancy *The Hunt for Red October*, and Steel *Passion's Promise*, and how such unknown authors journeyed against all odds onto the best-seller lists is a story that rivals their fiction.

CHAPTER 1

A Matter of Mystery

T he trouble all began on a summer evening in July of 1918 when twenty-one-year-old Scott Fitzgerald met eighteen-year-old Zelda Sayre, that captivating, southern belle tomboy who was already sneaking a smoke, a drink of corn liquor, and necking; Zelda, who had been voted the "prettiest and most attractive" girl in the Montgomery, Alabama, high school graduating class.

Or, to be more exact—as Fitzgerald was—the trouble began when he "fell in love on the 7th" of September, as he noted in his journal,[1] and concluded that to win the hand of this "whirlwind" he had to draw on his "ace in the hole" and complete the novel he had been spinning in his head.[2]

To be even more precise about it, the trouble really started when his sophomoric scheme worked: when his novel was accepted for publication and was an instant hit.

Before he took leave of his senses and dreamed up this plan to win Zelda, Scott Fitzgerald had been working for ninety dollars a month with the Street Railway Advertising Company, "writing the slogans that while away the weary hours in rural trolley cars,"[3] finding in this humdrum world that "all the confidence I had garnered at Princeton and in a haughty career as the army's worst aide-de-camp melted gradually away."[4] With a sense that time was running out, he quit his advertising job, left New York City and "crept home"[5] to St. Paul, Minnesota, announcing to his family that he was going to write a novel. "Through two hot months I wrote and revised and compiled and boiled down."[6] It seemed never once to have crossed Fitzgerald's mind that his book, like almost all first novels, was destined to oblivion. "This is a definite attempt at a big novel and I really believe I have hit it," Fitzgerald wrote on July 26, 1919, to Max Perkins, a young editor at Scribner's, the publishing house Fitzgerald hoped would accept his manuscript. "Now what I want to ask you is this — if I send you the book by August 20th and you decide you could risk its publication (I am blatantly confident that you will) would it be brought out in October, say, or just what would decide its date of publication?"[7] The novel was mailed off to New York City at the end of the summer, and Fitzgerald, "an empty bucket, so mentally blunted with the summer's writing," had taken a job repairing car roofs at the Northern Pacific shops.[8]

Suddenly, on September 15, 1919, the postman rang. A special delivery letter. And there he goes! Look! There goes Scott, now F. Scott Fitzgerald, running "along the streets, stopping automobiles to tell friends and acquaintances about it — my novel, This Side of Paradise, was accepted for publication."[9]

Fitzgerald was pretty oblivious to the nature of the miracle that had just befallen him, pressing Perkins to get the book out at once. Zelda was almost trapped in his net. The day he received word of his book's acceptance by Scribner's, he dashed off a note to Perkins: "Would it be utterly impossible for you to publish the book Xmas — or, say, by February? I have so many things dependent on its success — including of course a girl — not that I expect it to make me a fortune but it will have a psychological effect on me and all my surroundings and besides open up new fields. I'm in that stage where every month counts frantically and seems a cudgel in a fight for happiness against time."[10] But even Perkins's hat full of miracles was limited, and he patiently explained why the book could not appear until, would you believe it, March. Fitzgerald understood. "I feel I've certainly been lucky to find a publisher who seems so generally interested in his authors. Lord knows this literary game has been discouraging enough at times."[11] My, my, at twenty-two. Wait a few years Scott; you ain't seen nothing yet!

The acceptance of This Side of Paradise had been anything but inevitable. One of Scribner's editors "could not stomach it all" and another found it "hard sledding." Old Charles Scribner himself was skeptical: "I'm proud of my imprint," he growled. "I cannot publish fiction that is without literary value." A senior editor obediently ratified his judgment, calling the book "frivolous."[12] At the height of the novel's popularity, one of Fitzgerald's best friends, the eminent critic Edmund Wilson, termed it "very immaturely imagined; it is always just verging on the ludicrous. And, finally, it is one of the most illiterate books of any merit ever published.... It is not only full of bogus ideas and faked literary references but it is full of English words misused with the most reckless abandon."[13]

If the manuscript had not won the support of Max Perkins, a contemporary of Fitzgerald's, that probably would have been the end of F. Scott Fitzgerald: author. But Perkins was captivated by the vitality of the book and somehow pushed it to publication. To top miracle with miracle, the book clicked instantly with the reading public, and Fitzgerald was that year's shining literary star, waking up every morning "with a world of ineffable toploftiness and promise," swept along on "that first wild wind of success and the delicious mist it brings with it."[14]

Of course he felt great. He had taken a shot right in the main vein of that potent blend of aphrodisiacs and amphetamines, of steroids, crack and cocaine, that most wonderful of all legal drugs: success. If its user has some talent, it is a drug that allows him to achieve even more, for it is a wonderfully powerful stimulant of the confidence gland. "For a shy man," Fitzgerald mused, "it was nice to be somebody except oneself again: to be 'the Author' as one had been 'the Lieutenant.'"[15] Fitzgerald happily gave interviews in which "I told what a great writer I was and how I'd achieved the heights," expressing his great regret to one interviewer, who had just turned thirty, that he had "let his life slide away without accomplishing anything."[16] And with that confidence that success breeds, the drug's user, sure in his own abilities, may feel within him the drive, the ability, the vision, the need for another rush, and so try to match the accomplishment that gave rise to his success, and not only to match it, but to exceed it.

The same day Fitzgerald received the acceptance letter that changed his life, he added in his note to Perkins: "I'm beginning ... a very ambitious novel called *The Demon Lover* which will probably take a year. Also I'm writing short stories."[17] Indeed he was. Riding the rush after *This Side of Paradise* was accepted, Fitzgerald saw short stories everywhere, writing eight of them in the next two months and selling all, in contrast to his dismal record from March to June of that same year when he wrote nineteen stories and "no one bought them, no one even sent personal letters."[18] His ninth story was purchased "by the same magazine that had rejected it four months before."[19] On November 1, he sold his first story to *The Saturday Evening Post*, and three months later he had sold the *Post* six more. "I had been an amateur before; in October, when I strolled with a girl among the stones of a southern graveyard, I was a professional and my enchantment with certain things that she felt and said was already paced by an anxiety to set them down in a story."[20]

Was it not this wonder drug that allowed Scott Fitzgerald to move beyond the youthful meanderings of *This Side of Paradise* to the clear professionalism of *The Great Gatsby* published five years later? "I feel I have an enormous power in me now, more than I've ever had," Fitzgerald wrote to Perkins in 1924.[21] His early success gave him the head of steam to keep on writing and perfecting his art. "I want to be one of the greatest writers who ever lived," he confided to Edmund Wilson.[22]

So what was the trouble with all this? The trouble was that everyone — every reader, every writer, every would-be writer, even Scott Fitzgerald himself — was deluded. Everyone mixed up this hole-in-one miracle, the wildly improbable success of *This Side of Paradise* — a novel written in two months, a contract in hand in two weeks, publication five months later, and, although he did not live happily ever after, the young Fitzgerald did find some fame and fortune and the hand of the girl he loved — with the real world of publishing. So compelling is his story, and so strongly do we want to believe in it, that it still shines brightly on the dusty shelf of exhibits, a false clue misleading each generation of authors struggling to solve the mystery of what makes a book sell.

Whenever the F. Scott Fitzgerald exhibit is re-examined, another musty file should be dusted off— the file containing the story of one of his contemporaries, a woman one year older than Scott. This woman's novel was a main selection of the Book-of-the-Month Club and achieved that which Fitzgerald could only dream about all his life: It was a runaway best-seller, firmly entrenched for months on the *New York Times* Best Sellers list. That one book sold more hardcover copies than would all of Fitzgerald's novels combined during his lifetime. Had he been around to witness it, Scott would surely have envied the media blitz that this book attracted — front page of the *New York Times* with a three-column headline and a two-column photograph of its author, coverage on the major television networks and in all the news magazines, *60 Minutes*, the works.

Now, there was a significant difference between these two authors. While success came to Fitzgerald at twenty-three, Helen Hooven Santmyer's novel, *"...And Ladies of the Club,"* became a bestseller when she was eighty-eight, blind in one eye with a cataract in the other, her eighty-pound body wracked by arthritis and emphysema, confined to her wheelchair in her book-filled room at Hospitality Home East, a nursing home in her hometown of Xenia, Ohio. Miss Santmyer's joy, naturally, was somewhat more subdued than that of the young Fitzgerald running up and down the streets of St. Paul, stopping cars to tell his friends the good news. "All this publicity was fun for a while," said the old lady, "but sometimes I wish it would go away. It gets very tiresome."[23] She celebrated her book's success by getting her first permanent wave.

Santmyer had graduated from Wellesley a year before Fitzgerald graduated from Princeton. She received a bachelor of letters degree from Oxford and began working as a secretary to the editor of *Scribner's* magazine. The two novels she wrote in the 1920s, in her twenties, were dropped down that bottomless literary well where lost books fall without even delivering the satisfaction of a splash when they hit the water.

As an energized Scott and Zelda were partying around Europe, living happily in their dream world which "every day in every way grew better and better,"[24] that fleeting moment, as Fitzgerald described, "when the fulfilled future and the wistful past were mingled in a single gorgeous moment — when life was literally a dream,"[25] Miss Santmyer became the dean of women at Cedarville College in Ohio and later a reference librarian, working in her spare moments on what would become *"...And Ladies of the Club,"* her sixty-four-year history of a women's literary club in a small town in Ohio. Completed when she was young, her book did not find a publisher until 1982, when Ohio State University Press brought out a $35 edition of the massive novel, which sold a total of 1,300 copies. One day an Ohio woman heard a reader tell a fellow library patron that the novel she was returning was the best she had ever read. Intrigued, the lady read it and agreed, sending it on to her son, a Los Angeles film director, who also agreed and showed it to an industry friend, who agreed and sent it to his agent, who brought it to Putnam's, which purchased it for $50,000, published it, and sold 410,000 copies.

Now, the history of "...And Ladies of the Club" is a pretty frightening story — waiting until you're eighty-eight for the world to discover that what you had written really was pretty good after all. How about now climbing the creaking steps to the attic of the house of publishing to see what else may befall a book?

What's that? That noise in the dark at the top of the steps? Too late — there's no turning back now. Here it is, the scary story of John Kennedy Toole, who at the age of twenty-five, completed his first novel, which he titled A Confederacy of Dunces. It was a book into which he had poured himself and his ambition and his talent; a book, his Book, that became for him the reason for life. Seven years later, he still had not been able to find a publisher willing to take it on, and, at the age of thirty-two, he was found asphyxiated in his car.

Toole's mother, Thelma, a retired teacher of the dramatic arts, had faith in her son's book from the start. "I've been reading since I was a little girl and I knew John's book was good," she said. "When he came back from the Army he gave it to me and I finished it the next night. It was great, I told him."[26] After his death, his mother began her crusade, taking her dog-eared, smudged carbon copy of the manuscript from publisher to publisher. Each of the publishing houses to which she submitted the manuscript turned it down. For seven years, Mrs. Toole sent the tattered manuscript off to publishers and waited. And eight times, she saw it come back. "Every time it came back, I died a little."[27]

Somehow Mrs. Toole, hurrying in with her walker, buttonholed novelist Walker Percy, who was teaching a seminar at Loyala University near Mrs. Toole's home, and begged him to read the manuscript. Rather reluctantly, he agreed.

Percy took one look at the "badly smeared, scarcely readable carbon"[28] of the manuscript and regretted that he ever had promised Mrs. Toole that he would read it. Nevertheless, he waded in and read on. "And on. First with the sinking feeling that it was not bad enough to quit, then with a prickle of interest, then a growing excitement, and finally an incredulity: surely it was not possible that it was so good."[29] Percy arranged for its publication in 1980 by Louisiana State

8

University Press. Louisiana State University Press? Yes. Even the press was astounded. "The book is absolutely marvelous," the editor there wrote to Percy, "but why is it still in manuscript? Hasn't anyone else seen it?"[30]

There were still doubts, even with this editor. "It didn't take long to recognize that there was something of quality here although I admit I felt it was a book that would only have regional appeal. Frankly, I was astonished at the national response."[31] Within a month of publication, the national media were lavishing praise on *A Confederacy of Dunces*; it was into its fourth printing, the Book-of-the-Month Club had purchased it, and Louisiana State University Press (which printed up shopping bags announcing "LSU Press brings home the bacon") had sold the paperback, foreign and movie rights. The paperback sold a robust 750,000 copies. And on April 13, 1981, Mrs. Toole was notified that her late son had won the 1980 Pulitzer Prize for fiction. If Walker Percy had not agreed to read it, she sighed, "I could not have gone on after being rejected by eight publishers. I was wrecked!"[32]

The title John Kennedy Toole had chosen for his novel became a particularly apt description of the story of its publication. It came from a sentence of Jonathan Swift: "When a true genius appears in the world, you may know him by this sign, that the dunces are all in confederacy against him."

"Why, the question nags, why on earth was it not published till now?" asked the *New York Times* in a review of the book. "Are we to believe that for a period of 15 years a confederacy of publishing dunces rejected the manuscript of a comic genius?"[33]

Well, that's a good question. Where now are those myopic editors who had been lurking in the haunted attic, who read or skimmed the manuscript, or said they did, and breezily scrawled their verdict on one of those rejection letters? Can't you just see them? "This is definitely not our cup of tea." "Maybe a short magazine piece." "No way, José."

"It isn't about anything. It could be improved, but it wouldn't sell," read the actual rejection letter from Simon & Schuster which Mrs. Toole said was written by "a creature.... Not a man. Not a human being. I hope I never meet him...."[34] "You can't stand the heartache of the correspondence," said Mrs. Toole about her son's letters back and forth to publishers.[35]

To round out the horror tales of Helen Hooven Santmyer and John Kennedy Toole, one more exhibit must be examined, just one more; and that, of course, is the rest of the file on F. Scott Fitzgerald, whose ghost haunts every American writer's imagination.

Later in his life, Scott Fitzgerald recalled a day soon after the publication of *This Side of Paradise* and his marriage to Zelda, "riding in a taxi one afternoon between very tall buildings under a mauve and rosy sky; I began to bawl because I had everything I wanted and knew I would never be so happy again."[36] He described this period of bliss, of euphoria, that he felt after the publication and success of his first novel as "a short and precious time — for when the mist rises in a few weeks, or a few months, one finds that the very best is over."[37] It certainly was for him. Life never again would be so good, and he never again would know the public's adoration or the financial rewards he assumed would be his.

Fitzgerald was sure that his third novel, *The Great Gatsby*, published in 1925 when its author had achieved the ripe old age of twenty-nine, was special. "My book has something extraordinary about it. I want to be extravagantly admired again."[38] A few weeks before publication, he was hopeful that it would sell over 75,000 copies. But the book was a disappointment to its author, selling only about 20,000 copies, just enough to cover Fitzgerald's advance. In 1929, Fitzgerald earned $27,000 for eight short stories published in the *Saturday Evening Post*, but only $31.77 in royalties from his books, including $5.10 for *The Great Gatsby*.

Sales of his next book, *Tender Is the Night*, were even worse, about 10,000, in a year when Hervey Allen's *Anthony Adverse* sold over one million copies. "Alas," Fitzgerald sighed in a letter to Perkins, "I may again have written a novel for novelists with little chance of its lining anybody's pockets with gold."[39]

"Cards began falling for us much too early," Scott wrote to Zelda as he looked back on his failure to achieve that early promise of success that seemed to be his.[40] His books weren't selling. His life had become a week-by-week battle to scrape together enough money to exist. "My birthday is two-column front page news as if I were 80 instead of 40 — and I sit worrying about next week's $35.00 hotel bill!"[41] How much worse could it get? Let's see. He spoke to the dean of Princeton about giving a series of lectures on fiction at the university. No thank you, Dean Gaus replied; why don't you try one of the eating clubs?

Here was an author who had written the very best books that he could write, books that he knew were very good indeed; yet these books were all but ignored when published. Is it any wonder this author would suffer a breakdown at thirty-nine?

Published after Fitzgerald's death in 1940 at the age of forty-four, *The Last Tycoon* was critically praised, but that was all. "I hope the book will sell," Zelda wrote to Max Perkins, "at least enough to repay your interest."[42] It didn't. It sold 3,268 copies that year.

It's always been assumed that Fitzgerald's books were out of print when he died. Fitzgerald was afraid this would happen; he had told Max Perkins how odd it would be when his daughter "assures her friends I was an author and finds that no book is procurable."[43] As Charles Scribner III noted, "The truth is sadder: they were all in stock at our warehouse and listed in the catalogue, but there were no orders."[44]

It was only after Fitzgerald's friend, Edmund Wilson, put together some of Scott's miscellaneous writings in a volume which he titled *The Crack-Up*—a volume, by the way, which was turned down by every major New York publisher before it was brought out by New Directions in 1945—that a Fitzgerald revival began and the importance of his writing began to be recognized. Today, Fitzgerald's place as one of the American masters is secure. Today, *The Crack-Up* is still in print. Today, biographies of Scott, of Zelda, of their friends, sell more copies than his own books did in his lifetime. Today, all his books are in print and all continue to sell. And sell, and sell. In 1990, Charles Scribner, Jr., remarked that year after year, *The Great Gatsby* "has had the biggest sales of any Scribner's book; in fact, it is the best-selling book in the history of our company."[45]

The question of course is why Fitzgerald's books didn't receive the recognition and the sales they deserved during his lifetime. He was, after all, a very visible author, an author in the public eye right from the publication of *This Side of Paradise* when he was only twenty-three years old. What happened? And what if Edmund Wilson hadn't published *The Crack-Up* and started a Fitzgerald revival? Would his novels have been lost forever?

Publishing is a mysterious business. It is a business that tries desperately to find, among the fifty thousand books published annually, those two hundred or so which will be the year's best-sellers; yet it does little, if anything, to encourage the development of the authors who will write those best-selling books. In fact, it does quite a bit to discourage them. It is an industry littered with what Anthony Trollope called "that huge pile of futile literature, the building up of which has broken so many hearts,"[46] an industry littered with ruined books and shattered dreams, of authors as disillusioned, embittered, as frustrated as the author who, in 1979, rented an airplane and buzzed the mid–Manhattan offices of his publisher (Harcourt Brace Jovanovich). With its inexplicable failures and freak successes, "the profession of book-writing," John Steinbeck said, "makes horse racing seem like a solid, stable business."[47]

Does a good book ultimately, eventually, inevitably find a publisher and then an audience?

Ernest Hemingway almost didn't make it. Frustrated and discouraged by the repeated delays in the publication of his first book, *In Our Time*, twenty-five-year-old Hemingway wrote to Ezra Pound: "Now we haven't got any money anymore I am going to have to quit writing and I never will have a book published. I feel cheerful as hell…. Fuck literature."[48] It took the collective pulling and pushing and persuasion of Ezra Pound, Scott Fitzgerald and Gertrude Stein to break him into print.

Tennessee Williams almost didn't make it. "Before the success of *Menagerie* I'd reached the very, very bottom. I would have died without the money. I couldn't have gone on any further, baby, without money, when suddenly, *providentially*, *The Glass Menagerie* made it when I was thirty-four."[49]

Theodore Dreiser almost didn't make it. As E.L. Doctorow has explained it:

> Dreiser wrote this magnificent novel [*Sister Carrie*]. It was published in 1900; it was then and is still the best first novel ever written by an American. It's an amazing work…. The book was a magnificent achievement but the publisher, Doubleday, didn't like it, they were afraid of it. So they buried it. And naturally it did nothing; I think it sold four copies. I would go crazy too in that situation. Dreiser rented

a furnished room in Brooklyn. He put a chair in the middle of this room and sat in it. The chair didn't seem to be in the right position so he turned it a few degrees, and he sat in it again. Still it was not right. He kept turning the chair around and around, trying to align it to what — trying to correct his own relation to the universe? He never could do it, so he kept going around in circles and circles. He did that for quite a while, and ended up in a sanitarium in Westchester, in White Plains.[50]

Hemingway. Williams. Dreiser. Just three examples of authors who did find a publisher, but who came very close to falling into the abyss. The whole mysterious business of publishing calls forth such doubts that when we see an author who does make it, we can only wonder: is that proof that the system works, or are there scores of other accomplished writers out there who never got the lucky break?

Actually, getting published is just the first break from Lady Luck. Once the book is in print, another big break is needed to get it to sell, to find its audience.

Why are certain books popular? No one seems to know. The secrets of what makes a book a best-seller have been well secreted behind false panels, down hidden staircases, up in dusty attics, under haunted bridges. "Predicting which those will be is almost as much a game of chance as roulette," Brigitte Weeks, the former editor-in-chief of the Book-of-the-Month Club, has said.[51] Robert Loomis, an editor with Random House for over thirty-five years who has an enviable list of best-sellers to his credit, admitted that he had never been able to unravel the secret of best-seller success.[52]

It doesn't take much sleuthing to discover that the mystery of what makes a book sell has the publishing industry baffled. Evidence of bafflement is in plain sight.

Consider Christina Stead's *The Man Who Loved Children.* In 1940 Simon & Schuster brought it out to mediocre reviews and modest sales, then let it go out of print. In 1965 the book was republished by Holt, Rinehart and Winston to great reviews and great sales.

Consider Henry Roth's *Call It Sleep*, published in 1934 to mixed reviews. The book quickly disappeared, and Roth gave up writing and became a manual laborer, psychiatric hospital attendant, factory worker. Thirty years later, *Call It Sleep* was reissued as a paperback;

Irving Howe on the front page of the *New York Times Book Review* hailed it as an American classic, and the paperback went on to sell more than one million copies.

Consider Edward Crankshaw's *The Shadow of the Winter Palace.* It never did well when it was published, yet it became one of the Book-of-the-Month Club's biggest sellers.

How about Dale Carnegie's book, *How to Win Friends and Influence People,* which had initial sales of 1,526 and then sold 750,000 in the next two years? Or Thomas Peters's *In Search of Excellence,* which had a first printing of under 10,000 and ended up selling 1.5 million hardcover copies? Or Robert James Waller's *The Bridges of Madison County,* with an initial printing of 15,000, which received no enthusiastic reviews and had little advertising? Thirty printings later, 1,365,000 copies had been sold and it had spent most of the year on the best-seller lists.

How about the horror story of Nathanael West, whose labor over the course of a decade on novels like *Miss Lonelyhearts, A Cool Million* and *The Day of the Locust* brought him a return of $1,280? Since West's death in 1940 these same books have sold hundreds of thousands of copies.

How about the twenty publishers who turned down Richard Bach's *Jonathan Livingston Seagull,* the twenty-six who rejected Irving Stone's *Lust for Life,* the twenty-seven who said no thank you to Dr. Seuss's *And to Think That I Saw It on Mulberry Street,* the twenty-eight who rejected John Grisham's *A Time to Kill,* the forty who passed on the opportunity to publish Nabokov's *Lolita*?

Even when books are accepted for publication, their publishers often have no idea of their worth. How about the $3,000 advance to Jacqueline Susann for *Valley of the Dolls,* the $5,000 advance to Tom Clancy for *The Hunt for Red October,* the $3,000 advance to Stephen King for *Carrie*? These publishers had not the vaguest notion of the mega-hits they had purchased.

How about *The Snow Goose* by Paul Gallico, which was advertised only once (in a three-and-a-half-inch ad) and sold over 300,000 hardcover copies? In contrast, *A Remarkable Medicine Has Been Overlooked* by Jack Dreyfus, with $1.5 million spent on advertising, sold less than 50,000 copies.

How about a book just like the latest best-seller? Just when

14

publishers think they have mastered the formula for a best-selling book, just when they have begun to distribute their advances accordingly to the authors of sure hits, along comes something that blows all their theories out of the water. How about *The Name of the Rose*, an intricately plotted novel set in fourteenth century Europe, interspersed with Latin passages, written by an Italian professor? Harcourt Brace Jovanovich had bought the book for a modest $4,000. The book sold over a million copies and the paperback rights were sold to Warner Books for $550,000. And, for heaven's sake, how about *A Brief History of Time* by British physicist Stephen Hawking, a guide to astrophysics and the nature of time and the universe, which graced the *New York Times* Best Sellers list for over two years, with more than four months at the highest spot?

How about sex? Kenneth Roberts's "pimply and stupid nephew" advised him "to put more sex in my books if I wished them to sell,"[53] and indeed that is the recommendation of every author's helpful advisors. But the novels of Tom Clancy, certainly one of the best-selling authors in the United States, and Jeffrey Archer, England's premier best-seller, hardly contain any sex at all. Stephen Hawking's best-seller certainly didn't, nor did Robert Fulghum's *All I Really Need to Know I Learned in Kindergarten*, to cite two of the biggest nonfiction best-sellers of recent years; nor did John Grisham's *The Firm*, *The Pelican Brief*, and *The Client*, a few of the biggest recent fiction best-sellers. Nor did such all time best-sellers as Harper Lee's *To Kill a Mockingbird*, John Knowles's *A Separate Peace*, John Steinbeck's *Of Mice and Men*: on and on we could go, listing the books that have not depended at all on sex to sell.

Samuel Butler said, "There are some things which it is madness not to try to know but which it is almost as much madness to try to know. Sometimes publishers, hoping to buy the Holy Ghost with a price, fee a man to read for them and advise them. This is but as the vain tossing of insomnia. God will not have any human being know what will sell."[54]

Maybe God's not telling, but anyone involved with writing and publishing eventually uncovers at least a few clues as to what makes books sell. If we sift through some of the shop talk of authors, publishers, editors and agents in interviews, diaries, notebooks, letters, journals, memoirs and biographies, we may find that evidence —

sometimes circumstantial, but evidence nonetheless — begins to surface: a clue here, a confession there. And so, the shadows of the magic through which writers transform their interests and insights into words that will possess readers become visible, and the alchemy through which their books find their way to readers begins to crystallize.

CHAPTER 2

Winning the
Genetic Sweepstakes

O n individual writers sitting alone in the world's attics, dreaming, thinking, writing, rest the twenty-six billion dollar a year book publishing industry; rest the livelihoods of agents and editors and copywriters, publicists and publishers and printers and binders; rest the book clubs, the independent bookstores, the book chains and everything and everyone connected. No matter how big or how consolidated or how commercial the publishing industry becomes, it will remain at its core a cottage industry, for the product it is selling is homemade, woven by hand by individual craftsmen, piece by piece, book by book. The publishing industry may be brought into modern times with every technique of automation and mass merchandising, but there will never be a way to mass-produce what this industry is selling.

Who knows when the next *The Catcher in the Rye* or *To Kill a Mockingbird* will come along? There will never be assembly lines to manufacture what the publishing industry sells, for the foundation of this industry rests on the fragile riddle of creativity.

Are great writers born to write, like Barbra Streisand was born to sing or Joe DiMaggio was born to play baseball? Is writing a talent a person is born with? Does it all boil down to genetics? That, after all, is why our greatest athletes and movie stars are paid so much, isn't it? They are nature's freaks. Through some quirk in the union of sperm and egg, they were born with a slightly different set of vocal cords than the norm, a slightly different set of muscles and hand and eye coordination, or a lot better looks.

Everyone thinks he or she can write a book. Said Leo Tolstoy,

"If you ask someone, 'Can you play the violin?' and he says, 'I don't know, I've not tried, perhaps I can,' you laugh at him. Whereas about writing, people always say: 'I don't know, I have not tried,' as though one had only to try and one would become a writer."[1] With disgust John Cheever described the remarks his neighbors made to his wife, Mary: "It seems that all my rich neighbors (in the advertising business to a man) consider themselves to be the peers of Milton. Sitting on their red leather chairs in their 17-room houses they say: 'Oh if I only had all the free time your husband has I would have written many novels.'"[2] John MacDonald shared this disgust: "It is the memory of the amount of work it took to learn my trade that oftentimes makes me less than tolerant with the stranger who says earnestly, as though we share something special, 'You know, I've always wanted to write!' When my mood is especially astringent, I answer, 'Really! I've always wanted to be a brain surgeon.' The lay person can remove a splinter from a finger and can write a nice letter to Aunt Alice."[3]

To be a writer is just not that simple. It's something that really can't be taught. Encouragement, yes. A shot of confidence? Yes, indeed. And that can be all-important. "What can a teacher give a writer in a creative-writing class?" an interviewer asked Anne Sexton. "Courage, of course," she responded without hesitation. "That's the most important ingredient."[4] A word of encouragement, a nod of approval is sometimes all it takes. Years later, John Updike remembered his high-school art teacher who "gave me an underlined 'excellent' in composition; it struck me as an authentic artistic compliment, one of the few I have received."[5] For E. L. Doctorow, there were "always some teachers around, and people in the family, to say, 'This isn't bad, keep at it, you're good at this.' I was very, very lucky as a kid to have that kind of help."[6]

That sort of encouragement can make all the difference to an aspiring writer. But how to write is something each writer must learn on his own. A formal education has little to do with it. Twain had little schooling. Louis L'Amour never finished high school; neither did William Faulkner. Neither Hemingway nor Capote went to college. Nor does any sort of systematic reading program necessarily have much to do with it. E. B. White admitted that he never had "a very lively literary curiosity.... It is a matter of some embarrassment to me that I have never read Joyce and a dozen other writers who have changed the face of literature. But there you are."[7]

No matter how hard they study and work at it, not everyone can be a violinist or a brain surgeon, or a writer. Just as DiMaggio and Streisand are freaks, so are writers—"two-headed calves,"[8] Truman Capote called them—which is what Nelson Algren meant when he said, "There is no way of being a creative writer in America without being a loser,"[9] and what William Gass meant when he remarked that "most writers are probably quarter-formed. Hopeless and helpless. One's complete sentences are attempts, as often as not, to complete an incomplete self with words. If you were a fully realized person— whatever the hell that would be— you wouldn't fool around writing books."[10]

Those who may be writers are selected through "a lucky break in the genetic sweepstakes,"[11] as Isaac Asimov put it. Their childhoods hone and polish those special genes to determine who will be writers, and it is this honing and polishing that the sweepstakes winners must survive.

"Happy families are all alike," wrote Tolstoy at the beginning of *Anna Karenina*; "every unhappy family is unhappy in its own way." Unhappy families may be the breeding grounds of both maladjusted and adjusted individuals, but they seem the perfect petri dish for breeding writers.

When asked about the best early training for a writer, Ernest Hemingway invariably answered, "An unhappy childhood." Thornton Wilder, too, was "convinced that, except in a few extraordinary cases, one form or another of an unhappy childhood is essential to the formation of exceptional gifts. Perhaps I should have been a better man if I had had an unequivocally unhappy childhood."[12] Gore Vidal, also, is sure of it: "Hatred of one parent or the other can make an Ivan the Terrible or a Hemingway; the protective love, however, of two devoted parents can absolutely destroy an artist."[13]

Take an extreme example. Few childhoods could have been more thoroughly messed up than that of Truman Capote, an only child whose parents divorced when he was four and who spent his early years shuttled between homes of eccentric relatives in the deep South. "Except for my cousins and relatives, there was a great absence of love in my childhood," he remembered.[14] "You're a pansy! You're a fairy.

You're going to wind up in jail! You're going to wind up on the streets!" his mother would yell at him.[15] Left by himself, he began writing when he was eight, coming home after school and writing for several hours each day. This writing, he later understood, was an attempt to escape "from the realities of my own troubled life, which wasn't easy. My underlying motivation was a quest for some sense of serenity, some particular kind of affection that I needed and wanted.... I never felt I belonged anywhere."[16] A writer was born.

Once Tennessee Williams and Gore Vidal were having dinner with Tennessee's mother, the overpowering Miss Edwina, depicted quite faithfully as Amanda in *The Glass Menagerie*. Several times during the meal, Tennessee cleared his throat.

"Why," demanded Miss Edwina of her son, "do you keep making that funny sound in your throat?"

"Because, Mother, when you destroy someone's life you must expect certain nervous disabilities."[17]

In his study *The Wound and the Bow*, Edmund Wilson propounded his theory that Ernest Hemingway's "wound" that resulted in his art was his insecurity about his masculinity. When one reads, however, an extraordinarily hateful letter fifty-year-old Hemingway wrote to his publisher about his seventy-seven-year-old mother, one senses that perhaps childhood days up in Michigan were not all fun and games:

> I hate her guts and she hates mine. She forced my father to suicide and, one time, later, when I ordered her to sell certain worthless properties that were eating her up with taxes, she wrote, "Never threaten me with what to do. Your father tried that once when we were first married and he lived to regret it." I answered, "My dear mother I am a very different man from my father and I never threaten anyone. I only make promises. If I say that if you do not do certain sound things I will no longer contribute to your support it means factually and exactly that." We never had any trouble after that. Except that I will not see her and she knows that she can never come here.[18]

Hemingway might well have been closer to the mark than Wilson. "Forget your personal tragedy," Hemingway wrote. "We are all bitched from the start and you especially have to be hurt like hell before you can write seriously."[19]

Harold Robbins grew up in a Catholic orphanage, was adopted by a Jewish family, and ran away at fifteen. J.D. Salinger's college classmates remember him as not being close to any students or professors; "loner" is the term most frequently used to describe him. John Cheever wrote in his journals about "the bitter and ugly quarrels of our parents, circling angrily around the toaster and the orange juice squeezer like bent and toothless gladiators exhaling venom, bile, detestation, and petulance in one another's direction! My parents were not happy, and I was not happy with them."[20]

Not all the ingredients needed to create an unhappy childhood are confined to the family setting. So many future writers have been the last chosen for their school softball games and touch football teams that savvy publishers should send recruiters to sit in school gymnasiums and sign up those who are left standing alone after all the good players (and fair players, and mediocre players) have already been chosen.

Gore Vidal once noted that Louis Auchincloss "had the bad luck, for a writer, to come from a happy family, and there is no leveler as great as a family's love."[21] But Auchincloss's childhood was far from serene. He arrived as a boarder at Groton two weeks before his twelfth birthday: "I was naturally unpopular. I was a hopeless athlete. I was bored by most of the things that interested other boys and naive enough not to conceal my boredom.... Was it good for me to be universally labeled an effeminate moron," later in his life he wondered, "a non-male, a repulsive, unsexed creature, all day, every day, for months?"[22] Well, yes, it probably was, for as John Berryman was convinced, any ordeal that doesn't kill a writer is terrific.[23] Without his ordeal at Groton, might Auchincloss have been just another Wall Street lawyer?

Auchincloss's boyhood at Groton sounds a lot like Anthony Trollope's at Harrow a hundred years before. Trollope's unsuccessful barrister father sent the lad to Harrow School at the age of seven where he confronted "a daily purgatory." He remembered the headmaster stopping him in the street and asking him "with all the clouds of Jove upon his brow and all the thunder in his voice, whether it was possible that Harrow School was disgraced by so disreputably dirty a little boy as I! No doubt my appearance was against me. I had no friend to whom I could pour out my sorrows. Of course I was ill-dressed and dirty. But, ah! how well I remember all the agonies of my young heart; how I considered whether I should always be alone; whether I could not find my way up to the top of that college tower, and from there put an end to everything?" It was no better as he grew older. "I was now over fifteen, and had come to an age at which I could appreciate at its full the misery of expulsion from all social intercourse. I had not only no friends, but was despised by all my companions."

Again, in the long run, this wasn't so bad. Trollope did not hurl himself from the college tower. He survived. And the surviving Anthony Trollope was a new person, a writer. "As a boy, even as a child, I was thrown much upon myself. I have explained, when speaking of my school-days, how it came to pass that other boys would not play with me. I was therefore alone, and had to form my plays within myself. Play of some kind was necessary to me then, as it has always been. Study was not my bent, and I could not please myself by being all idle. Thus it came to pass that I was always going about with some castle in the air firmly built within my mind."[24] And so were sown the seeds of the forty-seven novels and sixteen other books that would constitute Trollope's oeuvre.

The cause of an unhappy childhood may sometimes be illness. Robert Louis Stevenson, an only child who suffered through "terrible long nights that I lay awake, troubled continually with a hacking, exhausting cough, and praying for sleep or morning from the bottom of my shaken little body,"[25] spent his days playing with his toy soldiers, his paint box and his writing tablet, the breeding ground of his creative imagination. When Eudora Welty was six or seven, she was taken from school and confined to bed for months for a "fast-beating heart." There, she says, "an opulence of story books covered my bed; it was the 'Land of Counterpane.' As I read away, I was Rapunzel, or the Goose Girl, or the Princess Labam in one of the *Thousand and One Nights* who mounted the roof of her palace every night and of her own radiance faithfully lighted the whole city just by reposing there, and I daydreamed I could light David School from across the street."[26] Tennessee Williams had the same sort of experience. "I was a born writer, I think. Yes, I think that I was. At least when I had this curious disease affecting my heart at the age of eight. I was more or less bedridden for half a year. Anyway, I took to playing

22

solitary games, amusing myself.... I mean I began to live an intensely imaginative life. And it persisted that way. That's how I turned into a writer, I guess. By the age of twelve, I started writing."[27]

For such children in the midst of experiencing in one form or another a troubled childhood, reading becomes an escape, an entry into fantastic new worlds. Books have a vivid impact on their imaginations. E.E. Cummings devoured *Treasure Island* "as a result of which, the blind pirate Pew followed me upstairs for weeks; while for months, if not years, one-legged John Silver stood just behind me as my trembling fingers fumbled the electric light chain."[28] And H.G. Wells happened upon Wood's *Natural History*, "copiously illustrated and full of exciting and terrifying facts. I conceived a profound fear of the gorilla, of which there was a fearsome picture, which came out of the book at times after dark and followed me noiselessly about the house. The half landing was a favourite lurking place for this terror. I passed it whistling, but wary and then ran for my life up the next flight."[29]

When children's imaginations have been thus haunted by the printed word, writing is a natural next step, a way of recasting life; a way of "transforming pain into honey," as Updike put it.[30]

Whether it is a genetic or a developmental characteristic or a combination of both, another common thread among writers seems to be an unusually acute sense that "Old Time is still a-flying." Writers seem to have a different feel for the passing of days than most people, to hear more clearly Time's winged chariot; and this sense that time is short, that (real or imagined) death is waiting around the next corner, is an impetus to their work.

"I am terrified that through illness or something the work may stop," John Steinbeck wrote in his journal as he worked on the manuscript of *The Grapes of Wrath*.[31] Does a lawyer, an accountant, a dentist, who is convinced his days are numbered, become obsessed with filing that final brief or tax return or filling that last tooth? Probably not. Perhaps knowing that time is short, they would schedule that long-dreamed-of trip to Bora Bora, or visit the Jersey shore to recall scenes of happier days. Not the writer. The writer becomes obsessed with racing death to finish that book. "Once the first draft is done," Steinbeck wrote again in his daily journal as he worked on *The Grapes of Wrath*, "it will be all right because someone could read

23

it even if I passed out of the picture. But I simply must get the draft done. Must avoid every side influence. Must get to be tough about so many things now. But once this book is done I won't care how soon I die, because my major work will be over."[32] This feeling hovered around him whenever he wrote. Later in his life, as he was working on *East of Eden*, he noted: "The design of this book, made so long ago, seems to hold.... My job seems to be to live long enough and strongly enough to set it down."[33]

Whenever he neared completion of a book, Hemingway quite regularly notified his publishers of just what to do if he died before publication. "If anything should happen to me by any bad luck," he wrote to Max Perkins when he was thirty-one and just finishing up work on *Death in the Afternoon*, "get it out with only a few illustrations. No color plates — give Pauline the money they would cost. Pauline could pick the illustrations and write very short captions."[34] Decades later, when he was fifty-one, he was writing in the same vein to his publishers about his work in progress, which would include *The Old Man and the Sea* and *Islands in the Stream*. "This book is, in total, some 1900 to 2000 pages in Mss. It is the book about the Sea, but there is no sense in arbitrarily labeling it as such.... This book about the sea could be broken up into four books and each one of them published separately.... The reason I told you that the four books which make up the whole could be published separately was in case of my death. Is this all clear?"[35]

Whether writers are sick or think they are sick, are dying or think they are dying, doesn't seem to make much difference; the sure knowledge that time is short is a spur to their work. In his collection of essays, *Partial Payments*, Jason Epstein has speculated that Anton Chekhov, who was a doctor as well as an author, knew he had tuberculosis and that with this knowledge, which he kept to himself, his "writing changed radically, becoming darker, more serious, denser, in every way better.... Chekhov, I believe, wrote with knowledge of his own impending death in his bones. It is what gave him his gloom, but his profundity too. Dr. Johnson said that the knowledge that one is to be hanged in a fortnight wonderfully concentrates the mind; the knowledge that one is carrying a fatal disease probably does something similar for the prose."[36] John Steinbeck could conjure up the feeling of death inevitable to help him write. "I have often thought that this might be my last book," he wrote as he began work on *East of Eden*. "I don't really mean that because I will be writing books until I die. But I want to write this one *as though* it were my last book. Maybe I believe that every book should be written that way. I think I mean that. It is the ideal."[37] Annie Dillard captures this same trick in her exhortations to writing classes at Wesleyan University: "Write as if you were dying. At the same time, assume you write for an audience consisting solely of terminal patients. That is, after all, the case. What would you begin writing if you knew you would die soon? What could you say to a dying person that would not enrage by its triviality?"[38]

Being especially aware of the passage of time, it is a writer's mission to stop it, to capture forever a moment, to preserve time in his work, "to arrest motion," as Faulkner described it, "which is life, by artificial means and hold it fixed so that a hundred years later, when a stranger looks at it, it moves again since it is life."[39] In his autobiographical novel, *My Secret History*, Paul Theroux has written that "all writing aim[s] at defeating time. No one could become a writer—no one would even care about it—until he or she experienced the impartial cruelty of time passing."[40]

In Hemingway's short story "The Snows of Kilimanjaro," Harry, a writer, lies dying of gangrene in Africa, remembering "the ranch and the silvered gray of the sage brush, the quick, clear water in the irrigation ditches, and the heavy green of the alfalfa," and thinking of the stories he had never written and now never would write. How similar is that short story, published when Hemingway was thirty-seven, to sections of *A Moveable Feast*, his sketches of Paris in the twenties on which he was working shortly before he killed himself at the age of sixty-two. Paragraph after paragraph near the end of the book begins with the words "I remember":

> I remember the snow on the road to the village squeaking at night when we walked home in the cold with our skis and ski poles on our shoulders, watching the light, and then finally seeing the buildings....
> I remember the trails up through the orchards and the fields of the hillside farms above the village and the warm farm houses with their great stoves and the huge wood piles in the snow....

I remember the smell of the pines and the sleeping on the mattresses of beech leaves in the woodcutters' huts and the skiing through the forest following the tracks of hares and of foxes.

I remember all the kinds of snow that the wind could make and their different treacheries when you were on skis."[41]

And isn't much of Hemingway's writing — certainly the best of it — like that? An effort to capture, to hold "the people and the places and how the weather was"?[42] And isn't that just like Mark Twain, middle-aged and living in Hartford, Connecticut, remembering his days on the Mississippi and writing about Huck Finn; and James Joyce, writing *The Dubliners* to preserve the dialogue of his father's friends; and J. D. Salinger, reworking his adolescence in *The Catcher in the Rye*?

Before he graduated from Princeton, Scott Fitzgerald brought to Dean Gauss the manuscript of a novel (which would become *This Side of Paradise*) to see if he would recommend it for publication. Fitzgerald, in fact, pleaded with Gauss, arguing that he probably would be killed in the war and that he therefore wanted to see his novel published, stating later that at that time he had been "certain all the young people were going to be killed in the war and he wanted to put on paper a record of the strange life they had led in their time."[43] Vladimir Nabokov remembered his privileged childhood in St. Petersburg before the Russian Revolution. He wrote to his mother:

> Mother dear, yesterday I woke up in the middle of the night, the stars, God: will I really *never return*, is it really all finished, wiped out, destroyed?.... In my sleep I saw black, eye-spotted caterpillars on vines of willow herb, then those yellowy-red wooden chairs, with fretwork backs like horses' heads which, remember, stood under the stairway in *our* house.... Mother, we must return, mustn't we, it cannot be that this has all died, turned to dust — such an idea could drive one mad? I would like to describe every little bush, every stalk in our divine park at Vyra.[44]

It would be in remembering, in reconstructing, in writing, that he would recreate, would hold on to, the world of his family's country estate he so loved.

Is it this sense of the rapid passage of time, and the consequent need to stop time in their writing, that opens writers' eyes to the world around them, that gives them a sense of wonder about everyday life? "Do any human beings ever realize life while they live it?— every, every minute?" Emily asks at the end of Thornton Wilder's play *Our Town*. "No," responds the Stage Manager, adding, "The saints and poets, maybe—they do some." And isn't that what makes writing possible, this ability to "realize life," to look at the commonplace and sense the miraculous? Isn't this just what John Updike meant when he said, "I describe things not because their muteness mocks our subjectivity but because they seem to be masks for God"?[45]

And so the gifted and bruised write books, creating through them an illusion that can seem more real than reality itself, an illusion that readers can live in, that may seem so real to them that it becomes a part of their experience. Counterbalancing all of the requisite sufferings involved in surviving the winning of the genetic sweepstakes, "his will be that acutest joy of all," Pearl Buck said of writers, "that rare, strange, secret, inexplicable ecstasy of joy, the joy of a god who one day took earth into his hand and created a man and a woman, and saw them live."[46] And it is that special gift that publishers can't manufacture or mass produce. As Hemingway said about writing: "It is impossible to hire out or contract to be able to do it, as to hire out to be an alchemist."[47]

CHAPTER 3

Sing, O Muse

*W*hat a writer knows, and what a writer writes about, isn't necessarily dictated by his direct experience. Henry James had a theory in which he posited a young woman who had led a sheltered life walking one day past an army barracks and hearing a fragment of conversation. If she was a novelist, James believed, she would be able to go home and write a novel about life in the army. His theory was not as farfetched as it might at first sound. Washington Irving, for instance, who wrote so hauntingly of the Catskills in his story of Rip Van Winkle, had not at the time set foot in the Catskills but merely had observed them from a Hudson River sloop one hazy summer afternoon. And Arthur Miller, in his early thirties, knew intimately the despair of Willy Loman.

An author's immediate inspiration may be triggered by anything — an overheard conversation, a slant of light, a stranger's expression, a jotted note that puts out roots and shoots and grows in meaning each time the writer returns to it. With such epiphanies do books begin. "Look," Norman Mailer has said, "novels don't always come your way. It's like falling in love. You can't say: 'Oh, gee, I think I'm ready to fall in love,' and then meet some woman who'd be perfect. When a novel comes, it's a grace. Something in the cosmos has forgiven you long enough so that you can start."[1]

John Fowles's *The French Lieutenant's Woman* began with an image that would not leave him: a woman standing at the end of a deserted quay looking out to sea. Who was it? Why did the image so possess him, he wondered, and in that wondering he began his book. While driving through the Adirondacks, E.L. Doctorow saw a road sign for "Loon Lake." "Suddenly an almost magnetic feeling for the place came to some point of shock when I sighted that sign, and I knew it was something for me."[2] Thinking of the sign, an image came to him: a private railroad train going through the mountains carrying gangsters. In that image, in that feeling, was born his novel *Loon Lake*. Eudora Welty found a short story when eavesdropping at the beauty parlor. Joyce Carol Oates has described the onset of an idea for a book in physical terms: "At times my head seems crowded, there is a kind of pressure inside it, almost a frightening physical sense of confusion, fullness, dizziness. Strange people appear in my thoughts and define themselves slowly to me."[3]

Authors have spoken reverently of their writing flowing so smoothly on occasion that the words and sentences seemed almost to be dictated to them by a muse sitting on their shoulders. Of his classic *Kidnapped*, Robert Louis Stevenson wrote: "The characters took the bit in their teeth; all at once they became detached from the flat paper, they turned their backs on me and walked off bodily; and from that time … it was they who spoke; it was they who wrote the remainder of the story."[4] The author blows some life into his characters, they rise, and off they go on their own. "My characters really dictate themselves to me," Joyce Carol Oates has said. "I cannot force them into situations they haven't themselves willed." And Faulkner, who wrote *As I Lay Dying* in six weeks, spoke of "running along behind" his characters "with a pencil trying to put down what they say and do."[5] As he once told Malcolm Cowley, "I listen to the voices, and when I've put down what the voices say, it's right. I don't always like what they say, but I don't try to change it."[6] Every now and then, it happened to Henry Miller: "Someone takes over and you just copy out what is being said."[7] And Francois Mauriac seems to have relied entirely on the voices in his head: "When I cease to be carried along, when I no longer feel as though I were taking down dictation, I stop."[8]

That's all well and good, but what happens when the dictation stops short? Or never starts? Sing, O Muse! Muse? O Muse, where are you?

Waiting for the muse can be a terrifying experience for the writer whose very being is tied to his writing and who, in slack periods, feels his talent waning. ("Could you live without writing, baby?" Tennessee Williams asked. "I couldn't."[9] Or, as he later put it, "I'm only really alive when I'm working."[10]) Inherent in being an artist is an altered state of consciousness, an ability to break free from self-absorption to see the magic of life, an ability to see the world in a slightly different way, which is perhaps the same thing as being tuned in to receive divine dictation. Writers have searched for ways to adjust their antennae and tuning dials to facilitate their entry into another world, the dream world reality of their own creation.

Being in love can do it — can alter people's perspective, heighten their senses, enhance their creativity. In such cases the muse is a living person. Just as Einstein developed his theory of relativity when he was in love, so Hemingway was convinced that "the best writing is certainly when you are in love,"[11] and indeed, his most memorable work, including his early short stories, *The Sun Also Rises, For Whom the Bell Tolls,* and *The Old Man and the Sea,* was created during the early days of his romances with Hadley, Pauline, Martha and Miss Mary, respectively. "Eased off on the book ... in May because Dr. said I worked too hard in April, and May fine month to fish and make love to Miss Mary," he wrote to his publisher. "I have to ease off on makeing [sic] love when writing hard as the two things are run by the same motor."[12] (Maybe women have two different motors. George Sands annoyed her lover no end by jumping right from their bed to her writing desk.) Anthony Burgess agreed that sex "has something to do with the creative process. I mean, you can't be a genius and sexually impotent.... I think art is sublimated libido. You can't be a eunuch priest, and you can't be a eunuch artist."[13] And Christopher Isherwood noted, "Some artists do say that during periods of intense creativity they find the sex drive has been ... I hate the word sublimated ... redirected."[14] It was for John Steinbeck: "Moment I stopped work," he wrote in his journal, "the drive became sexual."[15]

Were Hemingway's multiple marriages, like the many wives of Norman Mailer, connected to a quest for artistic stimulation? Other writers have been able to duplicate the consciousness-expanding effects of being in love with fewer alimony headaches by loving from afar. May Sarton found, "I'm only able to write poetry, for the most part, when I have a Muse, a woman who focuses the world for me. She may be a lover, may not. In one case it was a person I saw only once, at lunch in a room with a lot of other people, and I wrote a whole book of poems."[16] Tennessee Williams said he could not write any story at all "unless there is at least one character in it for whom I have physical desire."[17]

When not in love, writers have tried to court the muses through varied rituals of self-hypnosis, ranging from walking (Thornton Wilder), to sharpening pencils (Hemingway, Capote), to Dr. Johnson who could drink in one sitting as many as twenty-five cups of tea, to Balzac who drank up to fifty cups of coffee each day, to Amy Lowell who needed cigars to think and bought a stash of 10,000. By far, however, the most traveled road for writers searching for the muse has been drinking.

William Faulkner told his *Paris Review* interviewer: "My own experience has been that the tools I need for my trade are paper, tobacco, food, and a little whisky."

"Bourbon, you mean?" the interviewer interrupted him.

"No, I ain't that particular. Between scotch and nothing, I'll take scotch."[18]

Truman Capote called himself "a completely horizontal author." "I can't think unless I'm lying down, either in bed or stretched on a couch and with a cigarette and coffee handy. I've got to be puffing and sipping. As the afternoon wears on, I shift from coffee to mint tea to sherry to martinis."[19] Kingsley Amis found that "a glass of Scotch can be very useful as a sort of artistic icebreaker … artificial infusion of a little bit of confidence which is necessary in order to begin at all."[20] E. B. White made the same discovery: "Before I start to write, I always treat myself to a nice dry martini. Just one, to give me the courage to get started. After that, I am on my own."[21]

The courage to start for some; creative insight for others. Hart Crane composed the first drafts of many of his poems while roaring drunk, but refined them and revised them when he was sober. The alcohol gave him the visions, while his own clear-headed labor made the visions into poems. Tennessee Williams — who, incidentally, admired the writing of Hart Crane — had a similar approach. "I go to my studio. I usually have some wine there. And then I carefully go over what I wrote the day before. You see, baby, after a glass or two of wine I'm inclined to extravagance. I'm inclined to excesses because I drink while I'm writing, so I'll blue pencil a lot the next day. Then I sit down, and I begin to write."[22] Irwin Shaw reported the same effects: "I never drink while I'm working, but after a few glasses, I get ideas that would never have occurred to me dead sober. And some of the ideas turn out to be valuable the next day. Some not."[23] Said James Dickey: "At times, a certain amount of alcohol helps. The point is to get to a certain *level* at which the creative flow can best take place."[24] Thornton Wilder, too: "I got through the First scene of the Third Act and then something began to block. I could make a pleasing Third Act, but I didn't see how I could make a big one. So I got a little drunk and some light began to come to me."[25] The poet John Berryman believed his "forest of bottles" was the source of his creativity. When later in his life he joined Alcoholics Anonymous, his work fell off.

A masterpiece like "Kubla Khan" does not always spring from the "sort of Reverie brought on by two grains of Opium taken to check a dysentery," as Samuel Taylor Coleridge described his famous poem's origin.[26] The trouble, of course, as legions of writers and would-be writers have discovered, is that there is a very fine line between the ability of alcohol or drugs to trigger the senses and creativity, and the point at which they impede a writer's work. To stay on the right side of that fine line calls for professional judgment that would do credit to a skilled anesthesiologist. Hemingway claimed that "when I read Faulkner I can tell exactly when he gets tired and does it on corn [whiskey] just as I used to be able to tell when Scott would hit it beginning with *Tender Is the Night*."[27] Truman Capote told an interviewer how he had found cocaine to be "a really quite suggestive drug" and that he was writing "a lot" on it, "good material," too. "I wrote a lot of *Answered Prayers*. The writing part was good."[28] But one of the literary mysteries of this century is where is *Answered Prayers*? Other than the few fragments that had been published before his death, no one has discovered these fabled passages, if they indeed existed anywhere but in Truman's intoxicated brain.

Author John Irving has blamed drinking on the decline of great talents, citing authors like Hemingway and Fitzgerald who "pickled their brains" and never developed their talents, so that their best books were written when they were in their twenties.[29]

Whatever triggers it, when the dictation starts to flow, are the muses truly at work? (E. L. Doctorow was amazed that his book *World's Fair* fell into place in seven months when it typically took him several years to write a book: "I think what happened in that case is that God gave me a bonus book. I imagine He just decided, Well, this one's been paying his dues, so let's give him a bonus book."[30])

Or is it the result of thinking about a book, consciously or subconsciously, over time, until the work jells in the author's mind? "Before you write," Gertrude Stein advised Thornton Wilder, "it must be in your head almost in words, but if it is already in words in your head, it will come out dead."[31] James Thurber said that he never quite knew "when I'm not writing. Sometimes my wife comes up to me at a dinner party and says, 'Dammit, Thurber, stop writing.'"[32] In 1939, Paul Horgan made some notes for a novel. "Until 1968 they acquired enrichments every time I re-read them. When at last they contained the whole scheme, I wrote the book in eleven weeks. If asked how long it took me to write that book, I can reply, twenty-nine years and eleven weeks."[33] Eudora Welty has said that "once you're into a story everything seems to apply — what you overhear on a city bus is exactly what your character would say on the page you're writing. Wherever you go, you meet part of your story. I guess you're tuned in for it, and the right things are sort of magnetized — if you can think of your ears as magnets."[34] William Goyen has had the same experience. "Even the clerk in Macy's suddenly speaks out of the novel that you are writing, it seems, or is a character in it. All the people in the world are suddenly characters in the novel you are writing. Everything contributes."[35]

A few of the greats have been able to sit down and, in a display of enormous powers of concentration and comprehension, write a novel from beginning to end.

Dickens could sit writing in a corner of a room, at the same time entertaining his guests with a stream of chatter. John Steinbeck commenced work on *The Grapes of Wrath* on May 31, 1938, and finished the book on October 26, 1938, two months ahead of the schedule he had set for himself. He wrote two handwritten pages, two thousand words, every day, working "very near to a kind of unconsciousness,"[36] rolling onward with few changes or cross-outs, deletions or changes, so that his pencil manuscript found its way pretty much intact into proof and then into book. Ernest Hemingway plugged away at his monumental *For Whom the Bell Tolls* at 700 to 1,000 words a day, finishing it in less than a year and a half. The heroically prolific Erle Stanley Gardner and Georges Simenon come to mind as other examples. (Once Alfred Hitchcock telephoned Simenon and was told that he could not be disturbed because he was writing a novel. "Let him finish his book," Hitchcock joked, knowing of the author's legendary speed; "I'll hang on."[37]) Updike is another example. "I write fairly rapidly if I get going, and don't change much, and have never been one for making outlines or taking out whole paragraphs or agonizing much. If a thing goes, it goes for me, and if it doesn't go, I eventually stop and get off."[38] As E.L. Doctorow has explained it: "Where it flows, where you find yourself going on and the writing generates more writing — there's your book. Mark Twain said at one point, 'I don't write a book now unless it can write itself.' That's what he was talking about."[39]

Other writers have scoffed at the notion of the muses dictating. They believe that the act of writing is a deliberate one. "That trite little whimsy about characters getting out of hand; it is as old as the quills," mocked Vladimir Nabokov, who compared his writing to filling in the gaps of a crossword puzzle at any spot that at the moment struck his fancy, writing random sentences on index cards until his novel was complete. "My characters are galley slaves."[40] It's surprising to learn that the facile John Cheever was another galley master: "The legend that characters run away from their authors — taking up drugs, having sex operations, and becoming president — implies that the writer is a fool with no knowledge or mastery of his craft. This is absurd.... The idea of authors running around helplessly behind their cretinous inventions is contemptible."[41]

The otherworldly Anthony Trollope, who commenced writing every morning exactly at 5:30 A.M., stopped precisely at 8:30 A.M., and, with a clock set before him during those three hours, wrote 250 words every quarter of an hour, was scornful of writers who claimed they had to wait until inspiration moved them. "To me it would not be more absurd if the shoemaker were to wait for inspiration or the tallow-chandler for the divine moment of melting.... I was once told that the surest aid to the writing of a book was a piece of cobbler's wax on my chair. I certainly believe in the cobbler's wax much more than the inspiration."[42] Who is Joyce Carol Oates but today's Trollope? "Generally I've found this to be true: I have forced myself to begin writing when I've been utterly exhausted, when I've felt my soul as thin as a playing card, when nothing has seemed worth enduring for another five minutes ... and somehow the activity of writing changes everything. Or appears to do so."[43]

Thornton Wilder once quoted a poet as saying that "one line in fourteen comes from the ceiling; the others have to be adjusted around it."[44] Inspiration may start the process, may cut loose a line from the ceiling, but all the other lines, as Hemingway discovered, may come only through an effort that seems like "drilling rock and then blasting it out with charges,"[45] an effort which sometimes found him spending a full morning's work on a single paragraph. But in the end, if the writer is a professional, that is to say, a writer who has found his voice, neither reader nor writer can tell which sentences came easily and which did not.

For most writers, a vision captured on paper, whether it is comprised of sentences that gently float from the ceiling or those that are blasted out of rock one by one, emerges only after a whole lot of hard work and endless revision. It is this act of revision, of rethinking, of reshaping, of focusing and refining, that allows a fairly ordinary writer to achieve an extraordinary result, to accomplish the improbable and sometimes the impossible, creating a work that seems comprised only of sentences that dropped from the ceiling with divine blessing.

There is a story told of Flaubert and how he was visited by some friends on a Friday to see if he would join them on a weekend picnic. He declined, explaining that he was too busy with his manuscript, which they glanced at before leaving. On Sunday night, the friends returned and asked Flaubert how his work had gone. Splendidly, he told them. Again they looked at the manuscript and were startled to see that he had made absolutely no progress since Friday, that he was still at the same sentence — stuck, indeed, at the same comma. No, no, he assured them, on Saturday he deleted the comma and replaced it with a semicolon, and on Sunday he struck out the semicolon and changed it back to a comma, so yes, he had indeed made wonderful progress.

That is how sometimes it seems. Joseph Conrad described his writing method: "I sit down for eight hours every day — and the sitting down is all. In the course of that working day of eight hours I write a sentence which I erase before leaving the table in despair.... I assure you — speaking soberly and on my word of honour — that sometimes it takes all my resolution and power of self control to refrain from butting my head against the wall.... I would be thankful

to be able to write anything, anything, any trash, any rotten thing —
something to earn dishonestly and by false pretenses the payment
promised by a fool."[46]

Tolstoy went through eight rewrites of *War and Peace*. James
Thurber said that his wife would look at his first drafts and sigh,
"Goddamn it, Thurber, that's high-school stuff." He went on: "I have
to tell her to wait until the seventh draft, it'll work out all right. I
don't know why that should be so, that the first or second draft of
everything I write reads as if it was turned out by a charwoman."[47]
This is not at all unusual. Fitzgerald compared his method of writing to mining uranium: "one ounce to the cubic ton of rejected
ideas."[48] "It takes me six months to do a story," Dorothy Parker
explained. "I think it out and then write it sentence by sentence —
no first draft. I can't write five words but that I change seven."[49]
Joseph Heller was frustrated that he couldn't write more than a page
a night on *Catch-22*. "It made no sense to me that somebody with a
college degree and the gift for writing, as I had, couldn't just sit down
and write four or five pages at a session."[50] Since then, he has come
to accept that, for him, a realistic objective is "How can I inch along
to the next paragraph? Inching is what it is. It's not: How can I handle the next chapter? How can I get to the next stage in a way that I
like?"[51] Bernard Malamud told John Gardner that he just kept writing and writing "until it comes out right."[52]

And maybe that's it. Perhaps talent really is only long patience:
cameo appearances of the muse, with a lot of hard work and a lot of
waiting between visits.

CHAPTER 4

The Writing Life

*M*use or no muse, books are paid for in time. Writers do what they do, creating through illusions a new reality by withdrawing from their own reality, withdrawing from their world, sitting alone with paper and thoughts. "Nothing," John Updike has said, "is more antisocial and nontribal than one individual sitting in a quiet room coding make-believe for another individual to decipher in a quiet room maybe tens of years and thousands of miles away."[1]

Those who do not write have a hard time understanding the writer's life or apparent lack thereof. "A book takes so long that people get tired waiting," Steinbeck once noted.[2] Writers pour time into their work, they lavish time on it, they who so acutely sense time's passage spend time as if it was without end. "The most interesting thing about writing is the way that it obliterates time," Gore Vidal remarked; "three hours seem like three minutes."[3] One day melts into the next.

Authors learn to become jealous of their writing time. While Paul Horgan was writing or preparing to write, he found that "a phone call is a minor catastrophe and a knock on the door a potential disaster."[4] William Maxwell has said that he resents "any social invitation that keeps me up after ten-thirty, so that I'm not bright as a dollar the next morning."[5] Writers have little use for the games and hobbies and pastimes of their non-writing friends. "It is not that I dislike them but that they bore me and in no way hold my attention," Steinbeck explained. "Nine-tenths of a writer's life do not admit of any companion nor friend nor associate. And until one makes peace with loneliness and accepts it as a part of the profession, as celibacy is a part of priesthood, until then there are times of dreadful dread."[6]

That is the price of admission to the writing life. It is a price authors gladly pay. Upon completing *Hawaii,* James Michener was asked if he would ever again have the energy to undertake such a major work. He answered:

> I would always like to be engaged in such tasks. Young people, especially those in college who should know better, frequently fail to realize that men and women who wish to accomplish anything must apply themselves to tasks of tremendous magnitude. A new vaccine may take years to perfect. A Broadway play is never written, cast, and produced in a week. The good work of the world is accomplished principally by people who dedicate themselves unstintingly to the big job at hand. Weeks, months, years pass, but the good workman knows that he is gambling on an ultimate achievement which cannot be measured in time spent. Responsible men and women leap to the challenge of jobs that require enormous dedication and years to fulfill — as does book writing — and are happiest when they are so involved.[7]

Such a strange style of living, if it may even be called that, does not go over very well with family and friends. Few mothers or fathers, and few acquaintances, consider writing a real job. John Steinbeck's mother wanted her son "desperately to be something decent like a banker.... Mother always thought I would get over it and come to my senses."[8] James Michener's mother was horrified that he was even considering leaving his editorial position to pursue such an insecure job as writing. "She predicted, not once but many times, that no good would come of it, and not even my winning of the Pulitzer Prize appeased her, for that was an evanescent one-time thing which had happened by accident." It was only when she saw a story of his published in the *Saturday Evening Post* that she was able to find some peace of mind. Michener overheard her telling a neighbor: "Well, he did sell a story to the *Saturday Evening Post,* and they don't fool around."[9] To friends and acquaintances, writing apparently does not constitute gainful employment. Anne Tyler once was waiting in the schoolyard for her child when another mother came up to her. "'Have you found work yet?' she asked. 'Or are you still just writing?'"[10]

An author's children have little idea, if any, what their writing parent does. "I had Bumby for ten days while Hadley was on a trip,"

Ernest Hemingway wrote to Scott Fitzgerald, "and one morning I took him to a cafe and got him a glace and a new harmonica and holding the harmonica and eating the glace he said, 'La vie est beau avec papa.' He is very fond of me and when I ask him what does Papa do, hoping to hear him say Papa is a great writer like the clippings, he says Papa does nothing."[11] Once, when Stephen King set off on a promotional tour, his wife asked their son: "Owen, do you know where Daddy's going?" Of course Owen knew: "Yes, he's going off to be Stephen King."[12]

John Cheever's eight-year-old son struck up a conversation with a woman on shipboard:

> She wanted to know if my father was "John Cheever, the writer." I didn't think so.
> "Does he sell short stories to *The New Yorker*?"
> I wasn't sure. He had a typewriter, I knew that.
> "Well," she said. "Cheever is an unusual name; if he has a typewriter and he lives in New York, he must be John Cheever the famous writer."
> "Oh, no," I said, "It couldn't be."[13]

Familial annoyance comes in endless variations, from the unsolicited advice Kenneth Roberts received from that "pimply and stupid nephew … a high school student [who] knew all about writing, and safely advised me to put more sex in my books if I wished them to sell,"[14] to the tip-toeing patronizing John Cheever experienced when he began his first novel: "The family makes it quite unbearable by asking me 'have you been writing to-day … isn't that nice … and what have you been writing today…' and telling everyone from the char to the president of the woman's club that I'm going to write a book."[15]

Not only may writers see little of their friends and family, but they cannot do what they would like most to do: talk to them about their work. Authors quickly learn that talking about an idea for a book may prevent the book from ever being written. As E.L. Doctorow explained it: "When you're talking about a story you're writing it. You're sending it out into the air, it's finished, it's gone."[16] And a book-in-progress talked about is a book in peril. A much more innocent comment than James Thurber's wife's "Goddamn it,

Thurber, that's high-school stuff" could spook a writer groping to capture a vision.

The act of holding the first copy of one's book, is, for an author, an experience equal in awe and joy to holding one's newborn. Indeed, it is an experience that may transcend the miracle of birth, for in most cases, the book's gestation has been much longer than nine months, the pain more persistent, the doubts and anticipation more consuming. The moment of holding that first book surpasses the moment of first holding a wet, red and curious-looking baby; it is the equivalent of giving birth to a god or goddess-like teenager in all their power and glory, and though later on the book may develop the acne of anemic sales and the halitosis of horrible reviews and may whine a lot, at that moment it is the queen of the prom, the captain of the football team. "For several days after my first book was published I carried it about in my pocket," James Barrie remembered, "and took surreptitious peeps at it to make sure the ink had not faded."[17] This is the moment the author most wants to share with those closest to him. Christopher Isherwood once said that "one of the most gratifying of all expressions on one's friends' faces is when they are genuinely surprised that you had it in you."[18]

This expression, however, is all too rarely seen. Too often, the reactions of family and friends can be less than satisfying.

It was not until three months after the publication of *Jane Eyre* that Charlotte Brontë, egged on by her sisters, worked up the courage to reveal to her father that she was its author.

"Papa, I've been writing a book," she casually said as she walked into Mr. Brontë's study carrying a copy of her novel and a handful of the reviews it had received.

"Have you, my dear?" he said, not glancing up from his reading.

"But Papa, I want you to look at it."

"I can't be troubled to read manuscripts," he said, brushing her off.

"But it is printed," she persisted.

"I hope you have not been involving yourself in any silly expense."

"I think I shall gain some money by it. May I read you some reviews?"

Would he read her book, she inquired when she had finished reading him the reviews. Leave it, he ordered; he might.

The next day at tea, Mr. Brontë called his family together.

"Children," he announced, "Charlotte has been writing a book — and I think it is a better one than I expected."

And that was all he ever had to say about *Jane Eyre*.[19]

Ernest Hemingway's parents proudly ordered six copies of their son's first book, *In Our Time*, read a copy, wrapped the "filth" back up, and quickly sent all six copies back to the publisher. His next book, *The Sun Also Rises*, fared little better in their eyes. "You surely are now famous as a writer and I shall trust your future books will have a different sort of subject matter," his father counseled him. "You have such a wonderful ability and we want to be able to read and ask others to enjoy your works." His mother was more direct. It seemed to Grace Hemingway "a doubtful honor" to have written "one of the filthiest books of the year." She was too embarrassed, she informed her son, to attend the meeting of her Current Books Study Group when the book would be discussed. "What is the matter?" she questioned. "Have you ceased to be interested in loyalty, nobility, honor and fitness of life — Why life is more wonderful and beautiful to me every day of my life — I have found *my* heaven *here*— in the opportunity to create beauty and exalt the nobility of life. I love you dear, and still believe you will do something worthwhile to live after you."[20] Years later, when her son was working on the manuscript of *For Whom the Bell Tolls*, Grace expressed her hope that it would be "something constructive for once."[21] There seemed little escape for poor Ernest. Where his mother left off, his son Gregory took over, opining that *The Old Man and the Sea* "was as sickly a bucket of sentimental slop as was ever scrubbed off the bar-room floor."[22]

At the height of the popularity of *Valley of the Dolls*, Jacqueline Susann telephoned her mother to tell her she was number one on all the best-seller lists. "Maybe now you should take a writing course," her mother counseled her.[23]

Talk about a wet blanket. Here's an entry from John Cheever's journal:

> In the afternoon mail there is a letter saying that two pieces have been bought. I am jubilant, but when I speak the good

tidings to Mary she asks, oh, so thinly, "I don't suppose they bothered to enclose any checks?" I think this is piss, plain piss, and I shout, "What in hell do you expect? In three weeks I make five thousand, revise a novel, and do the housework, the cooking, and the gardening, and when it all turns out successfully you say, 'I don't suppose they bothered to include any checks.'"[24]

The critical reactions of relatives and friends who feel compelled to give their honest opinions about an author's latest book can be distressing. Maybe they are too close and cannot separate author from book. Maybe this lack of appreciation is the prophet-without-honor-in-his-own-country syndrome. "In my district of Gascony," Montaigne wrote, "it is thought a joke to see me in print. The further from my home the knowledge of me travels, the higher I am valued."[25]

Over the course of four days, Flaubert read aloud his first novel, *The Temptation of St. Anthony*, to two of his closest friends. When he was finally through, Flaubert turned to them. Ok, what did you think? he prodded them. "We think you should throw that in the fire and never talk about it again."[26] Nor did James Joyce's brother temper his evaluation of *Finnegans Wake*: "It is unspeakably wearisome…. The witless wandering of literature before its final extinction. I would not read a paragraph of it if I did not know you."[27] Louis Auchincloss's brother was equally blunt when Louis showed him his first novel: "Why it looks like a real book," he said in astonishment.[28] At least James Joyce's brother read his books; Kurt Vonnegut's relatives don't bother. They tell him "that they are glad I'm rich, but that they simply cannot read me."[29]

George Santayana knew what he was talking about when he said, "It is the part of prudence to thank an author for his book before reading it, so as to avoid the necessity of lying about it afterward."[30] May Sarton left her first book of poems at Virginia Woolf's doorstep, along with a small bouquet of flowers. Woolf responded with a short note: "Thank you so much, and the flowers came just as someone had given me a vase, and were perfect, and I shall look forward to reading the poems."[31] Woolf thereby gracefully sidestepped having to comment on the poems. That's how it should be done.

Such are the pleasures of the writing life that dealing with such obtuseness of family and friends seems a small price to pay. Picture the serene images of writers at work: Hemingway on a wet, rainy morning in Paris, seated in "a pleasant cafe, warm and clean and friendly," sipping a rum St. James and opening his notebook to write about a day up in Michigan;[32] Karl Marx, deep in thought in the quiet of the reading room of the British Museum; Barbara Tuchman seated in a hushed library, silently opening a forbidden box of raisins hidden between her index cards; Rachel Carson, her dungarees rolled up to her knees, her peaked fisherman's cap shielding her eyes as she peers into one of her beloved Maine tidal pools, taking the notes that would become her poetic sea prose. Who could ask for anything more?

Just before he started writing, William Faulkner met Sherwood Anderson. "We would walk about the city in the afternoon and talk to people. In the evenings we would meet again and sit over a bottle or two while he talked and I listened. In the forenoon I would never see him. He was secluded, working. The next day we would repeat. I decided that if that was the life of a writer, then becoming a writer was the thing for me."[33] Anthony Trollope wrote that "there is perhaps no career of life so charming as that of a successful man of letters.... Who else is free from all shackle as to hours?"[34] "It is," Annie Dillard has declared, "life at its most free."[35]

This is why John Steinbeck would write in his journal: "Tomorrow is the 4th of July. I do not see any reason to take it off."[36] And why Stephen King works every day except his birthday, the Fourth of July, and Christmas. And why Louis L'Amour really meant it when he said, "I have no hobbies. Hobbies are for idle time and I have none. All my activities: hiking, shooting, tracking, learning about plants and animals are geared to my work. Writing and all that attends it is my greatest pleasure; my schedule might seem very rough to some, but to me it is the essence of living."[37] And how Washington Irving could mean it when he wrote, "I have never found, in anything outside of the four walls of my study, an enjoyment equal to sitting at my writing desk with a clean page, a new theme, and a mind awake."[38] As did William Burroughs, who, a century later, expressed the same sentiment when he said, "I don't make myself work. It's just the thing I want to do. To be completely alone in a room, to know that there'll be no interruptions and I've got eight hours is just exactly what I want — yeah, just paradise."[39] This is what Joseph Heller meant when he said, "If I retired, I would live exactly the way I live now, assuming my health was good. Sleep as late as I want to, which is about eight in the morning, have a leisurely breakfast, and begin writing fiction. That's what I want to do."[40] And "how happy" Ernest Hemingway felt "to have put down properly 422 words as you wanted them to be. And days of 1200 or 2700 were something that made you happier than you could believe."[41] And how David Updike, son of John, has written of his father: "At night, as he sat reading books for review, or going over proofs with the same stubby golf pencil that had recorded his score that afternoon, he gave off an impression of leisure and repose, of doing exactly what he wanted to do."[42] And how Tennessee Williams could say to Gore Vidal with a great smile: "I like my life."[43]

Winston Churchill counted writers among "fortune's favored children," noting that "for them, the working hours are never long enough. Every day is a holiday and ordinary holidays, when they come, are begrudged as an enforced interruption in an absorbing vocation."[44]

To be sure, the act of writing itself may not always be pleasant. In fact, writers have given us horrifying glimpses of the most deranged forms of torture in describing their horrible agonies in putting words on paper.

Kenneth Roberts has said that "childbirth is sheer delirious joy by comparison with the task of wrenching a novel from the brain and transferring it to paper."[45] Rebecca West found writing "a nauseous process."[46] All you do is sit in a little room and stare at a blank sheet of paper "until the drops of blood form on your forehead," Gene Fowler has told us, or, alternatively, as Red Smith has described it, sit at the typewriter and open a vein.[47] Capote called it "a very excruciating life, facing that blank piece of paper every day and having to reach up somewhere into the clouds and bring something down out of them."[48] Joan Didion reaches a point where she believes she has suffered a small stroke, finding herself incapable of putting one word after another. John McPhee finds that "maybe, maybe, two minutes a day of writing are enjoyable. I go off the edge of a cliff and into the deepest swamps of gloom you ever heard of."[49] Even the prolific Danielle Steel is terrified that she won't finish her latest book, and then terrified that she will never be able to start another one.[50]

Georges Simenon was convinced that "writing is not a profession but a vocation of unhappiness. I think that every one who does not need to be a writer, who thinks he can do something else, ought to do something else."[51] Anthony Burgess concurred: "I think that the mental strain, the worry, you know, the self-doubt, are hardly worth the candle; the agonies of creation and the sense of responsibility to one's muse — all these various things become more than one can live with."[52] "Let's face it," William Styron concluded, "writing is hell."[53]

Maybe. But if ever an author's writing becomes a twisted knot that will not untangle, if ever he begins to miss the collegiality of the office water cooler and doubts begin percolating as to whether he ever should have left his real job, he should just hop into the car and sit for a while in the rush hour tie-up on the freeway. And then drive to the train station as the evening commuters are disgorged. And look. Look at their clothes, sweaty, disheveled, look at their eyes, as blank and vacant as that next piece of paper in the typewriter, though without the promise; look at their walk, the plodding gait of zombies in leaden wingtips; and remember, as Swiss author Blaise Cendrass knew, that writing is

> a noble privilege compared with the lot of most people, who live like parts of a machine, who live only to keep the gears of society pointlessly turning. I pity them with all my heart. Since my return to Paris I have been saddened as never before by the anonymous crowd I see from my windows engulfing itself in the Metro or pouring out of the Metro at fixed hours. Truly, that isn't life. It isn't human. It must come to a stop. It's slavery ... not only for the humble and poor, but the absurdity of life in general.[54]

No rat-faced boss. Work at home. Come as you are. Write when you want. No need to be nice to people you don't like. Sound good? Authors know just what they have. As John Updike has written: "Writing is surely a delicious craft, and the writer is correctly envied by others, who must slave longer hours and see their labor vanish as they work, in the churning of human needs."[55] And hear May Sarton: "When I can wake up and watch the sun rise over the ocean and know that I have an entire day ahead, uninterrupted, in which to write a few pages, take a walk with my dog, lie down in the afternoon for a long think (why does one think better in a horizontal position?), read and listen to music, I am flooded with happiness."[56]

No, the writing life isn't bad. And the real agony is not in the writing, but rather in trying to make the writing pay.

CHAPTER 5

Your Stupid Book Stinks

S ome pretty big fish have slipped through publishers' nets—indeed, so many groupers that it sometimes seems a wonder that any of Western civilization's great works ever made it into print. Daniel Defoe's *Robinson Crusoe*, Edgar Allan Poe's "The Raven," Lewis Carroll's *Alice's Adventures in Wonderland*, Upton Sinclair's *The Jungle*, William Thackeray's *Vanity Fair*, Hans Christian Andersen's *Fairy Tales*, Harriet Beecher Stowe's *Uncle Tom's Cabin*—the list of great works rejected by astigmatic publishers goes on and on. Some of the stories of rejection are real beauts.

Irving Stone submitted the manuscript of his first book to Alfred Knopf. "They never opened it — the package with the manuscript got home before I did."[1] A reader at one of the twenty-six other publishing houses to which Stone submitted the manuscript and which in turn rejected it, pigeonholed his story of Vincent Van Gogh as "a long, dull novel about an artist."[2] The Doubleday sales department concluded that "there is no way to sell a book about an unknown Dutch painter."[3] Irving Stone's biographical novel, *Lust for Life*, at last found a home, and went on to sell twenty-five million copies and establish Stone's reputation as a best-selling novelist.

In 1926, Kenneth Roberts broached with Harper & Brothers his plan for a book that would become the first of his acclaimed historical novels. The editor with whom he spoke "shook his head sadly and told me frankly that there was nothing for anybody in such a book as I proposed."[4]

Patrick Dennis recalled that his *Auntie Mame* "circulated for five years, through the halls of fifteen publishers, and finally ended up with Vanguard Press, which as you can see, is rather deep into the alphabet."[5] Within six weeks of publication, it was a best-seller.

Pearl Buck's first manuscript came right back to her with a note: "Regret the American public is not interested in anything on China."[6] So many publishers rejected a book by E.E. Cummings that when finally it was published, he penned the following dedication: "No Thanks to: Farrar & Rinehart, Simon & Schuster, Coward-McCann, Limited Editions, Harcourt, Brace, Random House, Equinox Press, Smith & Haas, Viking Press, Knopf, Dutton, Harper's, Scribners, Covici, Friede."[7]

James Michener, who had been a textbook editor at Macmillan before World War II, returned from service and submitted the manuscript of his *Tales of the South Pacific* to his former employer, who halfheartedly brought it out in 1947. Shortly after its modest publication, Michener submitted to Macmillan the manuscript of his next novel. Enough was enough. The head of Macmillan called Michener into his office to inform him that his future wasn't as an author, but as a textbook editor, and that he really should keep his eye on the ball; besides, he didn't think that Macmillan should be publishing the books of its employees. So Michener took the manuscript of *The Fires of Spring* to Bennett Cerf at Random House. Within two weeks of Michener's signing on with Random House, *Tales of the South Pacific* had won the Pulitzer Prize, and soon Rodgers and Hammerstein turned several of Michener's tales into their musical *South Pacific*. The rest, as they say, is history, and Michener faithfully abided by Macmillan's edict and never again submitted a manuscript to his former employer. For years thereafter, when the head of Macmillan bumped into Bennett Cerf, he would grumble, "You lucky bastard!"[8] James Michener seemed too much of a gentleman to have had such thoughts, but certainly he would be forgiven if he had grumbled to the head of Macmillan, "You stupid jerk!"

Herman Wouk had published with Simon & Schuster in 1947 a novel called *Aurora Dawn*, which sold a not-so-bad 30,000 copies and was a selection of the Book-of-the-Month Club. The next year, Simon & Schuster published his novel *City Boy*, which sold only 6,000 copies. Some years later, Wouk described to his editor the plot of the new book he was working on that would become *The Caine Mutiny*. His editor's reaction was simple and straightforward: "It sounds very much like a novel we turned down last week!"[9] Alfred A. Knopf also refused it. Doubleday took it on. "I thought it was a gamble," remembered the Doubleday editor who accepted it. "I believed it would be a major book club selection and that it would sell about 50,000 copies in the trade. I was wrong on both counts."[10] Doubleday's book club, the Literary Guild, turned it down, as did the Book-of-the-Month Club, "because," as the founder of the club remembered it, "our first reader's reaction happened to coincide with the original *unexcitement* on the part of the publisher."[11] Every magazine to which it was submitted declined to buy first serial rights. Initial reviews were lukewarm and sales were slow for the first three months; but readers loved it. Published in March of 1951, *The Caine Mutiny* was on the best-seller lists by August and stayed in first place on the *New York Times* list through most of 1952 (in fact, sharing the honor with Michener's *Hawaii* as the novel to have held the number one spot on the *New York Times* best-seller list the longest ever), winning the Pulitzer Prize twenty-three months after publication and achieving sales of well over one million.

Okay, enough! What's going on here? Authors have always felt that unless a writer is known to a publishing house, a proven name, a submission receives only the most perfunctory attention. Some interesting literary experiments certainly justify this sort of paranoia.

In 1978, writer Chuck Ross conducted an experiment to test publishers' receptivity to unsolicited manuscripts. He typed Jerzy Kosinski's novel *Steps*, which had been published by Random House ten years before and had won the National Book Award for Fiction, and submitted the manuscript to all the major houses. Each publisher rejected it. Random House, by the way, rejected it, too, as did Kosinski's then current publisher, Houghton Mifflin.[12]

In 1982, an unemployed writer changed the title of "Casablanca" to "Everybody Comes to Rick's" and changed the names of the characters. Everything else remained the same. He submitted his screenplay to 217 Hollywood agents. Only 31 of the 217 even acknowledged it. Of those 31, all rejected it, with a few adding such helpful hints as "try something that really grabs you" or suggesting that it was not right for film but how about making it into a novel?[13]

In years past, chapters of *War and Peace* and of William Faulkner's novels, for example, have been neatly typed and resubmitted, and the reaction is quite predictable: rejection. Does a novel by an unknown author stand a chance?

And then there was Joyce Carol Oates, who bypassed her agent and regular publisher and submitted her manuscript to Simon & Schuster under the name of Rosamond Smith. "When it was accepted," she said, "I felt the same excitement as when my first book was published."[14] The only trouble was, the advance was a paltry $10,000. One suspects that if she had substituted the three words "Joyce Carol Oates" for the two words "Rosamond Smith," the advance might have been larger by a significant factor.

The name. Ah, the name! "I finished my first book seventy-six years ago," George Bernard Shaw once remarked. "I offered it to every publisher on the Englishspeaking earth I had ever heard of. Their refusals were unanimous: and it did not get into print until, fifty years later, publishers would publish anything that had my name on it."[15] Once Stephen Crane's *The Red Badge of Courage* was a success, his first novel, *Maggie: A Girl of the Streets*, which had sold a grand total of one hundred copies, was reissued and became a hit. As Stephen King noted about his pseudonym, Richard Bachman, "The fact that *Thinner* did 28,000 copies when Bachman was the author and 280,000 copies when Steve King became the author, might tell you something, huh?"[16]

The problem, though, is not just manuscripts by unknown, "no-name" authors. Most name authors have experienced the same frustrating vagaries of rejection.

In 1949, when he was finishing work on a novel, William Shirer sat down with his editor, who asked him what he planned to write next.

"For once in my life," Shirer replied, "I not only know what I'm going to write; I even know the title. It's going to be called *The Rise and Fall of the Third Reich*."

"Bill, please God," his editor whined, "don't ask us to publish a book called *The Rise and Fall of the Third Reich*."

"Will you put that in writing?" Shirer asked.

Yes, he certainly would. That day, the editor dashed off a letter to Shirer stating that his publishing house was not interested in such a book.[17]

Shirer shopped the book around to other houses, but it met with no enthusiasm. At last, Simon & Schuster agreed to take a chance, and rather reluctantly handed Shirer an advance of $10,000, which had to last the ten years it would take to complete the manuscript. Upon publication, Simon & Schuster was still unenthusiastic. The first printing was small, and the company's book salesmen expressed their concern that they couldn't dispose of even that number of books. An editor at Simon & Schuster gently advised Shirer: "You'd better think of making your money somewhere else."[18]

The book, of course, was a huge best-seller, and became the all-time best-seller of the Book-of-the-Month Club.

Nevertheless ... nevertheless. In 1991, the publisher of William Shirer's final volume of memoirs, *A Native's Return*, refused to run post-review ads for the book, so Shirer paid for them himself. And Little, Brown turned down his proposal for his next book, *The Last Days of Tolstoi*. The octogenarian author seemed unfazed; Little, Brown had also had the opacity to reject one of his earlier books: *The Rise and Fall of the Third Reich*.

As great a writer as Henry James had a hard time finding an outlet for his work. After *The Portrait of a Lady*, his next two novels were commercial disasters, and the *Atlantic* rejected his short story "The Pupil." The commercial success of hack writers drove him wild. "What you tell me of the success of [Frances Marion] Crawford's last novel sickens and almost paralyzes me," he wrote to the editor of the *Atlantic*.[19]

Not even Nobel Prize winners are exempt from rejection. "All my life I have received rejection," said Isaac Bashevis Singer, "before I won the Nobel Prize and after."[20] Saul Bellow, another Nobel laureate, still on occasion has his short stories rejected. "I discovered that rejections are not altogether a bad thing. They teach a writer to rely on his own judgment and to say in his heart of hearts, 'To hell with you.'" *The New Yorker*, for instance, turned down his short story "Cousins." "One would think that after 40 years in the trade one could at least expect *The New Yorker* to publish a story like that. I was astonished. Then I was indignant. Then I said, 'The hell with them.'"[21]

John Cheever, even after recognition as one of the twentieth-century masters of the short story, had the same problem with *The New Yorker*. As he wrote to a friend in a letter from October of 1965:

> I wrote a short story, a couple of weeks ago, the first in over a year, and sent it to the New Yorker. Silence. At dusk on

Saturday a fiction editor appeared here, looked at me sadly, patted me gently, said that the story was a ghastly failure and implied that I had lost my marbles. The story went to the SEP [*Saturday Evening Post*] on Monday who took exactly ten minutes to pick it up for three thousand. This cheered me.[22]

Seven years later, it was still the same:

The New Yorker turned down my new story. Esquire wants to buy it but they'll only pay fifteen hundred. Considering the length of time it took, this is less than Susie [his daughter] makes on the Tarrytown paper. Harpers is out and the Atlantic still doesn't know about orgasms and that's that.[23]

At least an established writer secure enough in his own abilities can have a little fun with rejection and go down in style, pumping out a few rounds as he spirals to earth. Vladimir Nabokov's letter to Edward Weeks, the editor of the *Atlantic Monthly* who declined to publish a section of Nabokov's memoirs, is the kind of letter every rejected writer would like to let fly at his tormentor:

Dear Weeks,

I have just received your letter of September 20 [1948] and can only excuse its contents by assuming that you were in your cups when you wrote it.... I never send editors anything that I consider to be of inferior quality. In fact, the piece I sent you is better than those I have published in the New Yorker so far. Your letter is so silly *and* rude that I do not think I want to have anything to do with you or the Atlantic any more. I am sending you a checque for $800 and shall send the rest as soon as I am able to.[24]

Three years later, in a letter to *The New Yorker's* Katharine A. White, who had rejected one of his stories, Nabokov squeezed out another round: "I am really very disappointed that you, such a subtle and loving reader, should not have seen the inner scheme of my story.... I am really quite depressed by the whole business."[25] Incidentally, on August 22, 1953, fifty-four year old Nabokov wrote to the Burma-Vita Company to offer them, of all things, a jingle for the Burma Shave roadside signs. "If you think you can use it, please send checque to address given above." It was not accepted.[26]

What is most amusing is not so much that so many of the classics or most popular books were rejected, or that they were rejected time and again, but rather the way the editors rejected them with pious pontifications justifying their misguided decisions.

Dr. Charles M. Sheldon, the author of *In His Steps*, which was published in 1897 and which sold some 30,000,000 copies worldwide, was turned down by the first two publishers he approached who told him that "the public was not interested in a religious story."[27] Of *The Diary of Anne Frank*, a rejecting editor wrote: "The girl doesn't, it seems to me, have a special perception or feeling which would lift that book above the 'curiosity' level."[28] About Julia Child's *Mastering the Art of French Cooking*: "What we envisage as saleable ... is perhaps a series of small books devoted to particular portions of the meal.... We also feel that such a series should meet a rigorous standard of simplicity and compactness, certainly less elaborate than your present volumes, which, although we are sure are foolproof, are undeniably demanding in the time and focus of the cook, who is so apt to be mother, nurse, chauffeur and cleaner as well."[29] Bruce Catton had published his first book, *War Lords of Washington*, to what he called "bad reviews and bad sales. Another book like that would not satisfy my need to write a book people would read, admire, and react warmly to—a story!"[30] He set about writing a nonfiction account of the Army of the Potomac, but was told by Harcourt Brace, where he submitted the completed manuscript, that it was impossible to sell Civil War books. That verdict was repeated at another house before, at last, Doubleday brought out *Mr. Lincoln's Army*, the first volume of Catton's famous Civil War series. One suspects that James McPherson more recently might have heard that same verdict — it's impossible to sell Civil War books — before his *Battle Cry of Freedom* was published and hit the best-seller lists, and that Ken Burns heard it before his *The Civil War* became a smash mini-series and best-seller, and that today an author would hear it if he proposed a Civil War book to a publisher.

Publishers are the censors of what books the public will or will not see. Manuscripts that in their estimation will be unpopular or unprofitable books will never see the light of day. Anything new — anything unique, which admittedly is going to include some pretty dreadful stuff as well as some works of genius — is likely to stymie an editor, who can't compare it to something already published. When editors must depend on intuition, on hunches, on educated guesses, on leaps of faith, they can go off the deep end. As John Gardner wrote: "One should fight like the devil the temptation to think well of editors.... By the nature of their profession they read too much, with the result they grow jaded and cannot recognize talent though it dances in front of their eyes."[31]

It is not surprising that James Joyce's *Dubliners* was turned down by twenty-two publishers. Dr. Seuss's first story for children, *And to Think That I Saw It on Mulberry Street*, was rejected by twenty-seven publishers as being silly and nonsensical, and "too different from other juveniles on the market to warrant its selling."[32]

An editor wrote of Norman Mailer's *The Naked and the Dead*: "All other considerations which this book presents are subsidiary to the problem posed by the profanity and obscenity of its dialogue. In my opinion it is barely publishable."[33]

Forty editors over a five-year period passed on the opportunity to publish Vladimir Nabokov's *Lolita* (which, when finally published, sold more copies more quickly than any book since *Gone with the Wind*). One editor wrote: "It should be, and probably has been, told to a psychoanalyst, and it has been elaborated into a novel which contains some wonderful writing, but it is overwhelmingly nauseating, even to an enlightened Freudian. To the public, it will be revolting. It will not sell, and it will do immeasurable harm to a growing reputation.... I can see no possible cause could be served by its publication now. I recommend that it be buried under a stone for a thousand years."[34] (Some thirty-five years later, *Lolita* is alive and well; one suspects that that particular unknown editor, whoever he or she might once have been, is neither.)

Can these way-off-base pontifications be blamed on a lack of intelligence? of literary insight? of artistic sensitivity? Maybe sometimes.

For many years, Whitney Darrow ran the trade department at Scribner. Charles Scribner, Jr., wrote of him:

> Unfortunately, his pronounced skepticism about literature in general undermined his credibility. He was so loudly unsympathetic to many of our important literary works that

his more justifiable criticisms of the firm went unheeded. His lack of competence in literature made him useless as an adviser. He complained, for example, that Marcia Davenport's last novel, "The Constant Image," was a dirty book because it described an extra-marital affair in Milan. He thought Hemingway's "Old Man and the Sea" was just a book about catching a fish; he couldn't understand how it would sell. And when Marjorie Kinnan Rawlings' novel "The Yearling" was published in 1938, he considered it a juvenile book and thought it was ridiculous to be publishing it on our adult list.[35]

That was the head of Scribner's trade department.

But misguided rejections and the accompanying pontifications certainly can't always be blamed on a lack of intelligence, literary insight or artistic sensitivity. Before becoming a full-time writer (who claims never to have had any of his work rejected), William Styron was an editorial assistant for McGraw-Hill, where he was "forced to plow my way daily through fiction and nonfiction of the humblest quality." Now, one would assume that the young man who became the great author would have done his plowing with special insight. Not necessarily so. One manuscript he rejected with a reader's report stating, "The idea of men adrift on a raft does have a certain appeal, but for the most part this is a long, solemn and tedious Pacific voyage." This was his considered assessment of Thor Heyerdahl's *Kon-Tiki*. "Maybe a university press would buy it, but it is definitely not for us," he concluded, painting himself even more completely into the corner of one of publishing's greatest blunders by helpfully suggesting that perhaps it was suitable for abridgement in the *National Geographic*. Years later, Styron said, "Watching this book remain first on the bestseller list for unbelievable week after week [thirty-three to be exact, a near record], I was able to rationalize my blindness saying that if McGraw-Hill had paid me more than 90 cents an hour I might have been more sensitive to the nexus between good books and filthy lucre."[36]

No, these outlandish rejections are not, by and large, the calls of literary numbskulls. Rather, it seems often a matter of the right book falling into the wrong hands, or falling into the right hands at the wrong time. Under the pressure of making a decision, it is all too easy to reject a proposal or manuscript because it is simply not one's cup of tea. *Kon-Tiki* was not a book that appealed to Styron; what he could not fathom at that time was that a book that did not appeal to his interests would appeal to hundreds of thousands of other readers.

Although he admits that he never thought of it as best-seller material, Robert Giroux had in his hands the manuscript of J.D. Salinger's *The Catcher in the Rye*, which he brought to his boss at Harcourt Brace. "I didn't realize what big trouble I was in until, after he'd read it, he said, 'Is Holden Caulfield supposed to be crazy?' He also told me he'd given the typescript to one of our textbook editors to read. I said, '*Textbook*, what has that to do with it?' 'It's about a preppie, isn't it?'" his boss replied.[37] The textbook editor didn't like it, and Harcourt Brace passed. Here the right book had clearly fallen into the wrong hands.

Simon & Schuster rather reluctantly ordered a printing of a few thousand copies of John Lennon's *In His Own Write*, not perceiving what Beatlemania would mean for the sales of the book. When the onslaught of orders materialized, the publisher turned on its full promotion machine to pump sales, before realizing that nothing could influence these buying patterns: The book had a life of its own. Beatlemania had been outside of the understanding of Simon & Schuster's Robert Gottlieb, who threw up his hands: "This is like standing on a beach and saying to the waves, 'Now come in, now go out.' It's senseless. Let's quit and continue to enjoy it and turn our attention to things upon which we can have an effect."[38]

Even Phyllis Grann, Putnam's president with the enviable nose for best-sellers, can at times call them wrong. "You turn down commercial books," she once said. "You're too tired that night or you're stupid. But not deliberately.... Every year there is a book on the lists that is killing me, because I was so stupid that I didn't think it would work."[39]

Although reluctant to lead the world to a new author, publishers excel at playing follow the leader. Once their eyes are opened by someone else, they see the light.

The young Ernest Hemingway did not have an easy time finding a publisher who appreciated what later would be recognized as a revolutionary prose style. "I had not been worrying, I thought. I knew the stories were good and someone would publish them finally at home. When I stopped doing newspaper work I was sure the stories were going to be published. But every one I sent out came back."[40] A friend of Hemingway's, an agent for the Hearst group of American magazines in Europe, had read a draft of Hemingway's short story "Fifty Grand" and sent it on to his boss, Ray Long, with a glowing letter of praise. Long read the story. "It left me cold. Absolutely cold. For the life of me I couldn't see why my associate had got so excited about it. I rejected the story."[41] The story made its way on to Scribner, where Max Perkins suggested it be cut. No cutting, Hemingway insisted, and snatched it back (even though, as he said, "I could use the 250 I could have gotten by cutting it"[42]). He sent it on to the *Saturday Evening Post,* which rejected it, and to *Collier's,* which also passed. Some months later, Ray Long picked up the *Atlantic* and saw the story there. Curious as to how the magazine had shaped it, he began to read. The *Atlantic,* he realized, hadn't shaped it at all; the story was just as Hemingway had written it. And as he read it, the moment he saw the story set in type, Ray Long saw in it "what the others, myself heading the list, had overlooked." The next day, he wired his European agent to ask Hemingway "to forgive me for the stupidest blunder I'd ever made as an editor. For 'Fifty Grand' was one of the best short stories that ever came to my hands."[43]

John Grisham's first novel, *A Time to Kill,* was rejected by twenty-eight publishers before being published by Wynwood Press and selling, very slowly, the 5,000 copies typical for a first novel. His second novel, *The Firm,* was facing a similar string of rejections until some copies made their way to movie producers, who went wild. Paramount paid $600,000 for the unpublished novel. "After that," as the author explains it, "eighteen publishers begged for the chance to publish it. It was a hoot."[44] Ah, the wonders of confirmation, of someone saying to a publisher, "Yes, sleep well, your judgment was correct." P.S.: With the dazzling success of *The Firm* and his next novel, *The Pelican Brief,* Grisham's publishers brought out a paperback edition of *A Time to Kill,* which stayed atop the *New York Times* paperback best-sellers list for over a year. (First editions of the hardcover no one wanted when first published now go for $3,900.)

Now, in even a quasi-rational world, a world with just a bit of rational fiber, a book accepted for publication by one quality publisher should receive some more nibbles, or maybe even a small showing of interest, from a few others. But of course it doesn't work that way.

When Mary Cahill's agent sent the manuscript of her first novel, *Carpool: A Novel of Suburban Frustration*, to three publishers in 1990 and received three rejections, the agent told Mrs. Cahill, "Put it in the drawer and write something else."

"I said, 'Hell, who quits after three lousy rejections?'"[45]

Mrs. Cahill was unsuccessful in her quest for a new agent, and so she had the manuscript copied and sent it out herself to seven publishers. Six quickly wrote back and said, no way; the seventh, Random House, accepted it. The Literary Guild made it its main selection, and Viacom bought the rights to make it a television movie.

How long should a writer sustain his belief that he is right and the rest of the world is wrong? How long can a writer maintain such a belief without concluding that he is either lacking in talent or crazy? "No pain, no gain" might be a good philosophy, but how long can a writer carry on while receiving nothing but rejection? For how long can he maintain the belief in himself that is necessary to be able to write? How many times does a shocked rat repeat the behavior that caused the shock before it gives up?

Not for very long, Robert Louis Stevenson believed: "Human nature has certain rights; instinct — the instinct of self-preservation — forbids that any man (cheered and supported by the consciousness of no previous victory) should endure the miseries of unsuccessful literary toil beyond a period to be measured in weeks. There must be something for hope to feed upon."[46] As Joyce Carol Oates has put it: "The only question for most writers must be: when to give up? — or should one *never* give up?"[47]

"Write without pay until somebody offers pay," Mark Twain advised. "If nobody offers within three years, the candidate may look upon this as the sign that sawing wood is what he was intended for."[48]

Bernard Malamud's advice was: "Teach yourself to work in uncertainty. Many writers are anxious when they begin, or try something new. Even Matisse painted some of his fauvist pictures in anxiety. Maybe that helped him to simplify. Character, discipline, negative capability count. Write, complete, revise. If it doesn't work begin something else."

"And if it doesn't work twenty or thirty times?" he was asked.

"You live your life as best you can," was his response.[49]
Had certain authors thrown in the towel after either three years or twenty or thirty times, the world would have been deprived of many books which proved immensely popular. John Toland was forty-two and had seen his six novels rejected, twenty-five plays fail to reach production, and over ninety short stories turned down before his first book was accepted for publication. The success of his nonfiction best-sellers like *Battle: The Story of the Bulge, But Not in Shame, The Dillinger Days, The Last 100 Days, Adolf Hitler*, and the Pulitzer Prize–winning *The Rising Sun* raises questions about the soundness of Twain's and Malamud's guidelines.

With a phone call explaining, "Look, they're not interested in a talking seagull,"[50] Richard Bach's exhausted agent returned to him the manuscript of *Jonathan Livingston Seagull* after a flock of more than twenty rejections from publishers who could not see that here was that decade's slim volume of obvious truths — like Kahlil Gibran's *The Prophet* before it and Robert Fulghum's *All I Really Need to Know I Learned in Kindergarten* after it — that would sell and sell and sell. In the same day's mail was a letter from an editor at Macmillan asking Bach if he had a book that Macmillan might be interested in. Well, yes, he did. The book was launched with no advertising budget, received few reviews *(Publishers Weekly* called it "ickypoo"[51]), building word of mouth over eighteen months and then exploding, with sales soaring from 5,000 copies a week to an unbelievable 60,000 a day.

What if that letter from Macmillan had never come to Richard Bach? What if Eudora Welty had not had an agent who stood by her for the six years it took to get one of her stories published in a national magazine and the fifteen years it took for either of them to earn any real money from her writing? "This is just a little note of woe to tell you we are having the damnedest time trying to sell your stories," Diarmuid Russell wrote to Eudora Welty in 1940. "I think the editors are just about crazy and in my own mind I have determined that if all efforts fail I would like to keep your stories here, get some more stories from you, and then when your reputation has been established, make all the mad editors pay through the nose for the stories they had formerly turned down."[52] Later, when their luck was still not running, he added: "Editors are kind of stupid people, and it takes some time for merit to dawn on them for most of their time is concerned with what is openly commercial."[53]

"I don't speak of the future much," Welty once responded, "but some day I swear I will write something, I don't know what, that is so fortuitously and so carefully done (both) that with the push from you it will simply leap over the boundary the publishers have set up to keep it out, and suddenly like magic turn into something both good and profit-making, and we will all be astonished and rich, and I couldn't say which the more."[54] Welty depended on her agent to keep her "bearings"[55] and his confidence in her work caused her "outreaching"[56] as she put it: to try to go beyond the achievements of her previous stories.

What if Diarmuid Russell had not been there for Eudora Welty? What if that letter from Macmillan had never come along to Richard Bach? These and other stories have happy endings, but are such happy endings guaranteed for those who don't give up, who stay committed, who hold that belief that dreams come true? What is always so striking in these stories is how fragile their happy endings are.

Publishers are the ultimate guardians of the gates, both directly by their choice of the books they will allow the public to read, and indirectly — but just as significantly — by the chilling effect their rejections may have on an author's confidence and hence his creativity and productivity.

Acceptance can do wonders for a writer's self-confidence and his ability to work. Remember Scott Fitzgerald running along the streets of St. Paul to tell one and all that his novel, *This Side of Paradise*, was to be published by Scribner. Or the young Truman Capote: "Of course no writers ever forget their first acceptance. One fine day when I was seventeen I had my first, second and third, all in the same morning's mail. Oh, I'm here to tell you, dizzy with excitement is no mere phrase!"[57] John Updike, whose first short story was accepted by *The New Yorker* the month of his graduation from college, spoke of the moment as "the ecstatic breakthrough of my literary life."[58] Each had found acceptance; each had taken a pop of that ultimate feel-good aphrodisiac; each was off to the races.

On the other hand, as author Cynthia Ozick, who waited almost twenty years for her first acceptance, has said: "One can never catch up to the confidence early publication instills; the missed train leaves a permanent loss."[59] The emotional and creative toll that rejection can take on a writer is a heavy one. "You can imagine the effect of delay on an author's estimate of his work,"[60] Henry David Thoreau wrote to a friend after his first book had been repeatedly rejected by publishers. Scott Turow spent four years on a novel that was turned down by twenty-five publishers. "I was freaked out. The failure made me realize that I wasn't one-tenth the writer I hoped to be. I could not sustain the vision of myself as a writer only." And so he went on to law school (before eventually writing *Presumed Innocent*), unhappy that he had "renounced" a writing career.[61] Helen Hooven Santmyer was like someone who had picked the winning lottery numbers when she was in her thirties and was not able to turn them in until she was eighty-eight. Had her "*...And Ladies of the Club*" achieved when she was younger the success it ultimately did, would she have been a more prolific author? John Kennedy Toole sat there with a Pulitzer Prize–winning manuscript that no one would publish; he first lost his belief in all possibility, and then lost his life. Surely there are others out there who didn't make it; others who, one way or another, threw in the towel and left magnificent manuscripts behind.

What did he think he'd be if he had not become an author, Stephen King once was asked.

He wasn't having an easy time of it before *Carrie* was accepted for publication. He and his wife were struggling to make ends meet with his teaching salary and her work at a Dunkin' Donuts, King coming home after school to squeeze into their trailer's furnace room and type on his wife's Olivetti portable perched on a child's desk. "I wish I could say today that I bravely shook my fist in the face of adversity and carried on undaunted but I can't."[62] He began drinking too much, betting recklessly in poker and pool with what little money they had. Their marriage was on the rocks. So what would he have been if *Carrie* had not saved the day (eight or nine years after he completed the manuscript)? Maybe a "mildly embittered high school English teacher" was his first response. And then he added, "On the other hand, I might very well have ended up there in the Texas tower with Charlie Whitman, working out my demons with a high-powered telescopic rifle instead of a word processor. I mean, I know that guy Whitman. My writing has kept me out of that tower."[63]

His *published* writing, he might have added.

CHAPTER 6

We're All Connected

*I*t's pretty well conceded that writing can't be taught. Nevertheless, aspiring writers — and indeed, most writers — need the help
of other writers to make the publishing process work. Unfortunately,
that help is rarely forthcoming.

To be sure, there are bright examples of authors who have lent
a helping hand. Ezra Pound performed major surgery on T.S. Eliot's
"The Waste Land." Hemingway sat at the feet of Gertrude Stein,
drinking her natural distilled liqueurs made "from purple plums, yellow plums or wild raspberries"[1] and eating her cakes and learning
about "the wonderful rhythms in prose."[2] Fitzgerald wrote to his
editor, Max Perkins: "This is to tell you about a young man named
Ernest Hemingway, who lives in Paris (an American), writes for the
Transatlantic Review and has a brilliant future."[3] Malcolm Cowley,
then a junior editor at *The New Republic*, advised the still teenaged
John Cheever: "Tomorrow, write a story of one thousand words. Sunday, write another, and Monday write another, three and a half pages,
and do the same thing on Tuesday. Bring them all in on Wednesday
and I'll see if I can't get you some money."[4] Dashiell Hammett helped
Lillian Hellman with her first play. Booth Tarkington sat with his
friend Kenneth Roberts evening after evening, helping him edit his
books rather than "playing backgammon … and getting beaten most
of the time."[5] John Barth taught for forty years "out of my attach-
ment to university life and the pleasures of coaching a small group
of selected advanced apprentices."[6] James Michener donated gener-
ously to graduate writing schools and programs that support aspiring writers.

Such examples of one writer helping another shine like beacons
through the dark, dismal night of author envy. "Writers today seldom

wish other writers well," Saul Bellow once noted.[7] William Wycherly was a little more direct: "Poets, like whores, are only hated by each other."[8] Ah, now we're getting there! He might well have expanded his aphorism to include not just poets, but all writers. With their special talents, they often turn this curious hatred into an art form on which they lavish more attention than on their writing.

Truman Capote was an easy mark. "Truman Capote has made lying an art," mused Gore Vidal — "a *minor* art." Tennessee Williams opined that "I think you judge Truman a bit too charitably when you call him a child: he is more like a sweetly vicious old lady."[9] To Katherine Anne Porter he was nothing but "the pimple on the face of American literature."[10] But Truman was himself a master of the cat fight, and sharpened his claws on each of his contemporaries.

On Saul Bellow: "I've known Saul Bellow since the very beginning of Saul Bellow and I think he's a dull man and a dull writer. Saul Bellow is a nothing writer."[11]

Philip Roth: "...quite funny in a living room but ... forget it."

Bernard Malamud: "Unreadable."

James Michener: "He's never written anything that would remotely interest me. Why on earth would I be interested in reading a book called *Chesapeake*?"[12]

Gore Vidal: "Gore has never written anything that anybody will remember. Talk about fifty years from today, they won't remember it ten years from its last paperback edition. See, Gore has literally never written a masterpiece."[13]

John Updike: "I hate him. Everything about him bores me."[14]

Joyce Carol Oates: "She's a joke monster who ought to be beheaded in a public auditorium or in Shea or in a field with hundreds of thousands.... To see her is to loathe her. To read her is to absolutely vomit."[15]

Truman Capote used the forum of "The Tonight Show" to ridicule Jacqueline Susann's *Valley of the Dolls* at the time it was getting as much attention as his *In Cold Blood*. Susann, on her next appearance, rolled out her best Truman Capote impersonation. Capote then let it be known that he believed that Susann looked "like a truck driver in drag,"[16] whereupon Susann threatened to sue him for one million dollars. "She was told she had better drop that lawsuit," Capote cackled, "because all they had to do is bring ten truck drivers into court and put them on the witness stand and you've lost your case. Because she *did* look like a truck driver in drag!"[17]

Capote, of course, did not originate this black art form, any more than he did the nonfiction novel. The habit of insulting one's fellow writers has been practiced for centuries and has even been known to bring out a writer's best skills. Plutarch lambasted Aristophanes, whose language, he said, "reeks of his miserable quackery: it is made up of the lowest and most miserable puns; he doesn't even please the people, and to men of judgment and honor he is intolerable; his arrogance is insufferable, and all honest men detest his malice."[18] Lord Byron had a few choice comments on the work of John Keats: "Such writing is mental masturbation — he is always fr-gg-g his Imagination. I don't mean he is indecent, but viciously soliciting his own ideas into a state, which is neither poetry nor anything else but a Bedlam vision produced by raw pork and opium."[19] George Bernard Shaw was never one to beat around the bush: "With the single exception of Homer, there is no eminent writer, not even Sir Walter Scott, whom I can despise so entirely as I despise William Shakespeare when I measure my mind against his."[20]

Another century, another author: "So you've been reviewing Edith Sitwell's latest piece of virgin dung, have you?" Dylan Thomas wrote. "Isn't she a poisonous thing of a woman, lying, concealing, flipping, plagiarizing, misquoting and being as clever a crooked literary publicist as ever."[21] Kindly, grandfatherly old Robert Frost drew some poisonous barbs: "He was a very mean man," Capote believed. "Everybody that ever knew him at all will tell you that."[22] And *very* mean he must have been, for in comparison, Capote said of Hemingway, "There was a mean man."[23] Maybe he was on to something about Frost, for James Dickey heartily concurred: "If it were thought that anything I wrote was influenced by Robert Frost, I would take that particular work of mine, shred it, and flush it down the toilet, hoping not to clog the pipes. A more sententious, hold-forth old bore, who expected every hero-worshiping adenoidal little twerp of a student-poet to hang on his every word I never saw."[24]

William Faulkner called Henry James "the nicest old lady I ever met." Of Faulkner, Norman Mailer said: "Faulkner said more asinine things than any other major American writer. I can't remember a single interesting remark Faulkner ever made." James Dickey called

Mailer "a second-rate writer [who] will sit around wondering what on earth it is that Hemingway had that Mailer might possibly be able to get."[25]

Vladimir Nabokov turned his contempt on American literary lights D.H. Lawrence and Ezra Pound: "I must fight a suspicion of conspiracy against my brain, when I see blandly accepted as 'great literature' by critics and fellow authors Lady Chatterley's copulations or the pretentious nonsense of Mr. Pound, that total fake."[26]

Yes, authors have elevated their scratching to an art form, though not always high art. "I loathe you," D.H. Lawrence wrote to Katherine Mansfield. "You revolt me stewing in your consumption.... The Italians were quite right to have nothing to do with you. You are a loathsome reptile — I hope you will die."[27] Okay, so much for artistic sophistication.

Ernest Hemingway's carefully controlled style slipped a tad when he got to talking about the competition. "I'll never forget Sinclair Lewis calling To Have etc. [*To Have and Have Not*] a 'thin screaming of only 67,000 words!' May have the number of words wrong. He himself writes a hoarse scream of never less than 120,000. But if I wrote as sloppily and shitily as that freckled prick I could write five thousand words a day year in and year out."[28] Thomas Wolfe's *Of Time and the River*, Hemingway reported to Max Perkins, their common editor, was "something over 60 per cent shit."[29] He didn't seem to admire James Jones's *From Here to Eternity* either. To Charles Scribner, their mutual publisher, Hemingway wrote:

> To me he is an enormously skillful fuck-up and his book will do great damage to our country. Probably I should re-read it again to give you a truer answer. But I do not have to eat an entire bowl of scabs to know they are scabs; nor suck a boil to know it is a boil; nor swim through a river of snot to know it is snot. I hope he kills himself as soon as it does not damage his or your sales. If you give him a literary tea you might ask him to drain a bucket of snot and then suck the pus out of a dead nigger's ear.... Best always, Ernest.[30]

Jacqueline Susann once said, "I've been a fan of writers all my life. I thought when I became a writer, it would be 'Hello Gore, hello Truman.'" It of course was not, with Capote comparing her to that

68

truck driver, and Gore Vidal quipping, "She doesn't write, she types."[31]

Isn't there any way one author may *help* another?

Let's focus on just one way: by writing a blurb for the author's new book. A few words of endorsement can be used on the book jacket, or in advertising, or, indeed, to convince a publisher to publish the book.

The right testimonial can yank a book out of the pack. When Donald Fine was the head of Arbor House, he published a book called *The City Primeval* by the then unknown Elmore Leonard, sending galleys to John D. MacDonald for an endorsement. "MacDonald called me and asked, 'Who is that guy? He's terrific' and we used that line in our advertising."[32] William Least Heat Moon has credited the success of his *Blue Highways*, which became a best-seller, to Pulitzer Prize winner Robert Penn Warren, who called it "a masterpiece." Christina Stead's *The Man Who Loved Children* was published in 1940 by Simon & Schuster, received mediocre reviews, and had tepid sales before it drifted into oblivion, until republished in 1965 by Holt, Rinehart, and Winston. The new publishers included a preface by the distinguished poet and critic Randall Jarrell, who said it was "as plainly good as *War and Peace* and *Crime and Punishment* and *Remembrance of Things Past* are plainly great."[33] Other reviewers joined the parade, and the book achieved national acclaim and commensurate sales.

Until recently it's been difficult to place a value on such blurbs. But now we know that the imprimatur of the right author is worth a bundle.

In 1991, John Le Carré submitted a telegram endorsing a first novel, *Just Killing Time* by Derek V. Goodwin, calling this spy novel a "literary gem." "Read this celebration of the human spirit," he wrote. "I have still not emerged from its awesome power and delightful spell." At the same time, Joseph Wambaugh submitted a letter praising the book: "This is a chillingly authentic account that could only have been produced by a career investigator who also happens to be a masterful writer. Hard-hitting, yet restrained.... For years it has been a standing rule of mine not to make such endorsements. You have produced that exceedingly rare book." Derek Goodwin's agent submitted these prize endorsements at the auction for the book, which led eight major publishers to bid on it. Simon & Schuster came in with the winning bid of $920,000, just about a record then for a first novel by an unknown author.

Several days later, both Mr. Le Carré and Mr. Wambaugh issued indignant public statements that they had never seen or heard of the book or its author, and that the recommendations attributed to them were fraudulent.[34]

Within two weeks, Simon & Schuster announced that it would not publish *Just Killing Time*. To Simon & Schuster, the value of those two endorsements apparently was precisely $920,000, for without them, the worth of the manuscript dropped to zero. Not $250,000. Not $10,000. Zero. Bantam Books valued the two endorsements slightly less, for it had bid $850,000 at the initial auction, and was the runner up to Simon & Schuster. When Simon & Schuster dropped the book, Bantam did not jump in to pick it up. Either these publishers were in a snit about being hoodwinked, or they had concluded that the book had no inherent value, that it was only those two blurbs that gave it a value of from $850,000 to $920,000. Evidently those endorsements from Mr. Le Carré and Mr. Wambaugh must have been valued by Simon & Schuster and Bantam at well over $100,000 per sentence.

But wait: An advance is just the beginning. Assuming that type of advance had been paid, the book would have been made a bestseller by Simon & Schuster or Bantam — no doubt about it, with that sort of investment — and earned its author millions more from royalties, book club deals, audio tapes, television projects, the works. Those two blurbs, therefore, were worth more than a million bucks.

Yes, blurbs can work mighty powerful magic. If there ever were any doubts about that, Tom Clancy's fairy tale should have erased them forever.

Clancy was a thirty-four-year-old insurance agent in Owings, Maryland, with a wife and four kids, who every weekend banged away on an IBM Selectric set on the dining room table, working on what he hoped would be a novel, as his wife nagged him not to waste his time and to get out there and hustle more insurance business. Clancy's only other writing, a three-page article about the MX missile, had been published in a magazine put out by the Naval Institute of Annapolis, Maryland. In February of 1983, when he finished his book, he therefore took his manuscript to the Naval Institute Press, which published naval history and naval textbooks, yes, but fiction? Never.

If you didn't know the ending, you would see it coming, wouldn't you? The form rejection letter from the press saying thank you, but we don't publish fiction. Never have, never will, dummy, so do your homework and submit your stupid manuscript to an appropriate publisher. Instead, for some curious reason — which was Clancy's first draw on blind luck — the press figured it would take a look and had a veteran submariner, Captain John Byron, read the manuscript. Captain Byron found it full of errors, scribbled "crap" across page after page, and noted that "Mr. Clancy has tackled a subject that cannot be discussed accurately at an unclassified level,"[35] recommending that the press not publish. Okay, now it's coming, right? Dear Mr. Clancy, thanks but no thanks.

But no. For some reason, miracles — yes, miracles — do happen, and sometimes in twos. The press accepted for publication *The Hunt for Red October* and paid Mr. Clancy a $5,000 advance, which pleased him no end. He hoped that the book might sell 5,000 copies. The Naval Institute Press ordered a first printing of an unheard of 15,000 (draw three on luck; was someone at the press stoned or something? It was now committed to pushing the book) and set a publication date of October 1984.

Perhaps at last realizing how far out on the limb it had stepped, the press opened wide its throttle to promote this book in a way one suspects it never in its history had promoted another book. "We started with a Washington strategy," explained Tom Epley, the director of the press. "We thought the book would appeal to military people, the military-industrial complex. We sent advance copies to a lot of government officials, and our sales force worked hard to get copies in the Washington and Baltimore bookstores. We got a story in *The Washington Post* about this being our first novel." The *Post* ran an enthusiastic review, calling the book "breathlessly exciting," and within a month it was climbing the *Post*'s Washington, D.C., bestseller list.

"We also had a subsidiary rights strategy," Epley continued. "We had to get the wholesale and bookstore chains to take seriously a first novel about a submarine. So, before publication, we auctioned the paperback rights to Berkley Books for $49,500, auctioned book-club rights to the Literary Guild's Military Book Club, and auctioned off the English rights. Then we used those sales to force the trade to pay attention."[36] This guy knew what he was doing. But he wasn't finished. Somehow the press obtained blurbs from best-selling novelists Jack Higgins and Joseph Wambaugh. (Considering all the books with which those two novelists must have been bombarded by publishers hunting for blurbs, why would they even have cracked the cover of one from — you've got to be kidding! — the Naval Institute Press?) The press placed an ad in the *New York Times*, and the book received a favorable review in the *San Francisco Chronicle* that helped boost it onto the best-seller list in that city. Six months after publication, the book had sold an astounding 45,000 copies.

Now right here, even before the mother of all miracles happened, something very unusual had taken place.

And then … a friend of Ronald Reagan gave a copy of *The Hunt for Red October* to the president for Christmas. Of all the books that must have been under the White House Christmas tree that year, he picked up this one (why this one?), sat down to read it, finished it, and loved it. Word began circulating throughout Washington that the president had read *The Hunt* and was recommending it to everyone. *Time* ran an article reporting that the president was praising the novel as "the perfect yarn"[37] (what a puff! The press used it) and that officials of his administration were reading it. The Soviet embassy in Washington even ordered copies. Within several weeks, the book was a national best-seller, eventually selling over 365,000 copies in hardcover and 4,300,000 in paperback

It is, by the way, endorsements from outside of the book world — especially by a leader of the free world — that can have the most dramatic effect on sales. British publisher Michael Joseph recalled that one of his authors, Mary Webb, received consistent praise for her novels from all the influential reviewers, but her sales did not take off until Prime Minister Stanley Baldwin mentioned her books in an after-dinner speech. It was Theodore Roosevelt's public praise of *The Virginian* that jump-started its sales; Woodrow Wilson's recommendation of a whodunit, *The Middle Temple Murder*, that launched that book; and Franklin Roosevelt's recommendation of James Hilton's *Lost Horizon* that boosted its sales from 2,500 a year to 6,000 a week. Eleanor Roosevelt's mention of *Gone with the Wind* in her column "My Day"—"I can assure you that you will find Scarlett O'Hara an interesting character"—proved one of the most important mentions the book received. President Kennedy's praise for *The Guns of August* brought Barbara Tuchman out of the ranks of writers of history books and into the ranks of popular writers.

The moral of the story: If ever you support the winning presidential candidate, don't ask to be secretary of state or chief of staff or ambassador to the Court of St. James; ask only for a few words praising your next book. You don't even need those few words if the president doesn't really like your book or doesn't have time to read it; just have him hold it. When President Eisenhower was photographed reading a book called *What We Must Know About Communism*, sales went through the roof. In fact, you don't even need a president; Walter Mosley's mysteries took off when, in 1992, presidential candidate Bill Clinton on the campaign trail called Mosley his favorite writer of thrillers.

"What happened to me was pure dumb luck—I'm not the new Hemingway," Tom Clancy candidly commented about his remarkable transformation from about-to-turn-forty insurance agent to blockbuster novelist.[38] "President Reagan made *The Hunt for Red October* a best-seller."[39] It was as simple and as miraculous as that: "President Reagan made *The Hunt for Red October* a best-seller." And *The Hunt for Red October* made Tom Clancy much, *much* richer, with a $3,000,000 contract with Putnam for his next three books, *Red Storm Rising*, *Patriot Games* and *The Cardinal of the Kremlin*, and then a $4,000,000 contract for his next book, subject at the time of the signing of the contract unknown. (It would be *Clear and Present Danger*.) And then $15,000,000 for the next, *The Sum of All Fears*, and then, and then and then. Thirteen years after his first $5,000 advance from the Naval Institute Press, the son of a Baltimore mailman was earning over $100 million for two novels and their spinoffs.

For the daring act of plugging a first novel by an unknown author published by a definitely out-of-the-mainstream publisher, Ronald Reagan will always deserve a ranking among the greatest of all our presidents. But, come on; should presidents plug the same author twice? "What are you reading?" George Bush was asked several months into his presidency while on a weekend vacation at Kennebunkport,

Maine. Why, Tom Clancy's latest techno-thriller, *Clear and Present Danger*, was his reply, and he liked it so much he was recommending it to White House staffers.[40] With everything he touched turning to gold, Tom Clancy at that point had no need of a presidential nod, whereas one suspects there were a number of other authors out there at the time who did. For this reason, there should be legislation — if a constitutional amendment is necessary, so be it — that a president, or successive presidents of the United States, may not recommend the same author twice.

The enormous power of the right nod of approval again became evident in 1996 when television talk show host Oprah Winfrey started her monthly book club with a sleeper by Jacquelyn Mitchard called *The Deep End of the Ocean*. It instantly soared to the tops of the bestseller lists and stayed there week after week. Oprah repeated her magic each month; for example, Sarah Ban Breathnach's *Simple Abundance* found itself in the number one spot three weeks after the author's visit with Oprah. (The author was grateful and shrewd enough to dedicate her next book "For Oprah with Love. Thank You," which elicited another invitation to appear on her show.) Oprah even raised books from the dead. Toni Morrison's *Song of Solomon*, first published in 1977, hit the paperback best-seller lists again twenty years later in 1997 after Ms. Morrison's visit on the Oprah Winfrey show, and in fact, sold more copies than it had when the author was awarded the Nobel Prize for literature. Like the leader of a children's game of "Simon Says," when Oprah says, "Do this!" hundreds of thousands of viewers do, going to their local bookstores and buying the book she has recommended.

So, those ubiquitous "the greatest book since sliced bread" blurbs can be potent magic in the publishing world, and an author, if he or she chooses, can do a fellow author a powerful favor by agreeing to write a blurb for his book.

Writing is all about writers helping each other, if not directly, then surely indirectly. Samuel Taylor Coleridge said that writers borrow from writers who have gone before them "in a series of imitated imitations — shadows of shadows of a farthing-candle placed between two looking glasses."[41] That's what writing is — striving to go a step higher by building on the foundation laid by others. Sometimes that borrowing can be quite direct. Robert Louis Stevenson looked back

74

at the ease with which he wrote *Treasure Island* and realized his debt to other writers:

> No doubt the parrot once belonged to Robinson Crusoe. No doubt the skeleton is conveyed from Poe. I think little of these, they are trifles and details; and no man can hope to have a monopoly of skeletons or make a corner in talking birds. The stockade, I am told, is from "Masterman Ready." It may be, I care not a jot. These useful writers had fulfilled the poet's saying: departing, they had left behind them
>
>> "Footprints on the sands of time;
>> Footprints that perhaps another — "
>
> and I was the other! It is my debt to Washington Irving that exercises my conscience, and justly so, for I believe plagiarism was rarely carried farther. I chanced to pick up the "Tales of a Traveller" some years ago, with a view to an anthology of prose narrative, and the book flew up and struck me: Billy Bones, his chest, the company in the parlour, the whole inner spirit and a good deal of the material detail of my first chapters — all were there, all were the property of Washington Irving. But I had no guess of it then as I sat writing by the fireside, in what seemed the springtides of a somewhat pedestrian inspiration.[42]

Few would disagree, however, that the elements of *Treasure Island*, borrowed or not, achieved new and unique life in Stevenson's classic and so became his own. "Every novel which is truly written," Hemingway said, "contributes to the total knowledge which is there at the disposal of the next writer who comes."[43] In fact, he also said, "Some writers are only born to help another writer to write one sentence."[44]

"I'm always conscious that literature is, primarily, a chain of connection from the past to the present," Gore Vidal has noted.[45] And certainly a part of that chain is the work of one writer inspiring another, sometimes even inspiring someone to become a writer. Young Scott Fitzgerald was moved to try his hand at a novel after he started reading a book by Hugh Walpole. "One day I picked up one of his books while riding on a train from New York to Washington. After I had read about 100 pages I thought that 'if this fellow can get away with it as an author I can too.' His books seemed to me to be as bad as possible."[46] Twenty-year-old James Jones wrote to his brother: "What time I haven't been writing, I've been reading: Thomas Wolfe, if you know who he is.... In my opinion, little as it's worth, he is the greatest writer that has lived, Shakespeare included. He is a genius. That is the only way to describe him. And in reading of his childhood, his youth, and his struggles to get out of him, the things he wanted to say, I can find an almost exact parallel with myself. Of course details are different, but the general trend is practically the same."[47] James Jones never met Thomas Wolfe, never spoke to him, never corresponded with him; yet Wolfe's work spoke directly to Jones, and through that inspiration, Jones became another link in the chain of literature.

Indeed, every writer is indebted to other writers in some way, and most quite willingly acknowledge the importance of their literary forebears. "There are all sorts of weird ways consciousness is changed by literature," E.L. Doctorow has written. "Certainly, I can't imagine my mind, or the mind of any of us, without Chekhov, or Joyce, or Mark Twain. All the writers I've ever read or admired constitute my brain, in part, or deliver me to some point in civilization that I wouldn't have reached otherwise. I have to assume that this is true of most people."[48] It certainly seems to be.

"What writers influenced me as a young man?" Tennessee Williams asked himself rhetorically. "Chekhov! As a story writer? Chekhov!"[49] Chekhov was an influence, too, on Truman Capote, Neil Simon, Eudora Welty and Scott Fitzgerald, among others, and Ernest Hemingway always paid tribute not only to Chekhov but also to Turgenev, Tolstoy and Dostoyevsky. "In Dostoyevsky there were things believable and not to be believed, but some so true they changed you as you read them; frailty and madness, wickedness and saintliness, and the insanity of gambling were there to know as you knew the landscape and the roads in Turgenev, and the movement of troops, the terrain and the officers and the men and the fighting in Tolstoi."[50] It was Dostoyevsky and Tolstoy for James Jones and Joyce Carol Oates, and for William Faulkner, too. "I've read these books so often that I don't always begin at page one and read on to the end," Faulkner said. "I just read one scene, or about one character, just as you'd meet and talk to a friend for a few minutes."[51] And Twain, don't forget Mark Twain. Ernest Hemingway wrote in *Green Hills of Africa* that "all modern American literature comes from one book by Mark Twain called *Huckleberry Finn*.... It's the best book we've had. All American writing comes from that. There was nothing before. There has been nothing as good since."[52] William Faulkner agreed that Twain was the father of modern American writers, and Rebecca West "longed, when I was young, to write as well as Mark Twain. It's beautiful stuff and I always liked him."[53] And then there's Hemingway himself. "There's nobody writing, under a certain age, who wasn't influenced by Hemingway," author Robert Stone has said,[54] and James Jones, Ralph Ellison, John Hersey, Norman Mailer and innumerable others have paid homage to him. John Cheever remembered "walking down a street in Boston after reading a book of his, and finding the color of the sky, the faces of strangers, and the smells of the city heightened and dramatized.... He put down an immense vision of love and friendship, swallows and the sound of rain. There was never, in my time, anyone to compare with him."[55]

There can be no doubt about it: All writers are connected. Browsing through any of the journals of the Authors Guild or the National Writers Union and reading some of the author horror stories that fill their pages (to which every author could contribute his or her special favorites) should be enough to convince all authors of the importance of standing together, of helping one another. Authors who won't — and there are lots of them ("Writers can be the stinkers of all time, can't they?" asked Lillian Hellman[56]) — authors who won't are ninnies, for without a little help from a friend, a writer stands out there alone, and alone it's pretty tough to make the publishing process work without a healthy run of luck. As Paul Horgan declared: "Vanity and a spirit of competitiveness in the arts are not even childish — they are simply idiotic."[57]

Barbarians Through
the Gates

*T*he initial hurdle to selling books — and it's a Matterhorn of a hurdle — is that nobody reads. Selling books in the United States is like selling videotapes in a country where 75 percent of the population doesn't own a VCR, and 25 percent of the population that does, hasn't a clue how to operate them.

Much as we would like to consider ourselves a civilized and literate people, there is a staggering mass of evidence to the contrary.

According to the 1990 census, the population of the United States is 250 million, with an average age of 32.5 years. That's a lot of people of reading age. Yet in a slow season, the sale of 50,000 books may be enough to propel a new title onto the national best-sellers lists. The sale of one million hardcover books over the course of a year, representing a readership of less than one half of 1 percent of the American public, constitutes a runaway best-seller. At a time when the public is consuming tens of millions of newspapers, magazines and comic books each week, the average hardcover sales of recent super best-selling authors over the course of a year are 1.3 million for Tom Clancy, 1.2 million for Stephen King, 1.1 million for Danielle Steel, 850,000 for the venerable James Michener, 475,000 for Jackie Collins, 450,000 for John Le Carré, and 330,000 for Ken Follett.

Such figures have not increased all that much from what they were years ago — in 1923, for instance, when Walter Page, one of the founders of Doubleday Page, bemoaned the fact that "the masses even of intelligent folk have yet hardly fairly begun to buy books. Go where you will among the people and you will find few books — pitifully few."[1] The ten best-selling novels in the period from 1919 to 1927 sold from 140,000 to 814,000 copies each, with the top nonfiction titles in the period ranging from 44,000 to 1,000,000, not too far from today's puny figures. Keep in mind that the population of the United States in 1925 was 110,000,000 — less than half what it is today. John Steinbeck was always amazed that the print run for one of his books in Denmark, with a population then of 5 million, would be just about the same size as the print run for the United States, with a population then of 130 million. Our great American novel *Gone with the Wind* has sold but 28 million copies since publication in 1936; think how many Americans have come and gone since then. The best-selling mass market paperback of all time is Dr. Spock's *Baby and Child Care*, coming in at about 20 million; the best-selling paperback fiction, J.R.R. Tolkien's *The Hobbit*, has sold 15 million, with classics like *The Catcher in the Rye* by J.D. Salinger now at 10 million, *A Separate Peace* by John Knowles at 8 million and Steinbeck's *Of Mice and Men* at 7.5 million.

Proportionately, these numbers seem all out of whack. It helps a little — maybe just a little — to remember that, as Aldous Huxley once put it, "the world ... is only just becoming literate."[2] H.L. Mencken pegged the "human race that had the ability to think at one-eighth of one percent."[3] A study prepared in 1978 indicated that 54 percent of American men and 46 percent of American women do not read books.[4] There is no reason to believe these figures have changed for the better since then.

Today, twenty-five million adult Americans cannot read or write, period. Forty-five million are functionally illiterate, cannot read a help wanted ad or recipe, write a check or address an envelope.[5] It is estimated that sixty million adult Americans can't read or write beyond an eighth grade level. This number is said to be increasing by 800,000 to one million each year. A 1993 survey released by the Department of Education found that ninety million Americans over the age of sixteen do not have the most basic reading and writing skills required for employment.[6] Every eight seconds of every school day, an American student drops out of school. Every year, 700,000 students graduate without the ability to read their diplomas.[7] Was there any surprise when a report funded by the National Endowment for the Arts found that literate reading has been declining among young adults during the last two decades?[8] Or when a survey by the National

Endowment for the Humanities revealed that more than half of all college seniors flunked a basic history and literature test?[9]

Illiteracy gets all the press, but just as sad a problem is aliteracy, which has been defined as the ability to read without the desire to do so. This affliction, even among high school and college graduates, is rampant.

How common it is, nowadays, to walk into a home, decorated as if *Architectural Digest* had just completed a six-page photo spread, and feel something wrong, something missing: not a book in the house, not a book to be seen anywhere.

These poor people, first of all, are missing out on a great decorating technique; Paul Horgan called a wall of books "the most pleasingly decorative side for a room after a mural painting or a tapestry by master hands."[10] In one respect, it doesn't matter what particular books line the walls, for any combination will look good; as James Michener has written, it is the concept of a book itself that is "one of the finest symbols of our civilization."[11] And these poor folk are also missing out on making their homes come alive, for, as Cicero said, "a room without books is a body without a soul."[12] There is something about just having the books there. "Books are a delightful society," William Gladstone wrote. "If you go into a room filled with books, even without taking them down from their shelves, they seem to speak to you, to welcome you."[13]

These people are, of course, missing out on something much more. Better to read the books than just to have them on the shelves, for reading provides more opportunities for happiness than are available to someone who has never discovered its joys. It is a way of experiencing life and of altering perceptions, thereby increasing the range and richness of our lives. As S.I. Hayakawa put it, "In a very real sense, people who have read good literature have lived more than people who cannot or will not read.... It is not true that we have only one life to live; if we can read, we can live as many more lives and as many kinds of lives as we wish."[14]

Think of your favorite books, the ones you enjoyed when you read them, the ones you didn't want to put down and could hardly bear to finish; the ones you thought about after you finished them. These are the books you take off the shelf to reread every few years, the ones you open to certain pages to read and read again. Think of the characters that you remember as vividly as you remember anyone you've ever met: Huck Finn, Jim Hawkins, Scarlett O'Hara, Holden Caulfield, Jean Brodie, Mr. Chips, Ebenezer Scrooge, Tony Fry, Jay Gatsby, Phineas, Scout Finch, Holly Golightly. "My library," wrote Shakespeare in *The Tempest*, "was dukedom large enough." There are people out there, educated people, many people, who have never met Huck or Holly. One wonders sometimes how they live without having made such acquaintance. A Parisian hostess once asked Benjamin Franklin his thoughts on what condition of man most deserved pity. After due reflection, Franklin responded: "A lonesome man on a rainy night who does not know how to read."[15] The failure to impart the joys of books and reading to more people is the most woeful failure of our educational system (and of publishers, who have thus failed to further their business interests). Reading is the foundation of all education, and education still is the best hope for solutions to all the problems society faces.

If the American people are not reading, what are they doing? Every day, 73 percent of all American thirteen-year-olds watch three or more hours of television, and one has to assume additional hours are spent with the VCR, CD player, Nintendo, Walkman and the latest electronic gadgets. The *Wall Street Journal* reported in 1990 that for the third straight year, students' weakening verbal skills pulled down their scores on the Scholastic Aptitude Test. The College Board, the *Journal* noted, which sponsors the SAT, attributed the continuing decline in verbal scores to an erosion of reading time. Stated Donald Stewart, the president of the College Board: "Reading is in danger of becoming a lost art among too many American students."[16]

There is an even scarier statistic: that 90 percent of *everyone* in the United States spends one third of their waking hours watching television. About 500,000 Americans will go out and buy a Judith Krantz hardcover novel, while 20,000,000 people will turn on their television sets to watch the same Judith Krantz novel turned into a mini-series. (As James Michener has said, "If I were a young man today, I think I would head toward Hollywood and the movies. That medium is so effective and commands an immense audience. I would think that none of my books ever came within 3 percent of the audience that a Spielberg movie gets, and that counts for something."[17])

When Johnny Carson was its host, twelve million Americans tuned in every night to watch the *Tonight* show; forty-five million viewers watched his final show. Forty-two million viewers watched Ellen DeGeneres come out as a lesbian on her weekly sitcom, *Ellen*. Thirty-eight million viewers saw sitcom character Murphy Brown have her baby. Thirty-six million Americans regularly watched *Roseanne*.

Michael Jackson's 1983 album, "Thriller," sold in one year over 40 million copies to become the most successful recording in history; his 1987 album, "Bad," sold over 22 million copies. The top three movies of 1990, *Home Alone*, *Ghost* and *Pretty Woman*, had revenues of $305 million, $417 million and $411 million, meaning that over fifty million people saw each of them. In 1991, Americans bought one billion movie tickets and rented 4.1 billion video cassettes. Each January, the Superbowl is attended by some 75,000 fans, and watched on television by over one hundred million Americans and hundreds of millions more viewers worldwide. So anxious are advertisers to reach this audience that they will pay $800,000 for thirty seconds of air time.

In New York City alone, there are estimated to be 250,000 heroin addicts. Are there 250,000 book buyers? Are there 250,000 book readers? As Gore Vidal repeatedly has noted, "The *audience* for the novel is demonstrably diminishing with each passing year,"[18] and his estimate that only 3 to 5 percent of our population reads books seems on the mark.

Critic Christopher Lehmann-Haupt asked Jack Shoemaker, the editor-in-chief of North Point Press in Berkeley, California, how many serious readers are out there. "I'm not certain that there is such a thing as a general serious literary audience," he responded. "If there is, it surely is not above 15,000 people in this country, and those would be people who want to keep abreast of books as various as James Cleick's *Chaos* or Barry Lopez's essays or a new piece of fiction by somebody of repute." Lehmann-Haupt pressed: Is this audience growing or contracting? "I think it's steadily getting older, and it shows no signs of growing. And I think that a quick survey of some of the big independent booksellers will confirm my sense that there is no meaningful audience in their teenage years or people in their twenties. These stores are largely supported by people in their late thirties to mid-fifties." Novelist Philip Roth's assessment is just as grim: "There's been a drastic decline, even a disappearance, of a serious readership," he has said; "we are down to a gulag archipelago of readers."[19]

"It is a mistake to think that books have come to stay," E.M. Forster once said. "The human race did without them for thousands of years and may decide to do without them again."[20] If, as it seems, book reading is an imperiled, disappearing activity, then it should be the books of mass appeal, the real mega-sellers, that first feel the pinch, as marginal readers drop by the wayside. Maybe it's too soon to look for trends, or maybe bits of evidence do not a trend make, but in any event, in the 1970s a huge best-seller like *The Godfather* would sell twelve million paperback copies. Today's blockbuster weighs in at several million fewer copies.

The barbarians are not at the gates; they have breached the gates. They are among us. They are us. As Eugene Ionesco simply put it: "People who don't read are brutes."[21]

Today, who reads? According to the numbers, those who do are so rare that they might just as well be enlisted for the sideshows.

Woe unto him who reads too often, or admits he does it at all. During his confirmation proceedings, Supreme Court Justice David Souter was made out to be some sort of freak on account of his reading habits. "To call Souter bookish would be like describing the Grand Canyon as a hole in the ground," *Time* analogized. "In the ramshackle farmhouse nine miles outside Concord where he has lived since he was 11, groaning shelves of books on philosophy, history and the law have won the battle for space. Souter jokes that the room looks like 'someone was moving a bookstore and stopped.' Vacations are devoted to rereading as much of the work of a particular author as he can; he has plowed through Dickens, Proust, Shakespeare and Oliver Wendell Holmes...." Certainly there was something suspect about all of this. Despite *Time*'s report that while a Rhodes scholar at Oxford, Souter and a group of friends "would return so late to their rooms after visiting the local pubs that they would have to climb a ladder to get over the locked gates" and that friends at Harvard Law School reported that no one they'd ever met "is more fun at a party," *Time* pondered what it considered a serious issue: "whether a man who seems to prefer books to people can empathize with and understand the problems of ordinary people."[22] Flash back a hundred years or so, and David Souter's reading habits would have been the stuff of legend, especially if he read beside a fire in a log cabin.

Gore Vidal has recounted a story that illustrates just how much the reading habits of our society have changed in those hundred years:

> For some years I have been haunted by a story of [William Dean] Howells and that most civilized of all our presidents, James A. Garfield. In the early 1870s Howells and his father paid a call on Garfield. As they sat on Garfield's veranda, young Howells began to talk about poetry and about the poets that he had met in Boston and New York. Suddenly, Garfield told him to stop. Then Garfield went to the edge of the veranda and shouted to his Ohio neighbors. "Come over here! He's telling about Holmes, and Longfellow, and Lowell, and Whittier!" So the neighbors gathered around in the dusk; then Garfield said to Howells, "Now go on."
>
> Today we take it for granted that no living president will ever have heard the name of any living poet. This is not, necessarily, an unbearable loss. But it is unbearable to have lost those Ohio neighbors who actually read books of poetry and wanted to know about the poets.[23]

People today — public people certainly — are reluctant even to admit that they read. Bill Moyers once quoted the poet Joseph Brodsky as having said that "you can tell a great deal more about a candidate for the presidency from the last book he read than the last speech he gave."[24] In his first presidential campaign, George Bush told the approving American public that he doesn't read many books. In a *New Yorker* profile of his closest advisor, Secretary of State James Baker, it was reported that Baker "is not much of a reader and he has little time for museums or the opera or concerts. 'His outlet is turkey hunting, not books,'" his pastor noted.[25] As Gore Vidal hinted, perhaps it's better that way. Vice President Dan Quayle presented his book reports to doubtful reporters as proof that he had read books: "I read Nixon's book, *1999* ... Nixon's book was about the Soviet Union and how we ought to handle them in the future, in 1999." He went on to describe *Nicholas and Alexandra* by Robert Massie:

> a really interesting book on the downfall of the Russian czar and the Empire and the coming of Lenin and how that whole thing just crumbled when his father passed on

85

unexpectedly and Alexandra had to take it and they had that child that had hemophilia. And it came through Queen Victoria and everybody sort of thought that hemophilia was from the high living and they didn't realize it was hereditary. It comes through the mother. And Alexandra was from Germany. And it was a very good book of Rasputin's involvement in that, which shows how people that are really very weird can get into sensitive positions and have a tremendous impact on history.[26]

Compare all this to John F. Kennedy, who turned his Harvard senior thesis into a best-seller, *Why England Slept*; who, while recovering from a back operation, wrote *Profiles in Courage*, another best-seller and winner of the Pulitzer Prize for biography; who brought historian Arthur Schlesinger, Jr., to the White House to advise on the historical precedents of current political problems; who was a speed reader devouring books by the bushel; who recommended to his staff books like Barbara Tuchman's *The Guns of August*.

The regard that today's society affords to authors is just about the same it affords to readers. Aspiring writers may live on fantasies of glory, but in real life, the glory is not there.

Where are the Oscars, the Emmys, the Tonys, the Grammys for authors? Where is that special television extravaganza to honor our best writers? Nowhere; in fact, there are no television programs about books. From 1975 until 1990, France had a weekly ninety-minute television show, *Apostrophes*, featuring authors discussing their latest books, a show that in France achieved the popularity that *Wall Street Week* has in the United States. "America is basically anti-intellectual," novelist William Styron has said, explaining why such a show wouldn't succeed here. "My own feeling is that Americans in general have so little regard for serious literature that a TV book show could never achieve truly wide popularity."[27] Nan Talese, editor at Doubleday agrees: "Americans aren't French, and we don't get excited about ideas."[28] In fact, when Johnny Carson's *Tonight* show was cut back in 1980 from ninety minutes to an hour, it was authors who first disappeared as his guests.

Annie Dillard has written that an author may excite in his fellow man "not curiosity but profound indifference. It is not my experience that society hates and fears the writer, or that society adulates the writer. Instead my experience is the common one, that society places the writer so far beyond the pale that society does not regard the writer at all."[29]

Saul Bellow has humorously recalled his encounters with politicians:

> American writers are not neglected, they mingle occasionally with the great, they may even be asked to the White House but no one there will talk literature to them. Mr. Nixon disliked writers and refused flatly to have them in, but Mr. Ford has invited them together with actors, musicians, television newscasters and politicians.... Questions of language or style, the structure of novels, trends in painting are not discussed. The writer finds this a wonderful Pop occasion. Senator Fulbright seems almost to recognize his name and says, "You write essays, don't you? I think I can remember one of them." But the Senator, as everyone knows, was once a Rhodes Scholar.
>
> It is actually pleasant on such an evening, for a writer to pass half disembodied and unmolested by small talk from room to room, looking and listening. He knows that active public men can't combine government with literature, art and philosophy. Theirs is a world of high-tension wires, not of primroses on the river's brim. Ten years ago Mayor Daley in a little City Hall ceremony gave me a five hundred dollar check on behalf of the Midland Authors' Society. "Mr. Mayor, have you read *Herzog*?" asked one of the reporters standing by. "I've looked into it," said Daley, yielding no ground."[30]

There once was a day when Americans lined up on the wharfs of Boston and New York awaiting the ships from England that would deliver the latest installment of Charles Dickens' *The Old Curiosity Shop*, when Thomas Paine's *Common Sense* sold 100,000 copies in ten weeks, when Longfellow's "The Courtship of Miles Standish" sold 10,000 copies in a day. There once was a day when reading was a popular form of entertainment, when books provided a shared experience for a diverse and fragmented population. Amazed publishers are reminded time and again that that day has gone, that their franchise slipped away from them while they weren't minding the store. "You publish a book under the notion that there are people who will share your tastes, share your enthusiasm," Sonny Mehta, the head of

Knopf, has said. "It's disheartening to find that, apart from the fellows in the office, there's potentially only a handful — 3,000, 4,000, 5,000 people — in the country."[31] Lawrence Henry Gipson's volumes of history concerning *The British Empire Before the American Revolution* received the most extraordinary praise and yet were selling fewer than one thousand copies per volume. "I am tempted to raise my hands above my head," exclaimed their dismayed publisher, Alfred A. Knopf, "expose my galluses, and exclaim in the immortal words of that great border-state keynoter: How long, America! Oh how long, America! Oh how long!"[32]

CHAPTER 8

Judging a Book
by Its Cover

O ne of the amazing curiosities about publishing is that, barring miracles, the fate of a book is set long before it is printed and makes its way to bookstores. It is sealed at a sales conference, months before publication date, when publishers try to guesstimate just how many potential book buyers there are out there and try to determine how to catch their attention.

At a publisher's sales conference — its launch meeting — the season's list of books is introduced by the editors, who, spending a few minutes on each new book, summarize them for the company's sales representatives and provide one-sentence handles that the reps will use in selling the books. Also at the sales conference, an advertising and promotion budget is set for each book, based on the size of the author's advance, the author's track record, any good things that have so far happened to the book (the receipt of blurbs, a sale to a magazine or book club, or a television or movie production deal), and a dollop of educated guessing. This seat-of-the-pants process floors agent Morton Janklow:

> There's no marketing input, or, if there is some, it's not extensive enough. You know how they set a printing for a novel? They sit around at the publishing house and a guy says, "I don't know—fifty thousand?" "Sounds like a hell of a lot." "How many do you think?" "Oh, I think that booksellers might take five thousand initially." That's the way they make decisions. Does anybody sit down and put a computer on and see what novels in this genre have done in the Midwest in the past three years? No![1]

This haphazardly determined print run dictates the commitment the publishing house will make to selling the book. A small run results in little or no promotion or advertising, which results in disappointing sales. No problem, an editor will tell the worried author, we can always go back for another printing if demand justifies it. Yes, but the chances that demand will develop with the deck so stacked against the book are slim indeed. If a substantial number of books are printed, the sales representatives will press to get them into the stores; if not, they won't, and sales opportunities quickly fade. As the vice president of a major publishing house once commented: "The best way to make a best-seller is to have fifty thousand copies in the stores."[2]

Armed with a quota the publisher would like to meet in each territory, the sales representatives set out to see what they can do. They are the descendants of Parson Weems, who pushed his book-packed cart along the dirt roads of the Atlantic seaboard during the late eighteenth century; of the street hawkers who sold Dickens's latest novel after hearing a pep talk from the publisher; of the men that Appleton sent out in the 1920s in Ford trucks filled with books to reach the smaller communities along the byways.

Today's book travelers cover large territories, some encompassing several states with over one hundred accounts, almost exclusively the independent bookstores. They must know enough about the new offerings on the publisher's list to advise each store manager how each book will do in his store. It is unlikely that the sales reps have read or even skimmed any of the books. The sum of their knowledge is based on the catalog copy, the jacket, and the sales conference briefing. Their props are the book catalog, and the book jackets; their pitch for each book, which can rarely exceed a minute and usually is less, often is nothing more than a short-hand evaluation, like "good jacket, good facing, heavy run." As a Doubleday sales representative described it: "I make it my business to pass on the kind of information that can decide — irrelevant to a book's literary quality — whether or not it'll be a money-maker: What kind of attention will Doubleday provide, meaning advertising expense; the track record of the author, the glitzy jacket, how other bookstores are ordering and the availability of the author for personal appearances. All this enters into getting the order."[3]

A *New York Times* reporter once tagged along with a sales representative of William Morrow to see how it is done, and recorded his handle for a number of books:

A book by Morris the Cat: "This is a terrific nonbook item. There are little asides about how cats manipulate people to get more food and all that."

A Sammy Davis, Jr., memoir: "Very gossipy. You know, the-day-I-told-Frank-Sinatra-to-go-to-hell."

A Victorian novel: "This is for the perm set."

A train thriller: "This is fake Tolstoy with a little Agatha Christie thrown in."[4]

When editors present their books at the sales conference, every book is a best-seller. The sales representatives take it upon themselves to evaluate the books. As one representative explained his current list:

> There are three books on this list that I will not sell to any of my retail accounts. That's because they have no redeeming value. They're not good pieces of trash. They're not good pieces of literature. I could sell some of them if I wanted to, but they would just come back and it would ruin my credibility. I think that it's psychologically important to have a few skips on the list. It builds trust. It's something you can giggle over with the buyer. "Hey, look at this dud!"[5]

So, to make his pitch credible, the sales rep will damn other books on the list with "quite forgettable" or "I'm sorry, I don't know why this is being published" or "I hope it vanishes from the face of the earth."[6] Thus, with a flick of his hand, snuffs out some author's dreams. Jacqueline Susann knew what she was doing when she wooed the sales reps!

With so much of a book's fate dependent on everything but what is between its covers, publishers have learned to treat a book's skin with loving care. Alfred A. Knopf always labored over the appearance of his books, the bindings, the paper, the jacket; it was quite an innovation when the first books he published had colorful cloth bindings and bright dust jackets. "I have found the prevalent idea that a good-looking book must necessarily cost too much to manufacture wholly fallacious. Good-looking books do cost — the publisher's time and thought. And so I have experimented with boards printed up in brightly colored Continental designs, with Italian handmade papers, with French papers, with a Russian artist's idea for a binding."[7]

Other publishers watched the success Knopf had with his books and learned that it indeed was worth their time and thought, that readers could and did judge a book by its cover. Today, the art director, editor, publisher, and marketing director routinely meet to discuss the best jacket for their books, what will be eye-catching to secure display space, what will attract readers, what will sell a book. Mass-market paperback publishers discovered that red covers sold books, and when the racks became full of red covers, discovered that theirs could be distinguished by using white covers instead. Something different always works for a while, from printing a book with six different colored covers, as was done with extraordinary results with Alvin Toffler's *Future Shock* (some were white, some yellow, some blue, some pink, some green and some tangerine; this so caught the imagination of booksellers that they prominently displayed all six) to high technology techniques using embossing and fluorescent inks. Crown Publishers strove to create a suitably sophisticated image for Judith Krantz's first novel, *Scruples*, right down to its fashionable jacket. As one of Morton Janklow's associates described the process:

> *Scruples* was completely packaged and jacketed to make it look very classy, which is one of the factors in this kind of image-making. A lot of readers of such books as *Scruples* are middle-class and upper-middle-class housewives. If you were to say to them about one of these books, "Do we have a dirty sex book for you!" you might have a problem. In the packaging of *Scruples* everything was done to upgrade the image of the book and make it classy.[8]

Nothing should be left to chance, not even the author's photograph on the book jacket. The young Truman Capote knew just what he was doing when he was snapped in that languid, seductive pose for the jacket of his first book, *Other Voices, Other Rooms*; it garnered unending publicity for him and his novel. Danielle Steel dreads the many-hour photo session necessary to get the perfect shot for the back of her next book. "I feel I'm expected to look glamorous as an author and I'm a sort of retiring person. The photo session is a huge pain in the butt, if you want to know."[9] But it does the trick; Danielle Steel's readers feel as if they know her.

The positioning of the photograph of the author on the book jacket can depend, a book publicist commented, "on the author's physical appeal: Is he or she gorgeous, handsome, appealing, or does he or she have what is known in the trade as 'a radio face'?" "With glamorous lady authors like Jackie and Joan Collins, the photo matters a lot and it will help sell books," said Michael Korda, editor-in-chief at Simon & Schuster. Other jackets go photoless. "We have some authors who say what they look like hardly matters," the director of publicity at Farrar, Straus & Giroux explained. "We've rarely used a Susan Sontag photo because it's not her style. Same with Philip Roth. In his thinking, the book stands on its own and speaks for itself."[10] That's what John Steinbeck also believed: "I am never photographed," Steinbeck told his agent to tell his publisher. "This is not temperament on my part, nor is it self-consciousness. I do not believe in mixing personality with work. It is customary, I guess, but I should like to break the custom. A public nauseated with personal detail would probably be more grateful than otherwise...."[11]

Can an author's photo really make a difference in the reception of a new book? No question. In his review of Erica Jong's first novel, *Fear of Flying*, John Updike seemed as smitten by her pose as by her prose, noting that "on the back jacket flap, Mrs. Jong, with perfect teeth and cascading blond hair, is magnificently laughing, in contrast to the somber portrait that adorns her two collections of poetry." Although he doesn't name names, Updike once admitted that his critical objectivity may have been impaired "in a few reprehensible cases [when] I may have dreamed of sleeping with the authoress."[12]

Everything about the appearance of a book can make a difference in sales, but woe to the author and publisher who treat perfunctorily the titling of a book.

Will a baby boy named Howard grow up to be the same man as if he had been named Michael? Would *Gone with the Wind* have met with the same success if it had been titled *Ba! Ba! Black Sheep*? "What's in a name?" Juliet asked Romeo. "That which we call a rose by any other name would smell as sweet." Or would it?

Can a book's title influence its sales? Sure it can, as the publisher of a cheap run of paperbacks discovered earlier in the century when he cavalierly retitled De Maupassant's *Tallow Ball*, which had been selling about 15,000 copies a year, as *A Prostitute's Sacrifice*, which promptly boosted sales to 55,000 annually. And publishers at the turn of the century believed that the stillbirth of Marie Corelli's latest novel was her own fault for entitling it *Holy Orders*; the book fell flat on its face after the popular success of her previous novel, *Sorrows of Satan*. James Michener has credited "one of the most titillating titles of recent decades"—*Naked Came the Stranger*—for the appearance of that book, composed as a lark by a group of writers, on the bestseller lists.[13]

There are titles that are functional but still do the trick: *The Rise and Fall of the Third Reich, Kon-Tiki, The Godfather, Hawaii, Inside Asia*. And then there are titles that contain a touch of music, of poetry, of magic: *The Naked and the Dead; The Agony and the Ecstasy; Gone with the Wind; Song of Solomon; The Garden of Eden; The Sound and the Fury; Look Homeward, Angel; The Last Hurrah; From Here to Eternity; Listen! the Wind*. There are titles that resonate in your mind, that call to you. Title intrigue was certainly a part of the great appeal of the Nancy Drew and Hardy Boys mystery series. What youngster could resist titles like *The Hidden Staircase, The Mystery at Lilac Inn, The Secret in the Old Attic, The Tower Treasure, Footprints Under the Window*? There are memorable, off-beat titles with a twist that sparks our curiosity: *Breakfast at Tiffany's, As I Lay Dying, Is Sex Necessary?, A Tree Grows in Brooklyn, Cheaper by the Dozen*, and *It Was on Fire When I Lay Down on It*. There are titles that through a single word, or an enchanted combination, capture a beauty, a feeling, everything about a time or place: *Tales of the South Pacific, Lolita, The Guns of August*. There are titles that prick our prurient interest—Jacqueline Susann was getting quite good at these before she passed away: *The Love Machine, Once Is Not Enough*. There are titles that a friend has to explain to you—"See, Mag, 'dolls' are pills, you know, uppers, downers, amphetamines." "Ohhh! *Valley of the Dolls*; I get it!" "*Portnoy's Complaint*: I get it"—and so begins word of mouth. Some titles even become a part of our common parlance: *Life Begins at Forty, The Power of Positive Thinking, Catch-22*.

"A good title is the title of a successful book," Raymond Chandler once commented.[14] After the fact, after the book is successful, its title seems the natural and obvious title for that particular book. But before the fact? That's another story.

When *The Catcher in the Rye* was chosen as the main selection of the Book-of-the-Month Club in 1951, the club's editorial staff approached J. D. Salinger about changing that curious title. No, Salinger wrote back, "Holden Caulfield wouldn't like that"[15]—and so the title remained, and today seems the only conceivable title for that special book.

How about *Mourning Becomes Electra*? In 1931 Eugene O'Neill's editor brought his latest play to the editor-in-chief of Liveright, a publishing house that in those Depression years was in dire need of the cash flow its famous playwright's latest work would initiate. The editor-in-chief "concentrated on the title page," as O'Neill's editor remembered the scene, "played for a while with the long black ribbon on his spectacles, cleared his throat as a preliminary to uttering a shattering profundity, shook his white-thatched head and exploded the word 'meaningless' with an implied exclamation mark at the end of it. As on cue, the editorial assistants and the publicity director embellished the verdict with even stronger adjectives, both commercial and semantic."[16] It was only when it was explained that the word "becomes" in the title in that context meant "suits" that the editor-in-chief understood the title's meaning, though he still felt it was not exactly right to properly market O'Neill's play.

When the author's name is printed on the book jacket in letters bigger than the title, then and only then is the title of little concern. Whether James Michener titled his book *The Lesser Antilles* or *Timbuktu* is really irrelevant. Michener in fact once noted that "to me titles have never had great importance, and I have not paid much attention to mine."[17] No problem; he didn't need to. In most other cases, however, an experienced author or editor understands the importance of just the right combination of words to cast a spell and haul in buyers.

Scott Fitzgerald had a way with titles, though his titles certainly didn't come easily. In draft form, his first novel was called *The Romantic Egotist*, a title with which he tinkered that fateful summer as he slaved away in St. Paul for the hand of the girl he loved, coming up with *The Education of a Personage*, and then later in the summer—he got it and he knew it—*This Side of Paradise*, even though his esteemed Princeton classmate, Edmund Wilson, wrote to him: "I don't think any of your titles are any good."[18] Would the book have created the sensation that it did with either of Fitzgerald's earlier titles? Is it only because the title is now so familiar and has worn a groove in our brains that it seems so right, or is there an inherent magic to it? *This Side of Paradise* as the title for a book coming out right after World War I, just at the beginning of the Roaring Twenties, had the same evocative, haunting quality as the titles of Fitzgerald's later books, *The Beautiful and the Damned* (which replaced his earlier stab, *The Beautiful Lady Without Money*) and *Tender Is the Night*.

The Great Gatsby was another story. On October 27, 1924, Fitzgerald sent to Max Perkins the manuscript of his third novel, which he alternately was calling *Trimalchio in West Egg* or *The Great Gatsby*. In his covering letter, he noted, "I have an alternative title: *Gold-hatted Gatsby*."[19] A week later, in his next letter, he was floundering: "I have not decided to stick to the title I put on the book, *Trimalchio in West Egg*. The only other titles that seem to fit it are *Trimalchio* and *On the Road to West Egg*. I had two others, *Gold-hatted Gatsby* and *The High-bouncing Lover*, but they seemed too slight."[20] A month later, he was still mulling over titles, including *Among Ash Heaps and Millionaires* and still *Trimalchio in West Egg*. "Maybe simply *Trimalchio* or *Gatsby*."[21] On January 24, 1925, in a p.s. to a letter to Perkins, he noted: "I'm returning the proof of the title page, etc. It's O.K. but my heart tells me I should have named it *Trimalchio*. However against all the advice I suppose it would have been stupid and stubborn of me. *Trimalchio in West Egg* was only a compromise. *Gatsby* is too much like *Babbitt* and *The Great Gatsby* is weak because there's no emphasis even ironically on his greatness or lack of it. However, let it pass."[22]

What a mistake! Too late he realized it, two weeks before publication date sending off to Perkins from the isle of Capri a frantic wire: "CRAZY ABOUT TITLE UNDER THE RED WHITE AND BLUE STOP WHAT WOULD DELAY BE?"[23] At that late date, what did he expect an editor to say? Too late, wired Perkins, no doubt breathing a sigh of relief that it was. Fitzgerald was troubled and wrote that "if the book fails commercially it will be from one of two reasons or both," listing first that "the title is only fair, rather bad than good."[24] Undoubtedly, he attributed *Gatsby's* pitiful sales to its uninspired title. And although Truman Capote, himself a master titlist, ranked it right up there among his favorite titles (which included *Wuthering Heights; Pride and Prejudice; Gone with the Wind; Remembrance of Things Past; The Sun Also Rises; Look Homeward, Angel; Tender Is the Night; The Heart Is a Lonely Hunter;* and his own *Other Voices, Other Rooms* and *Answered Prayers*[25]), *The Great Gatsby* seems to miss the mark by a mile. It is a title without melody or music and, on top of that, not a very apt reflection of the book, as Fitzgerald himself realized.

That remarkable book succeeded, eventually, in spite of its title. Over the long run (and John Maynard Keynes was right, in the long run we're all dead, and in this case Fitzgerald was very dead), the worth of the novel emerged until the book became the biggest annual seller of any Scribner book. Would *The Great Gatsby* sooner have achieved the success for which it was destined with a better title? In retrospect it seems that nothing else was holding it back from assuming its rightful spot among the masterpieces of American literature. "A brilliant book cannot be put down by a bad title," Joni Evans, founder of Turtle Bay Books, has said; "it will not get lost."[26] Maybe not, but it sure can get misplaced for an awfully long time, as Fitzgerald's masterpiece illustrates. Not until some thirty years after publication and fifteen years after his death did recognition, and sales, of *The Great Gatsby* really begin. Assume *The Great Gatsby* had been Scott Fitzgerald's only published novel: In today's market, where the fate of a book is decided in a couple months or weeks, would such a poorly titled book have vanished forever? It certainly seems possible.

Would *Treasure Island* have succeeded with Robert Louis Stevenson's first title, *The Sea-Cook, or Treasure Island: A Story for Boys?* Maybe not.

A sales rep stopping at a bookstore with nothing but Willy Loman's shoeshine and smile, a mock-up of the book jacket and a fifteen-second message about the book had better have a title that catches the buyer's attention. "When books succeed, it's because their titles are intriguing to us," Simon & Schuster's Michal Korda has said, a sentiment endorsed by many publishers and editors. Jonathan Segal, a senior editor at Knopf, noted that "a title is important because it speaks to the reader when he's in the store. You can advertise and promote, but the best advertisement is the title."[27]

Often, once an author hits upon it, bingo! a title will feel just right. "By the end of May," Kenneth Roberts wrote in his memoirs, "I had finished twenty chapters and given the book a name —*Northwest Passage*. I thanked my lucky stars that no one had ever before thought of using those pregnant words as the title of a novel."[28] Max Perkins worked with Marjorie Rawlings through "The Flutter Mill," "The Fawn," "Juniper Creek," "Juniper Island," and "Yearling" before reaching *The Yearling*. Peter Benchley and his editor endlessly batted back and forth titles for his first novel. Should it be "A Stillness in the Water"? "The Summer of the Shark"? "The Jaws of the Leviathan"? "The Terror of Leviathan"? "The Terror of the Monster"? "The Year They Closed the Beaches"? "Why Us"? On and on, until one day at lunch Benchley asked, "Why not just 'Jaws?" and his editor at once was certain the right title had been found.[29]

"How about this for a title," Hemingway wrote to Max Perkins:

For Whom the Bell Tolls
A Novel
By Ernest Hemingway

"I think it has the magic that a title has to have," he debated as he continued his letter to Perkins. "Maybe it isn't too easy to say. But maybe the book will make it easy. Anyway I have had thirty some titles and they were all possible but this is the first one that has made the bell toll for me. Or do you suppose that people think only of tolls as long distance charges and of Bell as the Bell telephone system?" Hemingway continued. "If so it is out. 'The Tolling of the Bell.' No. That's not right. If there is no modern connotation of telephone to throw it off For Whom The Bell Tolls can be a good title I think."[30]

A few years later, in 1943, in writing to Perkins about wife Martha's efforts to find just the right title for her new book, Hemingway set out some of his thoughts on hunting for titles:

> Getting a title is a lot like drawing cards in a poker game. You keep on drawing and they're all worthless but if you can last at it long enough you always get a good hand finally. She's having a tough time, though, because each year there are fewer good titles since the mines have all been worked for a long time. There are still some wonderful ones in John

Donne but two people in the same family become self-conscious about digging into that wonderful lode. So many people have robbed the Bible that nobody minds that and I think we ought to start Marty digging into Ecclesiastes or Proverbs where there are still very valuable properties buried.[31]

Other writers have staked out their own mother lodes to pick around in, like Tennessee Williams, who always reread the poetry of Hart Crane to search for titles. Others — like Margaret Mitchell, who struggled mightily to name her Civil War opus — flail in every direction. "Tomorrow Is Another Day," which Mitchell's publishers liked, didn't quite seem to do it for her, and she made lists of other possibilities:

Tote the Weary Load

Milestones

Jettison

Ba! Ba! Black Sheep

None So Blind

Not in Our Stars

Bugles Sang True

And then, one day, she was reading one of her favorite poems, Ernest Dowson's "Non sum qualis Eram bonae sub regno Cynarae" (a title taken from an ode of Horace). In this poem she happened upon a line that grabbed her — "I have forgot much, Cynara, gone with the wind, flung roses, roses riotously with the throng" — and there was her title, the right title, the only title. It was *Gone with the Wind*, that felicitous union of sound and sense that echoed the theme of her book through all its pages.[32] (When Warner Books published the sequel to Mitchell's classic, the publisher favored "Tomorrow Is Another Day" as its title, but the results of repeated surveys mandated that it be *Scarlett*.)

John Steinbeck admitted, "I have never been a title man."[33] It was his wife, Carol, who while typing the manuscript came up with the winning title *The Grapes of Wrath*, lifted from Julia Ward Howe's "The Battle Hymn of the Republic." Steinbeck immediately knew it was right: "I think that is a wonderful title," he wrote in his journal.

"The looks of it — marvelous title."[34] "I like it better all the time," he wrote several months later. "I think it is Carol's best title so far. I like it because it is a march and this book is a kind of march — because it is in our own revolutionary tradition...."[35]

As an aside, we should consider *The Grapes of* Wrath as evidence that one title doth not necessarily a book make. Witness Mary Harriott Norris's *The Grapes of Wrath: A Tale of North and South*, published in 1901, and Boyd Gable's novel, *Grapes of Wrath*, published in 1917, both of which were long ago interred in the cemetery of forgotten books, while Steinbeck's *Grapes* since publication has sold over 14 million copies, and is today, year in and year out, still selling over 100,000 paperback copies.

The daily journal Steinbeck kept while writing his next major novel records in detail his struggle to find the right title. One day, in the midst of his work, one of his wife's distant relatives stopped in for a visit, and asked what he was writing. Steinbeck explained it was to be a long novel about his country for the last fifty years, which he was calling "Salinas Valley."

> "I think your title's wrong," the relative said.
> "What do you mean?"
> "Well," he said, "nobody who doesn't live there is interested in the Salinas Valley. You had the title yourself. Everybody is interested in my country. Call it that. Then they can connect it with their country.
> And you know — maybe he makes sense. But since it is not about the whole country — how would "My Valley" be. It's a wonderful-looking title.... It has the personal quality I am trying to put in the book. Think of it before you discard it. It is a wonderful jacket title too. MY VALLEY. The balance of letters, two y's and two l's, and the M balances the V. And it has great warmth and simplicity too.

Several days later, Steinbeck was still struggling. "I don't give a dam [sic] what it is called. I would call it Valley to the Sea which is a quotation from absolutely nothing but has two great words and a direction. What do you think of that? And I'm not going to think about it any more."

But he couldn't think of anything else but titles.

I thought about the book a great deal yesterday — what it is about and what its title should be. It is not local. It is not primarily about the Salinas Valley nor local people. Therefore it should have a general title. Now — its framework roots from that powerful, profound and perplexing story in Genesis of Cain and Abel.... With this in mind I went back to Genesis. I do not want a direct quotation but if I can find a symbol there which is understood on sight and which strikes deep, I will have my title.... So I suggest as a title for my book Cain Sign. It is not a direct quote, it is short, harsh, memorable and nearly everyone in the world knows what it means. And it is a pretty good-looking title too. What do you think of it?

Several more weeks of brooding and he had it: "And now I had set down in my own hand the 16 verses of Cain and Abel and the story changes with flashing lights when you write it down. And I think I have a title at last, a beautiful title. EAST OF EDEN. And read the 16th verse to find it. And the Salinas Valley is surely East of Eden."[36]

So on they go, on with their quest for that mellifluous combination of four or five or six words that will summon readers to their books, a quest not unlike a search for the winning numbers of a Pick-6 lottery. Steinbeck, critically eyeing the balance of letters in the words of a title. Hemingway, debating with himself: should it be "The Tolling of the Bell"? or "For Whom the Bell Tolls"? Margaret Mitchell, wondering if "Tomorrow Is Another Day" is better than "Ba! Ba! Black Sheep," or is "Gone with the Wind" the best of the lot? Wise authors all, they realized that the payoff for the right combination of words can be rewarding indeed.

CHAPTER 9

De Gustibus

O nce a book has made its way upstream beyond the swamps of initial evaluation by agents and publishers, past the boulders and around the sunken logs of editors, over the rapids of the sales conference, it must once again strike out alone against the surge, out of the control of its author, agent, editor and publisher, seeking a nod from the reviewers, and a favorable nod at that. To a frightening degree, on that favorable nod now rides the fate of the book — frightening, because whether the nod is favorable depends so much on the vagaries of chance.

John Updike and Paul Theroux — prolific writers, sophisticated authors, certainly distinguished men of letters — both reviewed Erica Jong's *Fear of Flying* when it was published in 1973.

Updike's review began: "Erica Jong's first novel feels like a winner. It has class and sass, brightness and bite. Containing all the cracked eggs of the feminist litany, her souffle rises with a poet's afflatus. She sprinkles on the four-letter words as if women had invented them; her cheerful sexual frankness brings a new flavor to female prose…. Fearless and fresh, tender and exact, Mrs. Jong has arrived nonstop at the point of being a literary personality…."[1]

Paul Theroux's comments were quite different: "With such continual and insistent reference to her cherished valve, Erica Jong's witless heroine looms like a mammoth pudendum, as roomy as the Carlsbad Caverns, luring amorous spelunkers to confusion in her plunging grottoes. On her eighth psychoanalyst and second marriage, Isadora Wing admits to a contortion we are not privileged to observe and confesses, 'I seem to live inside my cunt,' which strikes one as a choice as inconvenient as a leaky bedsitter in Elmer's End." And on he goes, calling the book a "crappy novel."[2]

It happens all the time. Look at Kenneth Roberts' diary entry for December 9, 1937: "Learned that *Northwest Passage* had been the choice of the English Book Society, and that they had spoken with enthusiasm of the English scenes in it. This was pleasing, since Allan Nevins, in his review of *Northwest Passage*, had pontifically said that my handling of the English scenes had been painfully inadequate, and that I wasn't competent to write about Englishmen of culture or refinement."[3]

Nabokov's *Lolita* was hailed by Elizabeth Janeway in her review in the *New York Times Book Review*: "The first time I read *Lolita* I thought it was one of the funniest books I'd ever come on…. The second time I read it, uncut, I thought it was one of the saddest…. Humbert is every man who is driven by desire, wanting his Lolita so badly that it never occurs to him to consider her as a human being, or as anything but a dream-figment made flesh…. As for pornographic content, I can think of few volumes more likely to quench the flames of lust than this exact and immediate description of its consequences." Orville Prescott had his say the next day in a review in the daily *New York Times*: "Lolita, then, is undeniably news in the world of books. Unfortunately, it is bad news. There are two equally serious reasons it isn't worth any adult reader's attention. The first is that it is dull, dull, dull in a pretentious, florid and archly fatuous fashion. The second is that it is repulsive … highbrow pornography."[4]

In the *New York Times* of Thursday, January 25, 1990, Christopher Lehmann-Haupt aired his disappointment in P.D. James's eleventh novel, *Devices and Desires*. He felt that the plot's "chain reaction of false leads, dead ends, subverted logic and clumsy comings and goings" reduced the novel "to a conventional who dunnit" with "lengthy descriptive passages that fail to justify the space they take up" and with "silly over-explanatory dialogue that reads like bloated word-balloons floating out of a void." How much worse could it get? Let's see. "Not even as a maze with no way out does the story make much sense…. We come to understand that the show must go on. But we find only a slight reason to attend it." So there!

But then, three days later, on the front page of the *New York Times Book Review*, appeared another review of the book. Now, to garner both a weekday and a Sunday *Times* review is the sign of an important book. And it is instructive to compare the two. The Sunday review was by the distinguished film critic Judith Crist, who has been a judge for the annual Edgar Awards of the Mystery Writers of America. Her opinion of the book was as clear in her opening sentence as Lehmann-Haupt's had been in his last: "Her newest mystery, *Devices and Desires*, is P.D. James at better than her best."

Whoa! Wait just a minute! Were Mr. Lehmann-Haupt and Ms. Crist sent the same bound galleys by P.D. James's publisher? Surely another publishing mix-up, right? Wrong. Ms. Crist goes on: "She offers her readers the satisfactions of an artfully constructed, beautifully written story of flesh-and-blood individuals in a time and place we get to know as well as the inhabitants. Not, mind you, that she ignores the conventions of the mystery story: the crime, the clues, the suspects and the puzzlement are there, but so absorbing a read does she offer that final revelations seem almost a bonus."

Assuming these two well-respected critics were reading the same book, who was right and who was wrong? Whose judgment was better? Hard to say; both reviews are well written and well reasoned. No matter to P.D. James, for both prominent reviews undoubtedly helped the sales of her book.

How can those two reviews be reconciled? Peter Benchley, whose *Jaws* did not receive the sort of reviews for which he had hoped, noted after the dust had settled, "I still don't understand how a book can get raves from one reviewer and be considered garbage by another."[5] *De gustibus non est disputandum*. Right. But tell that to the author of a first novel who doesn't get two reviews in the *New York Times*, who gets one short review if he's very lucky (the *New York Times Book Review* can only feature about 2,500 books each year), and that one review happens to be like the Christopher Lehmann-Haupt review of *Devices and Desires*, with no Judith Crist riding in on a white steed to save the day with another view. Then what? Barring a miracle, that is the end of that book, and might well be the end of that writing career.

It does not take a whole lot of evidence to demonstrate just how outlandishly wrong eminent critics have been, as Bill Henderson deliciously has shown us in his books *Rotten Reviews* and *Rotten Reviews II*.

For example, reviewers had no clue of what to make of *The Great Gatsby*, though the *Saturday Review of Literature* was sure that "Mr.

F. Scott Fitzgerald deserves a good shaking.... *The Great Gatsby* is an absurd story, whether considered as romance, melodrama, or plain record of New York high life." The *New York Herald Tribune* agreed: "What has never been alive cannot very well go on living. So this is a book of the season only...."[6]

Writing in *The New Yorker*, Clifton Fadiman called William Faulkner's *Absalom, Absalom!* "The final blowup of what was once a remarkable, if minor, talent."[7]

The *New York Times Book Review* concluded that Joseph Heller's *Catch-22* "gasps for want of craft and sensibility.... The book is an emotional hodgepodge; no mood is sustained long enough to register for more than a chapter."[8]

And Stanley Kauffmann, writing in *The New Republic*, dismissed Truman Capote's *In Cold Blood*: "One can say of this book — with sufficient truth to make it worth saying: 'This isn't writing. It's research.'"[9]

If eminent critics can miss the boat, can one review really make or break a book?

Alfred A. Knopf recalled that when he was a young man, "Mencken, William Lyon Phelps, Heywood Broun, Burton Rascoe, and Henry Sell — the latter two writing in Chicago — to name only five, *could* secure an almost immediate hearing for a book in which they believed — sometimes, as in Mencken's case, by denouncing it so brilliantly and provocatively that people rushed to read it."[10] Anais Nin was publishing her books with a home printing press, and then through tiny presses, when Edmund Wilson got hold of one and wrote a glowing review for *The New Yorker*. "It launched me," Nin declared. "Immediately all the publishers were ready to reprint both books in commercial editions."[11] And Malcom Cowley didn't attribute the revival of an interest in Faulkner's work to his *Faulkner Portable*, but rather to a front page review of the book in the *New York Times* and a major review in *The New Republic*.[12] So yes, a review can make a book.

But a bad review in the *New York Times* will not always break a book. The panning in the *New York Times Book Review* of *Scarlett*, the sequel to Margaret Mitchell's *Gone with the Wind* ("My best advice to GWTW fans is 'Don't bother.... This is dreadful.... You'll be really mad at yourself if you waste money buying it"[13]) put not a dent in the enormous sales of the book (According to the *Wall Street Journal,* "no other novel in the history of the printed word sold so many copies as quickly"[14]—1.2 million hardcovers sold in six weeks). Nor could all the reviewers' sticks and stones break any bones of a James Michener (a review of Michener's *Journey* in the *New York Times Book Review* noted that it "is not absolute junk. But I suspect no one but James Michener could get it published"[15]), or a Judith Krantz or a Danielle Steel or a Stephen King (a snide review in *Time* of his novel *The Dark Half*—"in each genre there is good trash and bad trash, and King's does not seem very good"[16]— probably didn't affect the sales of the first printing of 1.5 million one bit). Their books have lives of their own. Reviewers can pound on them as much as they wish and not harm their sales.

On the other hand, one review in the *New York Times* indeed may break a book. It is true that the editor-in-chief of a publishing house once remarked: "I greatly welcome a review in the *Times* no matter whether it is favorable or not; any review [in the *New York Times*] sells books."[17] But tell that to John Cheever, whose third novel, *Bullet Park,* was picked apart on the front page of the *New York Times Book Review* of April 27, 1969, by Benjamin DeMott, a professor of English at Amherst. "The manuscript was received enthusiastically everywhere," Cheever reported, "but when Benjamin DeMott dumped on it in the *Times,* everybody picked up their marbles and went home."[18] The book sold only 33,000 hardcover copies. Tell that to Gore Vidal, who early in his career saw the power of the *New York Times* to make or break a writer. His first novel, *Williwaw* (1946), was praised by the powerful *New York Times* critic Orville Prescott. "I was made," Vidal remembers.[19] Two years later there appeared his next novel, *The City and the Pillar,* which dealt with a homosexual relationship. Prescott read the book and was horrified, telling Vidal's publisher, "I will not only never review another novel by this disgusting writer, but I will never read one."[20] Vidal's next five novels were never reviewed in the *Times.* "I was unmade. For ten years I did television, theater, movies" before returning to the novel.[21]

Vidal saw the same power of the *Times* years later, in 1976, when he reviewed Tennessee Williams' *Memoirs.* "We had been friends from the late forties to the early sixties…. When next we met, he narrowed his cloudy blue eyes and said, in tones that one of these biographers would call 'clipped,' 'When your review appeared my book was number five on the nonfiction best-seller list of *The New York Times*. Within two weeks of your review, it was not listed at all.'"[22]

Any review in the *Times* is a beneficial review? Tell that to the producers and actors in Broadway shows that received raves from some critics but were panned by Frank Rich, for many years the leading theater critic of the *New York Times*. Some of those shows closed within a week. Rich's likes and dislikes determined which plays got on Broadway and which plays stayed there. A direct correlation was found between his reviews and box office sales. "No *Times* critic is going to hurt Neil Simon," said playwright Wendy Wasserstein. "But if a young playwright has a play at [such off-Broadway theaters as] Playwrights Horizons or Manhattan Theater Club and everybody likes it but Frank Rich, it probably won't move to a bigger theater. If he does like it, all the producers will rush to see it."[23]

"Time is the only critic without ambition," John Steinbeck once said.[24] And maybe time, and not the *Times*, is the real critic, the real judge of a book's worth. After all, Malcolm Cowley's *Exile's Return* was shattered by hostile reviews when it was published in 1934, selling a grand total of 983 copies; it was reissued in 1951 and took off, becoming a classic. James Agee's *Let Us Now Praise Famous Men* shared a similar history, selling a handful of copies when published to bad reviews in 1941, but recognized as a masterpiece by the 1960s.

In today's publishing world, however, a book may disappear — yes disappear from the face of the earth — before time has had its chance to render its verdict. "I cannot greatly care what the critics say of my work," John Updike has said; "if it is good, it will come to the surface in a generation or two and float, and if not, it will sink, having in the meantime provided me with a living, the opportunities of leisure, and a craftsman's intimate satisfactions."[25] Now maybe that's true for John Updike (though Mary McCarthy revealed that she almost didn't read Updike's *Rabbit, Run* because of the reviews, but when she did get around to it she found it "the most interesting American novel I've read in quite a long time"[26]), but if all of Updike's readers were put off by a negative review, he perhaps would find his books providing him more intimate satisfactions and less of a living.

As May Sarton succinctly put it, "A bad review keeps readers from buying a book, it is as simple as that."[27]

Not so long ago, a new book might remain in a store for a year, eighteen months, two years, before being sent back to the publisher. Not so today — when, as Calvin Trillin reminds us, the average shelf life of a trade book is "somewhere between milk and yogurt."[28] Promotion and word of mouth have to work pretty darn fast to get a book selling, and a well-placed, ill-natured, silly review can bludgeon a good book to death.

How? Very simply. Most major publishers don't implement their advertising plans for the majority of their books — those not by a name author, not by a celebrity, and not focused on the events on today's front page — until the reviews start coming in. If an early review in a key publication (the *New York Times* is the prime example) is unfavorable, the publishers are spooked, stop publicity and promotion and move on to another book. As a result, the bookstores stop ordering, the radio and television talk show hosts stop calling, the newspaper and magazine interviewers look elsewhere for stories, the reviewers stop reviewing, paperback houses and television and movie studios don't bid, and the public, never having had the chance to hear about the book, doesn't buy it. Just like that, the book an author has slaved over for years is no more. According to John Cheever, Knopf had anticipated that his *Bullet Park* would be a best-seller. "There was a hostile review in the *Times* and the publisher stopped all advertising."[29] And so, the book was not a best-seller or even a fair seller.

This is the catch-22 of publishing. Many publishers have concluded that advertising, to be effective, must follow sales, that sales don't follow advertising; so a book must prove itself without advertising before it can get a piece of a publisher's advertising budget. Yet how, without advertising, can anyone know the book exists? The answer, of course, is reviews.

So authors bite their nails, and wait: "I should be working, but now I wait for reviews," John Cheever wrote, anticipating the first notices of one of his novels. "I not only wait for them: I write them. I've written them all, even the Albany Times-Union."[30]

And they feel rotten when the reviews aren't good: "I never felt worse in my life," Kurt Vonnegut recalled when every review — from the *New York Times,* to *Time, Newsweek, The New York Review of Books,* the *Village Voice,* and *Rolling Stone* panned his *Slapstick.* "I felt as though I were sleeping standing up in a boxcar in Germany again."[31]

And they fall into despair. Upon reading some hostile reviews, Thomas Wolfe wrote from Geneva, Switzerland, to his editor, Max Perkins: "Will you please have Mr. Darrow [Whitney Darrow, vice president of Scribners] send me a statement of whatever money is due me? I shall not write any more books, and since I must begin to make other plans for the future, I should like to know how much money I will have."[32]

Ernest Hemingway had the same reaction. "I am tempted never to publish another damned thing. The swine aren't worth writing for. I swear to christ they're not. Every phase of the whole racket is so disgusting that it makes you feel like vomiting."[33] As did Malcolm Cowley. "It all seems amusing in retrospect, but the impression it gave me of being exposed and helpless, a criminal chained and taunted in the marketplace, was a shattering experience while it lasted.... I reviewed for the *New Republic*—with rather more kindness to authors than I had shown in the beginning, I wrote essays and poems, but for years I couldn't bring myself to write another book."[34]

And so, sometimes, just in this way, a bad review may bludgeon not only a book, but also a writing career.

CHAPTER 10

Non Est Disputandum

*W*hat recourse does an author have when hit with an unfair review? Well, if you're Norman Mailer and receive such a review, as he did in 1991 from John Simon in the *New York Times Book Review* for his novel *Harlot's Ghost*, you can request (and get) a meeting with the editors of the *Times* to demonstrate how the reviewer was biased against you, and demand (and get) "prominent play" for a lengthy rebuttal. Nevertheless, that prominent play — in which Mailer marshalled more than sufficient evidence to demonstrate that Mr. Simon hated his guts — could not reverse the precipitous slip of the magnum opus, on which he had labored for seven years, from its fingerhold on the *Times* Best Sellers list; nor could it prevent the final word by "The Editor" at the end of his prominent play: that Mr. Simon "wrote a fair and balanced review that met the standards of this newspaper."[1]

Now suppose a criminal defendant were gagged during his trial and not represented by counsel. Suppose that the jury promptly found this defendant guilty and the judge sentenced him to seven years imprisonment — all without a word in his own defense. You can bet that the *New York Times* would be all over that one, front page coverage, editorials, op eds, the works. Yet the *Times* has no problem letting a reviewer serve as prosecutor, judge, jury, and executioner of a book on which an author has toiled for seven years, with the author effectively gagged and unable to say so much as, "Now just a minute."

Unless he's Norman Mailer — and even for Mailer things didn't work out so well — there's precious little an author can do (author Dan Moldea sued the *New York Times* — ultimately to no avail — when the *Book Review* in 1989 trashed his book *Interference: How Organized*

Crime Influences Professional Football) or maybe even should do, for there is nothing to be gained by answering a critic. It's a waste of psychic energy, a waste of time, and, as Saul Bellow recognized when he quoted the Jewish proverb that any fool can throw a stone into the water which ten wise men can't recover,[2] oftentimes an impossibility.

The brutalized author, though, need not just sit there and take it. Jean Kerr, author of *Please Don't Eat the Daisies*, had the best idea of how to deal with such assaults: "Confronted by an absolutely infuriating review it is sometimes helpful for the victim to do a little personal research on the critic. Is there any truth to the rumor that he had no formal education beyond the age of eleven? In any event, is he able to construct a simple English sentence? Do his participles dangle? When moved to lyricism does he write 'I had a fun time?' Was he ever arrested for burglary? I don't know that you will prove anything this way, but it is perfectly harmless and quite soothing."[3]

At one time or another, most authors have followed this formula for relief. "Critics are like horse-flies which prevent the horse from ploughing" said Chekhov. "For over twenty years I have read criticism of my stories and I do not remember a single remark of any value or one word of valuable advice." These truths have persisted from Chekhov to Grisham: "I've sold too many books to get good reviews anymore," John Grisham has said. "There's a lot of jealousy, because [reviewers] think they can write a good novel or a best-seller and get frustrated when they can't. As a group, I've learned to despise them."[4]

"Reviewers are usually people who would have been poets, historians, biographers, etc., if they could," wrote Samuel Taylor Coleridge. "They have tried their talents at one or at the other, and have failed; therefore they turn critics."[5] This sentiment was set to verse by James Russell Lowell:

> Nature fits all her children with something to do;
> He who would write and can't write, can surely review.[6]

Brendan Behan said of drama critics, "Critics are like eunuchs in a harem. They're there every night, they see it done every night, they see how it should be done every night, but they can't do it themselves."[7] The eunuch as metaphor seems regularly to recur in authors' descriptions of critics. Early on, Ernest Hemingway concluded that "all Criticism is shit anyway. Nobody knows anything about it except yourself. God knows, people who are paid to have attitudes toward things, professional critics, make me sick; camp following eunuchs of literature."[8]

Criticism is a tricky business, because what we bring to the reading of a book will shape our reactions to it. *When* a reader reads a book can be of significance, not only the particular day or time of day — a book might seem meaningless drivel if read in an oral surgeon's reception room, as it might seem truly enchanting if read on a lazy summer afternoon in a comfortable chaise under the shady branches of a tree — but also the particular time of life. A reader first encountering *The Catcher in the Rye* as a junior in high school might have no idea what Holden Caulfield's problem was. By the next year he could be Holden. When rereading the book in his thirties, he might be dazzled by Salinger's art, by his extraordinary creation of life, something he had not appreciated in his first two readings. A fifty-eight-year-old reader picking up the book for the first time might discover little to recommend it, undoubtedly just why the reviewer for the *New York Herald Tribune Book Review* concluded about Salinger's novel: "Recent war novels have accustomed us all to ugly words and images, but from the mouths of the very young and protected they sound peculiarly offensive.... The ear refuses to believe."[9]

"For a book to be great in a reader's life," John Updike has said, "it is not enough for the book to be great; the reader must be ready."[10] Certain kinds of novels, he noted, "especially nineteenth-century novels, should be read in adolescence, on those dreamily endless solitary afternoons that in later life become so uselessly short and full of appointments, or they will never be read at all."[11] Similarly, Truman Capote believed that "between thirteen and sixteen are the ideal if not the only ages for succumbing to Thomas Wolfe — he seemed to me a great genius then, and still does, though I can't read a line of it now. Just as other youthful flames have guttered: Poe, Dickens, Stevenson. I love them in memory, but find them unreadable."[12] Capote remembered that "I also didn't like *Moby Dick* the first time I read it, but then I was about thirteen. The second time I read it I was about thirty and somewhere along the line I liked it a great deal."[13] Critic Joseph Epstein has said it best: "In place of capsule comments telling readers what a book is about, I should tell them where a particular book might best be read: in airports, in bed, in bathtubs, at solitary meals, in the country, on the subway, etc. My list would specify at roughly what age a book ought to be read; no F. Scott Fitzgerald beyond thirty; no Chekhov before thirty; no Proust before forty; no James Joyce after fifty."[14]

Even an author's evaluation of his own work can shift. Chaucer and Kafka questioned the very worth of their writing. Others really didn't understand the place of their work; Melville was convinced that *Pierre; or, The Ambiguities* would be a popular best-seller to match his previous *Typee* and *Omoo*. He died believing himself a failure: "No man," he despaired, "ever hitched his wagon higher to a star or fell so low."[15] Dickens thought of *Great Expectations* as something of a comedy. Fitzgerald believed *Tender Is the Night* to be a more experimental work of prose than James Joyce's *Ulysses*. Joyce believed *Finnegans Wake* a simple novel. Leonard Woolf had to snatch Virginia Woolf's manuscripts away from her before she tore them to pieces. John Steinbeck found his work at times "to have the high purpose I set for it, and at other times it seems pedestrian and trite."[16] As he worked on the last chapter of his masterpiece, *The Grapes of Wrath*, he was discouraged: "I am sure of one thing — it isn't the great book I had hoped it would be. It's just a run-of-the-mill book. And the awful thing is that it is absolutely the best I can do."[17] James Dickey observed that "your opinion of your own work fluctuates wildly. Under the right circumstances you can pick up something that you've written and approve of it; you'll think it's good and that nobody could have done exactly the same thing. Under different circumstances, you'll look at exactly the same poem and say, 'My Lord, isn't that boring.'"[18]

Let's face it: There are books — good books, great books — that each of us will never appreciate. For whatever reason, they are simply not our cup of tea. "Three times in my life I have read through Shakespeare and Goethe from end to end," sighed Leo Tolstoy, "and I never could make out in which their charm consisted."[19] Others have felt the same way about Tolstoy's writing. Anthony Trollope wrote that *War and Peace* had "absolutely no plot — no contrived arrangement of incidents by which interest is excited."[20] And Rebecca West admitted she was "a heretic" about Tolstoy. "I really don't see

War and Peace as a great novel because it seems constantly to be trying to prove that nobody who was in the war knew what was going on. Well, I don't know whoever thought they would ... that if you put somebody down in the wildest sort of mess they understand what's happening."[21] Unlike Truman Capote, Gore Vidal never came to appreciate Melville. "I do detest *Moby Dick*," Vidal has declared, "and I never finished *Pierre; or, The Ambiguities.* But then, I don't like Melville's writing. It is windy and pretentious, it is bogus Shakespeare."[22] Katherine Anne Porter could not stomach the writings of F. Scott Fitzgerald: "I couldn't read him then and I can't read him now.... Not only didn't I like his writing, but I didn't like the people he wrote about. I thought they weren't worth thinking about, and I still think so."[23] Henry James found *Crime and Punishment* so dull he could not finish it, while Robert Louis Stevenson called it the greatest book he had read in ten years. Stephen King cannot read James Michener. And so it goes.

Now, consider this: What if *Moby Dick* were Herman Melville's just-published first novel, and the *New York Times* selected Gore Vidal to review it? What if it selected Truman Capote but before he was old enough to appreciate the book? What if the *Times* selects Katherine Anne Porter to review a first novel by an author named F. Scott Fitzgerald? What if the reviewer assigned a first novel is running out of time to meet the deadline to have his review in to the *Times*, and takes the manuscript with him to his appointment with the oral surgeon and continues reading in the reception room? Bad luck! In today's publishing world, those reviews would probably mean the death of those books and perhaps the disappearance of those authors.

It gets even worse. As thoughtful a critic as John Updike ("I became a reviewer in part to assuage my sense of indignation about some of the reviews I've got, so that I would sort of show what a fair review should be") has catalogued how his personal feelings of the moment sometimes have seasoned his reviews: "Here and there filial affection for an older writer has pulled my punch. Fear of reprisal may have forced a grin or two.... In other cases irritations of the moment added their personal pepper." A review he did of Dostoevsky was composed "during a mysterious attack of tendonitis; I could not sleep, and sat up all one night, watching dawn infiltrate Menemsha Bight, my throbbing left wrist held above my head while my right hand confidently advised Dostoevsky to keep trying."[24] What if Updike is assigned a first novel to review and has another attack of tendonitis as he reads the book and writes his review? If Dostoevsky came up short, who wouldn't?

"'Tis the good reader that makes the good book," Emerson said. It's not as if Updike and Porter, Capote and Vidal, and for that matter probably most critics, are not good readers. The question is, what are these readers bringing to the book at that moment they review it? Thus the author whose book has been sent out to be reviewed sees his pages riffled by the fickle hand of fate.

Books can be medicines for the soul; but if medicines made their way to the ill the same way that books make their way to the reader, human civilization would have been wiped out long ago by epidemics of typhus and cholera. For what are critics but the Food and Drug Administration for readers, telling the stores what to stock, telling us what is good for us and what is not? The big difference is that the FDA has developed a very structured screening process for bringing new drugs to market, whereas a critic may be you or me or that troglodyte down the street who may say anything he pleases about the book he reviews. Those 79,000 souls in need of a new novel about teen-age angst may never learn that such a book exists if a critic does such a demolition job on it that its publisher cuts promotion and bookstores don't stock it.

The foremost purpose of criticism should be to give books the readership they deserve, for a book unread is a book that doesn't exist. As Henry Seidel Canby, the former chairman of the board of judges of the Book-of-the-Month Club, said, "The primary object of all writing about books, we take it, is to give them currency. For the best book in the world is worth nothing at all if it never finds a reader."[25] "Better to praise and share than blame and bury,"[26] is the way John Updike has put it.

Reviewers who have authored books understand this. Anthony Burgess has said, "In my capacity as critic I never stab anybody, for I know how life-denying it is to be stabbed. Writing a book is damned difficult work, and you ought to praise a book if you can." This opinion is shared by Kurt Vonnegut: "I have long felt that any reviewer who expresses rage and loathing for a novel is preposterous. He or she is like a person who has just put on full armor and attacked a hot fudge sundae or banana split."[27] James Atlas, an editor of *The New York Times Magazine*, dished out his share of nasty reviews until his novel was banged up a bit, at which time he made a vow: He would still tell the truth about a book, but he would tell it "in a gingerly way and with genuine remorse," because, he explained, "they think we can take it, but we can't."[28] And John Irving:

> I write only favorable reviews.... If I get a book to review and I don't like it, I return it; I only review the book if I love it. Hence I've written very few reviews, and those are really just songs of praise or rather long, retrospective reviews of all the writer's works.... Another thing about not writing negative reviews: grown-ups shouldn't finish books they're not enjoying. When you're no longer a child, and you no longer live at home, you don't have to finish everything on your plate. One reward of leaving school is that you don't have to finish books you don't like. You know, if I were a critic, I'd be angry and vicious, too; it *makes* poor critics angry and vicious — to have to *finish* all those books they're not enjoying. What a silly job criticism is! What unnatural work it is! It is certainly not work for a grown-up![29]

So read that book, reviewer. Read it like a reader. What was the author trying to do? How close did he come to succeeding in what he attempted to do? Quote from the book to support your assessment. Where are you, the critic, coming from? Within what framework are you reading and analyzing the book? Did you like it? What did you like? What didn't you like? If you have a predisposition against a book, don't review it. (A major review in *The New Times Book Review* of Anaïs Nin's diary *A Journal of Love* began: "My idea of hell is to be stranded on a desert island with nothing to read but Anais Nin's diaries, but some people, apparently, can't get enough of them. Her publishers, for instance."[30] That's just silly. How did the *Times* pick this reviewer? Why didn't the reviewer disqualify herself? Why did she bother to write this review? Why did the *Times* publish it?)

Ask yourself: Who would like this book? Who wouldn't like the book? Is your review free of ridicule, disparagement, prophetic pronouncements from Olympus? Be interesting, be entertaining, certainly; but being clever, being cute, is not the role of the critic. John Steinbeck claimed he knew critics "who, thinking up a wise crack —

wait happily for a book to come along to apply it to. This is creativeness — not criticism."[31] Telling what a book is about; telling who would, or would not, like it; describing why the author succeeds or does not succeed in what he has attempted to do; this is criticism.

"Literature" said Jules Renard, "is an occupation in which you have to keep proving your talent to people who have none."[32] As satisfying a thought as this might be, it does not convey the real problem. These are not people without talent, these people who mistakenly reject manuscripts or who write rotten reviews. The real problem is that the manuscript, or the completed book, by chance has fallen into the wrong hands — the hands of a William Styron who is just not into books like *Kon-Tiki;* or the hands of a publisher or reviewer who, at that point in his or her life, does not really understand a book like *The Catcher in the Rye;* when a colleague down the hall might be a great lover of sea adventures or be a parent with two Holden Caulfields living at home.

When the review copies are mailed out a month or six weeks before publication date, the author had better cross his fingers tightly and pray for a run of luck, for at that point he has stepped up to the table and said to the croupier, put it all — the blood, toil, sweat and tears of the last several years of my life — put it all on twenty-seven.

CHAPTER 11

Make a Joyful Noise

A book is written; a book is edited; a book is published. How do readers find out about it? By wandering up and down the aisles of a bookstore, coming across it by chance? What an uncertain, improbable way to discover a new book. Is this how we learn about a new breakfast cereal, fabric softener, deodorant? By happening across it in a supermarket and risking our stomachs, our underwear, our underarms, with some unknown product? Of course not. Yet this is precisely the way that publishers try to sell the majority of their wares.

"Yes, but" — publishers have always responded — "selling a book is a lot different from selling soap." To that "but," a legendary best-selling author, a prominent literary agent, and a top editor have all replied: Maybe it's not so different.

Jacqueline Susann felt that the selling of a book was exactly like the selling of detergent. "Why the hell not? It works."[1] Agent Morton Janklow has said, "My opinion is that Procter & Gamble could hire a smart acquisitions editor and go into the paperback business tomorrow." And editor Michael Korda reports that he has learned from experience that "books can be merchandised, just like anything else."[2]

The role of advertising in selling books has been pondered by publishers forever. An editorial in the *New York Times* in 1885, titled "Authors and Advertisers," noted: "Authors frequently complain that their books do not sell, and they do not seem to understand the reason for this unpleasant state of things. The reason is plain. Publishers have no real conception of the art of advertising and consequently few books sell. They do not seem to understand that anything that is advertised will sell. The appearance a day or two ago in this city of 'sandwich' men advertising a new novel shows that at least one publisher has learned how to conduct business."[3] Even after decades of mulling over the relationship between advertising and selling books, the best and brightest in publishing remain mystified by the impact of advertising.

In 1923, Walter H. Page, one of the founders of Doubleday, Page & Company, threw up his hands in despair: "About the advertising of books, nobody knows anything."[4] The usually unflappable Max Perkins was frustrated: "The problem of book advertising is a very difficult one. It often seems as if it were stupidly handled but, so far, neither we nor any other publisher have [sic] been able to make it very effective."[5] Even the brilliant Alfred Knopf was perplexed: "It is a source of perpetual puzzlement to me to know why people buy our books," he wrote in 1961 after forty-six years as a highly successful publisher. "We spend a great deal of money advertising them, largely in *The New York Times Book Review* but also in *The Reporter, The Atlantic, Harper's, The New Yorker,* and many daily and Sunday papers. I have never been able to convince myself that any of this advertising does actually sell books.... I would therefore greatly welcome postcards from readers of any Borzoi book which would tell me just what led them to beg, borrow, buy, or steal the book in question. Should any reader have been influenced by an advertisement, it would be of special interest to me to know where that advertisement appeared."[6]

Unlike most publishers who have only sighed about the difficulties, the impossibilities, of advertising books, Alfred Knopf at least was asking some questions which, if pursued, might have helped solve this mystery.

The problems are real enough. "Book-advertising," Max Perkins came to believe from his experience at Scribners, "is deprived of the great principle of general advertising — repetition. An advertiser of any other product can go on for several years, and lose money by it, and yet be a great gainer in the end as the result of persistent repetition. But, as each particular book is a separate product, it is impossible to apply to any one, except to a very limited extent, this great fundamental advertising principle."[7] In addition, whether a book is published by Scribners or Doubleday or Knopf makes no difference to the reader; book consumers have no brand loyalty to a manufacturer-publisher. A consumer who buys a pair of Nike sneakers will wear them out and, if he was satisfied, will consider buying another pair of Nike sneakers; in contrast, the consumer who enjoyed a particular book published by Farrar, Straus & Giroux will not ordinarily go and look for another book published by that house.

But isn't all that equally true about movies? How do we find out about a new movie? By driving past the movie theater every day to see what is playing? Perhaps some people do, just as some roam the aisles of bookstores. But many learn about a new movie through the relentless newspaper advertising during the relatively short life of a movie, advertising which either makes them aware of a new movie or reinforces what they have already heard about it. Those people who want to go to a movie know just where to look to see what's playing. Why shouldn't publishers conclude that those people who want to read a book should know just where to look to see what's available? Why shouldn't they determine that they could reach the widest audience for their new books through a number of small ads in, say, the book page of newspapers? Would it be more effective to spend a limited advertising budget on one full-page ad in the *New York Times Book Review*, or to run a series of less expensive ads in some of the nation's major dailies? No one seems to know.

"But every book is a different product," our publisher persists. "What works for one book might be worthless for another; books aren't like a line of dishwashers." Surely the same could be said of movies or Broadway shows (other products with a very limited shelf life), yet advertising is the lifeblood of movies and plays. Indeed, time and again, Serion, Coyne, the leading ad agency for Broadway shows, triumphantly overcame a bad review by Frank Rich in the *New York Times* by using targeted advertising to build a market.

With a little research and study, wouldn't publishers recognize patterns in promoting a contemporary novel, or a book of historical nonfiction, or a book about the sea, and know precisely which of the hundreds of newspapers and hundreds of magazines to target with exactly what types of ads? If they don't know this — if the advertising of each new book really is a new puzzle, or if they apply the same advertising formula to every new book — then the publishing houses haven't been doing their homework, or perhaps they are entrusting one of the most critical components of their work to their most inexperienced employees. Charles Scribner, Jr., remembered how, when he joined his family's publishing house in the late 1940s, "advertising and marketing in those days were rather amateurish. I, who knew nothing, was in charge." Scribner wrote the copy for the ads, "most of which, I must say in all modesty, were painfully bad."[8] It's no different today; even at major publishing houses, promotion and advertising sometimes seem an afterthought.

What else? What other problems with book advertising? Well, a soft drink manufacturer, for example, might bring out one new product that it wishes to promote over the course of a year. Not only can it target its advertising budget on that one new product, it can keep advertising the product, week after week, month after month, until the consumer gets the message. Each major publishing house, in contrast, is bringing out scores of new products — new books — each spring and fall season (what if Coke or Pepsi pushed twenty-eight new soft drinks this spring?), and the shelf life of these books is alarmingly short.

But aren't we talking about two very different types of advertising? The "quicker-picker-upper," "hold the pickles, hold the lettuce," "don't leave home without it" messages that over the course of time begin to hum in the noisy static of our minds, are all forms of advertising by repetition, which aims to drum a message into our heads until it enters our subconscious. There is also another type of advertising: the kind that lets the world know that a new product has arrived. Given the limited life of a book and the limited revenues that may be devoted to promoting it, this would seem to be precisely the type of advertising on which publishers should concentrate their resources.

For all their protestations about the dubious value of advertising in selling books, publishers do run ads, and ads do sell books, though to be sure, the process is not as simple as it might seem.

Although the use of television and radio advertising of books has been increasing, publishers still believe that newspapers and magazines are the most cost-effective media for reaching the book buying audience. And the *New York Times Book Review*, with its several million well-educated, probably book buying Sunday readers, is the publication of choice for most of the major houses. What could be simpler?

The *Times* once ran an ad featuring a testimonial by Arbor House publisher Eden Collinsworth: "The *New York Times* was invaluable in the Arbor House marketing campaign for Elmore Leonard's novel, *Glitz*. The full-page ads we ran in the first section of the daily *Times* and the double-page spread in *The New York Times Book Review* resulted in reorders totalling more than 30,000 copies. Arbor House can say — without hesitation — that *The Times* advertising campaign had an undeniable strong impact on the sales for this book. I cannot recall a better return on investment." The *Times* appended its own ad, trumpeting that "word of mouth about an exciting new book can do wonders in spreading the news. But for sheer power in moving a title off the shelves into the buyer's hands and onto the Best Seller list it's *The New York Times* every time."[9]

Ms. Collinsworth and the *Times* both neglected to note that two little words in those ads might have had quite a significant impact in moving those 30,000 copies, and those two words were "Elmore Leonard." A substitution of those two words with "Johnny Jones" or "Tom Smith" would have been an interesting control to run before concluding it was the advertisements alone that resulted in the reorders of 30,000. Can anyone doubt the result? The solution to the riddle of the role of advertising in selling books is not so simple, for if it were, a well-funded publisher would become a very rich publisher indeed.

Still there should be no doubt about it: Advertising can sell books.

An extremely attractive, long-named lady, Mrs. Emma Dorothy Eliza Nevittee Southworth, walked into a publisher's office one day in 1854 with her long manuscript entitled "The Lost Heiress." She candidly admitted that several publishers had already rejected it. One suspects that this particular publisher might have found Mrs. Southworth's personal charms at least as compelling as her romantic novel. In any event, the publisher not only accepted her manuscript for publication, but signed a contract for her future books, and committed to spending $6,000 on advertising before publication, an amount equivalent to a healthy promotion budget today of perhaps $75,000. *The Lost Heiress* was an instant success. It would seem that only advertising did the trick, and if it did, it was money well spent. Mrs. Southworth was now a name author. Her publisher bought the plates for her previous books and reprinted them all, and all sold well. Fifty of her novels were still selling into the 1930s, and most sold over 100,000 copies.

The same story was repeated at the turn of the century with author Harold Bell Wright, whose publisher catapulted his novels to sales of hundreds of thousands of copies with advertising budgets of $75,000 per book.

Over the years, as advertising has progressed from the mere listing of a publisher's new books as was the custom early in the twentieth century, innovations in book advertising have often met with remarkable success: the use of pages at the end of a volume to tease the reader with a taste of another volume; creative copy for the ads; the first full-page ads; the first two-page spreads in the *New York Times Book Review*. Anything a little bit different to attract attention has worked. Miss Caro M. Clark, a no-nonsense young woman from Unity, Maine, set up a publishing house in Boston at the turn of the century, signed a contract with Charles Felton Pidgin to publish his manuscript, "Quincy Adams Sawyer," and made sure that "it was advertised as no other American novel was ever advertised." She ran frequent newspaper and magazine announcements; she used billboard space; she traveled to ten cities in eleven days, selling numerous copies during the three to five hours she allotted for each city. Through all this frenetic activity she managed to sell some 250,000 copies. Her profitable C. M. Clark Publishing Company succeeded through advertising. As Miss Clark explained it:

> We have arrived at the conclusion that the main point is to keep on advertising in some manner, avoiding the beaten paths of other publishers and accomplishing something enough different to attract more than ordinary attention. When we launched our first book, "Quincy Adams Sawyer", one of our first thoughts was to secure a striking poster, by sight of which all might become familiar with the title. We happily hit upon the old white horse driven by a man in a chaise along a country road. We stamped it on the cover of the book, we printed it on the paper wrapper of the book, we had it on posters to display in bookstores, and we had it in "one-sheets" and in "eight-sheets" for the billboards. We plastered the dead walls of Boston, Philadelphia, New York, Chicago, and San Francisco with them. We covered

124

the country from Portland, Maine, to San Francisco with our red posters. When we went into the newspapers, it was with the idea that unless our advertisement was much bigger than that of any other publisher it would not attract the necessary attention. No newspaper advertisement was put out that did not contain a cut of the horse and chaise."[10]

There could be no doubt that Miss Clark was on to something: Advertising does sell books. Or does it?

There are books which have become runaway best-sellers without a lick of advertising. Knopf's publication in 1923 of *The Prophet* by Kahlil Gibran is a classic example. Knopf had published three previous books by Gibran which had mediocre sales, and so printed a small run of his latest, *The Prophet*, which fulfilled Knopf's low expectations by selling only 1,300 copies in twelve months. But behold! The next year it sold 2,600 copies, and over 5,000 copies the third year, rising to 10,000 copies a year, and then to 70,000, and then to 175,000. In the first four decades of the history of this book, Knopf had advertised it only once, and a bemused Alfred Knopf noted that sales slackened after that one ad, which he never repeated. Another example was the publication of *The Snow Goose* in November of 1941 by British publisher Michael Joseph, a book which again was advertised only once, in a 3½ inch ad that also listed some other current books. *The Snow Goose*, by an unknown Paul Gallico, received only twelve reviews in its first six months, none of them in England's major papers; yet it went through twenty editions, selling over 300,000 hardcovers.

Just as there are books that achieved enormous sales despite the absence of any advertising, so there are terrifying tales of books that fall flat despite a surfeit of advertising. Random's Bennett Cerf was convinced that "you can take a full-page ad in the *Times* for a book that's dead and it won't sell fifty additional copies." And he knew; more than once he had found out the hard way.

Although publishers have never stated publicly that they run ads to foster good relations with a particular publication, many publishers have conceded that their advertising is sometimes run as much because of pressure from an author or an author's agent as it is to sell books. To placate valued authors and agents, Cerf had taken out large ads for books he considered dead. "The ad will come out and we watch the daily sales. Invariably, a full week later, we haven't sold a hundred copies of the book all over the country, meaning that the ad is absolutely worthless."[11] Max Perkins, too, had learned this was so. He compared advertising a book to pushing a car that's stuck. "If the car is really stuck in the mud, ten people can't budge it. But if it's moving even a little bit, one man can push it on down the road. By the same token, if a book is absolutely dead, all the advertising in the world isn't going to help. If it's got a glimmer of life, if it's selling a little bit maybe in only one or two spots, it's moving enough to be given a push."[12] As Perkins found, "we can hardly ever accomplish anything by advertising any books but new ones."[13]

Why this should be so is inexplicable. A thriller we haven't read is as new to you and me as it was on publication day. If someone is interested in Louis Comfort Tiffany, why should it matter whether a book about him was published yesterday or eighteen months ago? Whatever the reason, it matters: With few exceptions, books either sell well from the outset or will never sell. Perhaps John Webster was right when he spoke of "ignorant asses visiting stationers' shops, their use is not to inquire for good books, but new books."[14]

What may well remain for all time the most horrifying cautionary tale is the story of Jack Dreyfus, founder of the Dreyfus Mutual Fund and a wealthy man indeed. When he was almost fifty, he suffered from depression, and, on a hunch, had his doctor prescribe for him a drug used in the treatment of epilepsy. His recovery was spectacularly immediate. Dreyfus spent the next fifteen years and over $20 million to sponsor medical research into the benefits and uses of this drug, but despite his heroic efforts, the drug never received FDA approval for anything but the treatment of epilepsy. And so Jack Dreyfus wrote a book, *A Remarkable Medicine Has Been Overlooked*, and being Jack Dreyfus, entered into an arrangement that must have made the executives at Simon & Schuster drool: If Simon & Schuster would publish his book and get it out into the nation's bookstores, he would pay all the advertising and promotional expenses; not only that, he guaranteed to Simon & Schuster that he would spend the extraordinary sum of one million dollars to publicize the hardcover edition; and not only that, he would forgo any earnings on the book — he wanted no advance, no royalties, no nothing. Would that all authors were so accommodating, the executives at Simon & Schuster must have thought as they watched their own Don Quixote set off in 1981 on his Rocinante while their presses spewed forth 50,000 copies of the book and spread them across the land.

Now it must be noted that it was generally conceded that the book was well written and that it concerned an intriguing topic, certainly a worthwhile topic. And Jack Dreyfus was true to his word. He spent $1.5 million on full-page advertisements, run time and again in every major newspaper and magazine in the country — the *New York Times*, the *Wall Street Journal*, *Time*, *Newsweek*, everywhere. Simon & Schuster sold almost all — note the word "almost" — of the 50,000 copies. One and a half million dollars divided by 50,000 comes to $30, the amount spent to sell each of those books, more than three times the retail price of the hardcovers: $9.15.

Still riding toward his next windmill, Jack Dreyfus then decided to bring out a paperback edition, and made the same arrangement with Pocket Books, whose executives, too, no doubt were salivating. Dreyfus spent another $1.5 million on advertising, and the paperback sold 150,000 copies. Again, as with the hardcover, not a bad showing in terms of sales, but a flaming disaster in terms of the promotion dollars expended. (One wonders what the result might have been if the same dollars had been spent not on a specialized book like *A Remarkable Medicine Has Been Overlooked*, but on, for instance, a critically acclaimed first novel.)

Without benefactors like Jack Dreyfus funding them, publishers always appear a little squeamish on the subject of advertising. They seem fearful of hearing their authors' ideas about advertising, convinced that these thoughtless professionals, mindful only of the royalty they receive on every book sold, will pressure them to advertise regardless of the cost to the publisher or the squeezing of the publisher's profit margins. Some publishers seem quite convinced that authors demand ads simply because they like to see their name in print, and that ads are really for the authors, their mothers and their agents.

British publisher Michael Joseph once said that "no class of reader is so attentive to publisher's advertisements as authors,"[15] that it was only the authors who ever really even noticed the ads. There might be an element of truth to this. Scott Fitzgerald was able to cite to Max Perkins line and verse of where *This Side of Paradise* had, or had not, been advertised: not once in that enchanted southern paradise of Montgomery, Alabama, where his true love lived; three times in his native St. Paul; eleven times in Chicago, where it sat on the best-seller list for eighteen weeks and "should have been advertised in 2 papers *at least* every other week," since books that were competing with his "had been advertised almost every week for 8 months in Chicago papers."[16] Ernest Hemingway was just as vigilant and just as quick to cry to Max:

> I cabled you yesterday because I had been seeing the N.Y. Times, Herald Tribune and Sat Review of Lit and they all were full of ads of a book of stories by Dotty Parker but nothing about this book [*Winner Take Nothing*]. There was an ad in Sunday Times and I believe Daily Times the week the book came out. Then nothing. No follow up at all. Saw no mention of book in Sunday Herald Trib in number it was reviewed in. An ad in with your fall list in the week after. Believe there was an ad in Herald Trib the day it came out. The advertizing is your business — not mine. But if a publisher seems to give no importance to a book and makes no Boom Ha Ha the public takes the cue from the publisher very quickly.[17]

And then, publishers worry, too, that authors will criticize the content of whatever advertising they do run. Max Perkins believed that authors and publishers would never agree on the subject of advertising; "authors generally have a completely unjustifiable faith in what book-advertising can do, and they get it largely from knowing what advertising in general can do."[18] Certainly this was true of Scott Fitzgerald, who began his career with a short tenure as "an advertising man" at the Street Railway Advertising Company.[19] Fitzgerald complained to Max Perkins that Scribners ads for *This Side of Paradise* "were small and undistinguished," and even worse, none of Fitzgerald's ideas for the ads "from among my nine or ten suggestions" were used. "The greatest selling point my book had, Mencken's statement quoted on the wrapper ... was allowed to be forgotten with *one* exception, *one* ad. Sinclair Lewis's remark in the *Tribune*, 'In Scott Fitzgerald we have an author who will be the equal of any young European' was *absolutely* unused."[20]

Bennett Cerf published his book, *Shake Well Before Using*, with Simon & Schuster, not with his own Random House, believing that it was most impolitic for a publisher to publish his own book. He could just hear his authors calling him: "I see that you have money to advertise your own book. Why didn't I have an ad in the *Times* this morning? You're spending your time exploiting yours instead of mine."[21] In addition, with another house bringing out his book, Cerf had the pleasure of lambasting another publisher for not properly promoting his book. He felt that Simon & Schuster was promoting a book by Billy Rose more aggressively than his own. "Like a typical author, I felt I was being neglected and I raised holy hell, as a result of which they took several full-page ads."[22] Cerf took a special delight in making a nuisance of himself with his new publisher. "It was like a minuet. We'd go through the routine of my grumbling about something and their giving me the precise answer that I give my own authors."[23]

Publishers worry, too, that authors will start comparing the ads for their books with the ads for other books, and, naturally, theirs will come up short every time. Ernest Hemingway groused to Perkins that "it did seem as though they laid off advertising *Men Without Women* when it was still going well just as much as they jumped out with enormous ads for Thornton.[Wilder]'s book [*The Bridge of San Luis Rey*] the minute it started going."[24] Young Scott Fitzgerald dashed off a letter to Max Perkins on July 30, 1921, when he saw an advertisement calling a new Knopf book, *Zell and Mooncalf*, "the most brilliantly successful first novel of many years." This was intolerable. "You've let everyone forget that my book once had this title," he fumed. "Knopf's statement goes quite unchallenged." *Mooncalf's* claim to the title, Fitzgerald was sure, was ludicrous since he knew that its sales had not reached 50,000. "Yet my novel so far as I have seen got not one newspaper ad, not one *Times* or *Tribune* ad or Chicago ad since *six months* after publication. And Knopf has forcibly kept *Mooncalf* in the public eye for *twice that long*. What notoriety my book has preserved as well as what notoriety it got in the beginning, it got almost unaided. Its ads were small and undistinguished and confined almost entirely to college magazines and to *Scribners*."[25]

And yet, as upset as Fitzgerald was at Scribners with what he considered the "ultra-conservatism in their marketing and editorial policies," doesn't the publication history of *This Side of Paradise* prove the point that it is not advertising alone that ultimately makes or breaks a book? Here he admits himself that the launch of *This Side of Paradise* was "almost unaided." Unaided, *This Side of Paradise* made more of a splash on publication than did *Zell and Mooncalf* with all that advertising behind it. And who today has read, who today has heard of, what was it? *Zell and Mooncalf*? Title unknown. Author forgotten. Taking the long view, Fitzgerald's *This Side of Paradise* has far outsold *Zell and Mooncalf.* And Fitzgerald himself is with us today, and one suspects that he will be for generations to come.

It is interesting that an older and wiser, or perhaps just more resigned, Scott Fitzgerald wrote to Max Perkins in quite a different vein thirteen years later about advertising for his latest book, *Tender Is the Night*: "Again I want to tell you my theory that everybody is absolutely dead on ballyhoo of any kind... The reputation of a book must grow from within upward, must be a natural growth."[26] Because Max Perkins was Max Perkins, he did not reply "I told you so," though he must have been pleased when another of his famed authors, Thomas Wolfe, recognized quite early in the game that "publishing is a very mysterious business. It is hard to predict what kind of sale or reception a book will have, and advertising seems to do very little good."[27]

But some form of advertising is essential for every new book, to make a joyful noise to let the world know a new book has arrived. This is not to say that every book needs a double-page spread in the *New York Times Book Review*, but something more than the publisher's catalog write-up is necessary. A small notice in the *Beekeeper's Gazette* might be just what is needed to get the word out about a new book about beekeeping. As much as publishers would like to rely on reviews to do the job of advertising, a book must be advertised to the trade to get the book into the bookstores, and it must be advertised to the public to get people into the bookstores to buy the book.

There is a market for any good book, and maybe for any bad book, too. A senior buyer for the B. Dalton chain once noted that "given a lot of display, *any* book will sell."[28] If ten thousand people buy a book, isn't it likely that in this great country of 250 million people there must be at least 10,000 more who would buy that book if they knew about it? Those 10,000 book buyers can make a big difference to author and publisher alike. The problem has always been to find those book buyers who are out there, somewhere, between sea and shining sea. The only way to do this is to advertise, to run some announcements to let the world know a new book has been born. If a publisher has no intention of advertising a book, that publisher should not have accepted the book for publication in the first place.

CHAPTER 12

Making the List

S ometimes best-sellers are consciously crafted. An agent once thought up an intriguing title for a book about airline stewardesses, "Coffee, Tea or Me?" hired a ghostwriter to write the book, found two attractive stewardesses to pose as its authors, sent them on a cross-country publicity tour, and landed a number one best-seller for Bantam.

Ophthalmic surgeon Dr. Robin Cook was not satisfied with the sales of his first book, a novel he wrote during medical school called *The Year of the Intern*, and so began a study of best-sellers, dissecting them to see just how they were constructed and cataloging their strengths on index cards. His string of hits that followed, including *Coma*, *Sphinx*, *Fever*, and *Harmful Intent*, showed that he learned his lessons well.

But these are rare instances. A search for best-selling formulas and the attempt to apply them to another book rarely results in a best-seller. It has been said that a publisher's idea of a good book is a book very much like another book that has sold well. But writers and publishers have found that more often than not, setting out to write a best-seller is just about the worst way to write a best-selling book.

Kenneth Roberts tried it a couple of times. Seeing the success of Alexander Wollcott's collection of essays, *The Wollcott Reader*, which sold 175,000 copies, he gathered together a collection of the essays he had published in the *Saturday Evening Post*. His publishers were convinced that the *Post's* two million subscribers would snap it up, but the book found only five thousand purchasers. Roberts later tried again, putting aside his work on *Northwest Passage* with the hope of matching the success of Irvin S. Cobb's *Speaking of Operations*, which had sold 200,000 copies. Roberts' *It Must Be Your Tonsils* sold, as he put it, "the conventional 5,000 copies."[1]

Joseph Conrad believed that only two types of books sold well: the very best and the very worst.[2] True enough, though "best" and "worst" are perhaps not the right adjectives to distinguish that always troubling dichotomy between art and commerce. Some best-sellers are meteorites, blazing through the dark with a brilliance which, for a moment, focuses all attention on them. Others are stars that will be there, shining in the night sky, long after the meteorites are ashes. And that is certainly a distinction between books that are great entertainment and books that are great entertainment *and* great literature: One is of the moment and one lasts longer, sometimes forever.

The best and the worst are also not the right labels, for it is certainly better that people be reading some book than no book at all. One book, any book, is a book in the house; it's a start. Stephen King has called his own books "the literary equivalent of a big Mac and a large fries from McDonald's."[3] John Grisham, author of a string of back-to-back-to-back number one best-sellers starting with *The Firm*, *The Pelican Brief*, and *The Client*, has acknowledged, "I write to grab readers. This isn't serious literature."[4] Judith Krantz has said, "I'm no Joan Didion—There are no intelligent, unhappy people in my books. I want to be known as a writer of good, entertaining narrative. I'm not trying to be taken seriously by the East Coast literary establishment. But I'm taken *very* seriously by the bankers."[5] These sorts of books are just what they are intended to be: great entertainment, great reads. They are also books with a short life, books we don't tend to care too much about a year or two after publication.

What is more flat, more lifeless, than old best-seller lists? Who today cares about Paul Erdman's *The Billion Dollar Sure Thing*, the number nine best-seller for all of 1973, or James Michener's *Centennial*, the number one fiction best-seller of 1974, or Marabel Morgan's *The Total Woman*, the number one nonfiction best-seller of the same year? Who today would pick up a book by Jacqueline Susann? *The Mammoth Hunters* by Jean Auel? *Whirlwind* by James Clavell? *Lucky* by Jackie Collins? *I'll Take Manhattan* by Judith Krantz? John Gardner once made the point by comparing Octave Thanet, the best-selling novelist of the nineteenth century, with Herman Melville.

134

Melville's novels never sold well compared to Thanet's, but no one today reads Thanet, or has even heard of her, while Melville is still with us. The same, he noted, was true of two novelists who were contemporaries: John O'Hara and William Faulkner. "John O'Hara outsold Faulkner, he circled Faulkner at the time they were writing. Ten years after his death, O'Hara's books are out of print. We all read Faulkner, nobody reads O'Hara."[6] Few books last. "Only three or four books in a lifetime give us anything that is of importance," was Marcel Proust's judgment.[7] "Until one has some kind of professional relationship with books," George Orwell wrote, "one does not discover how bad the majority of them are."[8]

Books that appeal to a mass audience, books that have the mega best-seller potential, will always be sought after by publishers. But what about the authors who write serious literature? What about the next Hemingway or Fitzgerald or Faulkner who could be writing books that will be read not only this season, but every season for the next hundred years? What chance do they have today? As John Updike has said, "If Henry James never quite realized that the price of excellence is a large neglect, James Joyce and Marcel Proust certainly did; the publication of their masterpieces required, respectively, heavy patronage and a private income."[9] Could they even find a publisher today?

Surely there must be times when John Updike envies the riches of Stephen King. Why doesn't he just dash off a Stephen King–type horror novel and rake in the cash? And surely there must be times when Stephen King is sick and tired of hearing that he is nothing but a schlock writer. Why not make the critics eat their words by publishing in *The New Yorker* an Updikean short story or two? The truth of the matter is that John Updike could probably no more write a Stephen King–like novel than Stephen King could write a short story like John Updike. "Those big-shot writers ... could never dig the fact that there are more salted peanuts consumed than caviar,"[10] Mickey Spillane once said in disgust, echoing the similar sentiments of Don Marquis: "If you want to get rich from writing, write the sort of thing that's read by persons who move their lips when they're reading to themselves."[11]

But the writers of immensely popular books aren't faking it, and writers who try to imitate their success seem invariably to fail. Even the writer of a bad book, W. Somerset Maugham was convinced, must believe when he is writing it that it is a great book. As Updike has said, "Each of us who claim to be writers should strive, I think, to discover or invent the verbal texture that most closely duplicates the tone of life as it arrives on his nerves. This tone, which induces style, will vary from soul to soul. Glancing upward, one is struck by the dispersion of recent constellations, by how far apart the prose masters of the century — say, Proust and Joyce, Kafka and Hemingway — are from one another."[12] Far apart? As Stephen King once said, "While Joyce Carol Oates and Harold Robbins are both writing English, they are really not writing the same language at all."[13] King has noted that some seem to think he writes the books he does simply as a money machine and "suspect that the minute my bank balance reaches the right critical mass, I'm going to put all that childish nonsense behind me and try to write this generation's answer to *Brideshead Revisited*. But the fact is that money really has nothing to do with it one way or the other. I love writing the things I write, and I wouldn't and *couldn't* do anything else."[14] One suspects that Updike couldn't either.

"I never really 'wrote down,'" Scott Fitzgerald explained, "until after the failure of *The Vegetable* and that was to make this book [*The Great Gatsby*] possible. I would have written down long ago if it had been profitable — I tried it unsuccessfully for the movies. People don't seem to realize that for an intelligent man writing down is about the hardest thing in the world."[15]

"Would you ever make a compromise in your books to gain more readers?" John Barth once was asked.

"I would, but I can't," he responded.[16]

A hypothetical questions was posed to publisher Alfred Knopf: If he were going to write a novel, deliberately setting out to make a million dollars from its sales, with his experience in publishing, what would that novel be about?

"I wouldn't know how to go about it," he answered, "because I think you've got to assume a very skilled technique. I wouldn't know how to set about writing a novel at all. But I know that when I was a young man I sensed in the case of certain authors an attempt to change their kind of story-telling to suit the market and most of the time they failed. The people that hit that kind of market were people who wrote with an honest conviction and not with tongue in cheek. They really believed in what they were turning out."[17]

Maybe every writer thinks, as he begins work on his next book, that *this* is the one that will capture the public's imagination; *this* is the one that will take off. "I have never yet," said James Landis of the William Morrow publishing house, "met a writer who, sharing his or her fantasies on the matter, didn't in this day and age, muse about glory, envision earning with one book a lifetime's money and at the same time enough critical praise to feed his ego and his family's ego for at least the day and a half that it takes a healthy ego to absorb and digest and eliminate all the world's praise, before hungering for more."[18] And maybe this has to be, for as Paul Horgan has written, "It is not possible to create the moderately good work without imagining the utmost great."[19]

What books sell well never fails to amaze, for the best-seller lists are invariably a mind-boggling mixture of commercial and literary books, always with a few unexpected thrown in for good measure.

There are numerous best-seller lists. *The Washington Post* has one; so do *The Los Angeles Times, The Wall Street Journal, Publishers Weekly,* and many regional and local newspapers. But for half a century, the *New York Times* Best Sellers list, "The List," has always been the place to be. When a book is on The List, it has arrived. Readers make their selections based on The List. Gift-givers scan The List for ideas. The chains offer bigger discounts for books on The List, and bookstores provide more prominent positioning. Subsidiary rights sell like umbrellas in a downpour. Royalties flow like gushers of liquid gold. Being on The List creates its own momentum. The higher toward Spot 1 on The List a book ascends, the more newsworthy the book becomes, so that the mass media, once courted by publisher and author as the book came out of the gate, now court the author for his time and thoughts and brand of breakfast cereal — the author as celebrity, the author as star. The more newsworthy the book becomes, the better it sells, and the better it sells, the more newsworthy it becomes. Daniel J. Boorstin has quipped that a best-seller is a book that "somehow sold well simply because it was selling well."[20]

It's surprising how few books need be sold to land a book on The List. Fifty thousand during a relatively short period of time is the figure usually bandied about, but there has been some intriguing evidence that that figure may be way too high.

Case 1: *The Washington Post* reported in 1990 that the Gannett Foundation had spent about $40,000 to purchase 2,000 copies of its chairman's new book, *Confessions of a S.O.B.* According to this article, to get the book onto The List, executives of the Gannett Foundation called editors at some of the eighty-three Gannett newspapers around the country and told them to go out and purchase the book at certain stores, with the Foundation to reimburse the editors at full retail price. *Confessions of a S.O.B.* dutifully jumped onto The List, remaining on it for seven weeks and reaching as high as position 5. The Foundation said the books it bought were to be donated to journalism schools; Allen Neuharth, the book's author and chairman of the Foundation, commented, "I wish I knew how to control the New York Times best-seller list, because if I did, my book would still be on it." Nevertheless, Benjamin C. Bradlee, executive editor of *The Post*, noted for the record that "my response is that the story speaks for itself— period."[21]

Hmmm ... Is there a way to manipulate The List?

Case 2: Professor Allan Bloom received a $10,000 advance from Simon & Schuster for his treatise, *The Closing of the American Mind*. The book had an initial printing of 10,000 copies. And then, *mirabile dictu*: While those 10,000 books were out there waiting to be purchased, the book, on May 3, 1986, appeared on The List. Now, the book did receive a so-so review in the Sunday *New York Times Book Review*, and then a rave from Christopher Lehmann-Haupt in the daily *Times*, but even so, could it appear on The List with only a measly 10,000 copies in print? Note we're not even talking 10,000 sold; we're talking 10,000 in print, with some in bookstores, some still cartoned in the warehouse, and others in transit. "The only logical explanation for the book showing up on The List as early as it did," one editor at another house commented, "is that it did incredibly well at a few bookstores that the New York *Times* weights heavily in its survey."[22]

Case 3: *Business Week* reported that the authors of *The Discipline of Market Leaders* purchased 10,000 copies of their book at stores believed to be those reporting to The List. Their book graced The List for fifteen weeks in 1995.

Interesting case studies.

William Peter Blatty, author of *The Exorcist*, once sued the *New York Times*— unsuccessfully — claiming that his 1983 novel, *Legion*, was ignored by the *Times* in making up The List despite its high sales, and that he thereby suffered economic loss because of lost hardcover sales, the loss of a potentially higher paperback rights price and the loss of possible film deals. Blatty alleged that to obtain sales figures from the bookstores it canvases, the *Times* sent to the stores a form which had printed on it a list of 36 best-selling books, and that the use of this form influenced bookstores to report only sales of those 36 books. The *Times* confirmed that it did in fact use the printed forms, but that it left a space on them for stores to write in other choices; in fact, the *Times* noted, every number one best-seller for one year started as a write-in.

Each week, The *New York Times* canvasses the sales figures of 3,000 bookstores, including chains and independents. Although the names of the stores surveyed are top secret and some of the stores are switched each year, a publisher just might want to spend some street money in such major independents as Shakespeare & Company, Coliseum Books and Endicott Booksellers in New York City, the Harvard Cooperative in Boston, Kramerbooks in Washington, The Tattered Cover in Denver, Cody's in Berkeley, A Clean Well-Lighted Place for Books in San Francisco, Powell's in Portland, The Library Ltd. in St. Louis, and Oxford Books in Atlanta.[23] And schedule author stops at these stores.

The *Times* editor who assembles The List is ready for such invasions, having developed "a standard procedure to detect and query sales activities that are out of the usual pattern for a typical store. If a store sold 70 copies where it would normally sell 5, or if a stranger came in and paid cash for 60 copies, that would ring warning bells and we would adjust our computer model to take account of it."[24] Despite this stalwart Maginot line, a creative publisher and author perhaps could devise ways to breach it.

What sorts of books make their way onto The List? Of the 50,000 new titles published each year, only about 200 ever touch The List, and only a handful of those really hit the jackpot. In 1989, for example, only 63 novels sold over 100,000 copies (beating the old record of 52 in 1987); only 27 novels sold over 200,000 copies; and only four novels sold over 1,000,000 copies. Only 78 nonfiction books had sales of 100,000 or more, and 33 topped 200,000 in sales. Interestingly, no first novels that year had sales of over 100,000, and no nonfiction books by no-name authors had sales of over 100,000, with books by politicians or thespians or athletes being the heavy sellers on the nonfiction list. Sometimes it seems that it's easier to make money writing books if you're not an author.

Of the books that land on The List, there are some that anyone could predict would be best-sellers, long before the first book comes off the presses. What does it mean, after all, when Doubleday and Bantam pay $10 million for the next three novels John Jakes is to write; when Farrar, Straus & Giroux pays Tom Wolfe over $5 million for his next novel when he has written neither a chapter nor an outline, and has no idea what the book will be about; when Simon & Schuster pays Mary Higgins Clark $10.1 million for her next five books ("Now all I have to do is write them," Mrs. Clark noted upon signing the contract[25]); when Dell Publishing agrees to pay $12.3 million for Ken Follett's next two novels, even though Mr. Follett acknowledged that he had "no plot, no ideas, no outline whatsoever"[26]; when Viking Penguin and New American Library pay Stephen King between $30 million and $40 million for his next four thrillers? "You don't have to see what Tom Wolfe, Stephen King or Ken Follett are going to write to sign them up," commented Arnold Dolan, associate publisher of NAL/Dutton. "They are almost guaranteed best-sellers — as guaranteed as anything can be."[27] These are authors with a superb track record and, more importantly, a predictable track record. Their books sell in the hundreds of thousands — in the millions in paperback. In a business that consists mostly of sailing highly unpredictable seas, these very few authors — perhaps two dozen — represent a safe harbor of certainty. Such record advances are front-page news, further contributing to the glamour surrounding these fabled authors and the sales of their awaited books.

Predictable, too, in an uncertain market is the success of celebrity memoirs: *Iacocca* (the best-selling hardcover nonfiction book in 1984 and 1985), Tip O'Neill's autobiography *Man of the House*, Nancy Reagan's *My Turn*. (It is interesting to note, however, that some presidential memoirs do well — Nixon's — while others, such as Johnson's, Ford's, and Carter's, have fallen flat. Interesting, too, how Barbara Bush's *Millie's Book*, which she wrote as if it were written by her dog, outsold them all and was number one on The List for weeks. One bookseller noted, "We did really well with Reagan's book, although not as well as with Millie's — but then, he's not a spaniel."[28]) Within three months of the Desert Storm victory, five publishers had bid between $2.5 and $5 million for the memoirs of General Norman Schwarzkopf. Bantam won with a bid of $5 million, the most ever paid for a work of nonfiction. The advances for the memoirs of Marlon Brando and of Sam Walton, chairman of Wal-Mart Stores, Inc., were not far behind. When Joan Collins's autobiography (Joan, mind you, not Jackie; we're talking Alexis here), *Past Imperfect*, and first novel, *Prime Time*, became best-sellers, Random House threw a $4 million contract to her for two more novels. Tell-all celebrity biographies like Kitty Kelley's *(Nancy Reagan)* and C. David Heymann's *(A Woman Named Jackie)* are also sure bets. There are over sixty books about Elvis and about the Beatles, each of which seems to sell well. "Personally, I think there is room for about 15 more Elvis books," joked an editor at Random House.[29] True crime stories, the more sensational the better — any manifestation of psychotic behavior, including patricides, matricides, and serial killers — have been among the hottest selling books, from Truman Capote's *In Cold Blood*, to Joe McGinniss's *Fatal Vision*, Norman Mailer's *The Executioner's Song*, Shana Alexander's *Nutcracker*, Jonathan Coleman's *At Mother's Request*, Linda Wolfe's *The Professor and the Prostitute*. Within days of the charge of Robert S. Chambers for the so-called "preppie murder" of Jennifer Dawn Levin in Central Park, Chambers's attorney received scores of calls from authors, agents and publishers. "Oh, to be young, attractive and under arrest in New York," sighed one agent in disbelief.[30] And after Charles Stuart was arrested in Boston for the murder of his wife, every major publisher received dozens of book proposals. Said Howard Kaminsky, the president of the Hearst Trade Book Group, "It seems that the perfect crime for our times will be to rob, murder or rape with a video camera in order to sell it afterward."[31]

Big advances make big news, and big news helps make big sales. And a big advance forces a publisher to push a book. "This is a business of self-fulfilling prophecies," agent Mort Janklow has said. "One of the reasons to drive for big advances is not to make authors and agents rich. It's to make the publisher aware of what he's bought. You've got to get them pregnant. They get up before their sales force and say, "We paid millions for this book. This is the biggest book we've got. *Drive* it into the stores."[32] Agents know this. And publishers know this. "The first thing we look at is how much did we spend on the book," reports Arlynn Greenbaum, marketing director of Little, Brown & Company. "If we have spent a lot, then we put a lot into promotion."[33] And authors know this. "I think I will have to get a large advance on my next book to insure it being advertised in florid and gigantic manner in order that Scribners must sell a large number of copies to get the advance back," wrote Ernest Hemingway to Max Perkins after the publication of *The Sun Also Rises*.[34]

Readers and potential readers in turn gauge the importance of a book by its publicity. So do the book buyers working for the chains and the independent bookstores. They are interested in two numbers when they place their orders: the publisher's print run, and the advertising and promotion budget. What faith does this publisher have in this book? What sort of muscle is the publisher putting behind it? Without that faith and muscle, chances are good that the book will never move off the shelves.

As we have seen, there are books whose success is easy to call: the next book by a name author, the celebrity biographies, the books on a hot topic. On the opposite side of the spectrum are the freak successes that not even the most insightful publisher could ever predict.

The American public possesses an infinite capacity to amaze. Just when you think all of America is watching *Roseanne* and *Monday Night Football*, along comes *The Civil War*, Ken Burns's critically acclaimed PBS 12-hour, five night, history lesson, a composite of archival material, old photographs, readings, location filmings, and interviews. Each night, fourteen million Americans tuned in. When the book based on this series, *The Civil War: An Illustrated History*, hit the bookstores, hundreds of thousands of readers materialized to buy copies at $50 each, making the book a number one nonfiction best-seller in 1990.

How do clearly noncommercial books like *A Brief History of Time* by British physicist Stephen W. Hawking, Professor Paul Kennedy's *The Rise and Fall of the Great Powers*, and Dava Sobel's

Longitude: The True Story of a Lone Genius Who Solved the Greatest Scientific Problem of His Time, get on and stay on the best-seller lists?

In 1985, Michael Kinsley, editor of *The New Republic*, conducted his own experiment to try to solve this mystery. He had a slip of paper inserted three quarters of the way through books of this sort — the improbable best-sellers — in a Washington, D.C. bookstore. The slips contained a message offering $5 to anyone who called to report that they had read to that point in the books. He never received a single call. Not one. "These books," he concluded, "don't exist to be read. They exist to be gazed at, browsed through, talked about. They exist, above all, to be reviewed."[35] They become cultural phenomena.

The independent bookstores often have been credited with initiating the groundswell sales of such out-of-the mainstream books. Following the groundswell, once a certain level of sales is attained, the public follows the fashion of the day and doesn't look beyond the best-seller lists. Thus a book that has sold 75,000 copies might well sell its next 100,000 because people know that 75,000 others have already bought the book. Once launched, best-sellers begin to pull readers into their orbits, whether or not readers really like the books or even understand them — or even read them. As Gore Vidal once wrote about Solzhenitsyn's *August 1914*: "Many people who do not ordinarily read books have bought this book and mention rather proudly that they are reading it, but so far I have yet to meet anyone who has finished it."[36]

These are the two extremes on the spectrum of new books: the sure hits and the freak hits. Most newly published books fall somewhere on the vast tundra in between. Publishers fantasize about seeing more of their books from the tundra on The List, but they don't always recognize the steps they must take to help make their fantasies come true.

CHAPTER 13

A Boy Has to
Peddle His Book

O ver the years, publishers have perfected the production of books, but they are still struggling with how to sell these books once they are printed and bound. Readers are out there, we know that, for sometimes at night they'll sneak down from the hills and buy hundreds of thousands of copies of the unexpected and hundreds of millions of copies of the expected, like the novels of Barbara Cartland, Louis L'Amour, Harold Robbins, Earle Stanley Gardner, and Georges Simenon. But exactly where these readers hide out by day, and how to reach them to let them know about the next book, remain mysteries. Rogers Straus III, managing director of Farrar, Straus & Giroux, has been candid about this: "One of the wonderful, sad and desperate things about this business is that nobody really knows how to sell books. Especially as the stakes have gotten higher, we are all thrashing around looking for some way to sell these books."[1] It used to be, he continued, "that commercialism was a bad word, you'd put all your energy into creating a book and when it came time to sell the product, everyone ran out of gas."[2]

John Knowles was having dinner with Truman Capote one evening in 1960, just before Knowles's first novel, A Separate Peace, was published.

"Do you know what's going to happen to this novel of yours when it comes out?" Capote asked him.

"What?"

"Nothing, that's what! Nothing ever happens to first novels unless you make it happen." Capote went on to describe to Knowles how he had secured success for his Other Voices, Other Rooms. He said he had arranged all the publicity, promotion and reviews himself. He encouraged Knowles to pursue the same route — "if you don't want your novel to drop like a pebble in the ocean and be instantly forgotten." Knowles got the message.

"So, upon reflection," wrote Knowles in *Esquire* magazine, "I exerted myself over *A Separate Peace* and found ways to draw what turned out to be crucial attention to it and to me, and it did not disappear like a pebble in the sea. Instead it sold nine million copies — so far — and I owe a great deal of that to Truman."[3]

Capote's theory was that all the work involved in publicizing and promoting a book had to be accomplished in six weeks, and that those six weeks were primarily the weeks before publication date; that all the planning and preparation before publication were worth much more than any amount of scurrying about thereafter.

On publication date, most books make their appearance not with a blare of bugles and a ruffle of drums, but quietly, like wisps of fog coming in from the sea: a review here, an ad there, maybe a display in a bookstore, an interview on talk radio. And whether these wisps will scatter and dissipate or whether they will gather and roll in and blanket the countryside can depend on how close together they appear. For the successful launch of a book, a rule of thumb has been that a potential reader must hear about the book a half-dozen times over the course of a week — he might see an ad, hear an interview on television, read something about it (be it a book review or off-the-book-pages piece), hear a friend talk about it, whatever. It is those multiple encounters within a short period of time that seem to lure a reader into a bookstore to buy a copy. Publishers therefore must plan a promotion campaign that makes everything happen at once: Bang!

Publishers on occasion have recognized the validity of the Capote promotion principle. Alfred Harcourt once noted that the important thing is first to get the right angle on a book and then give it build-up before publication. Jack McKeown, publisher of trade books at Simon & Schuster, has said, "As publishers, we are all very conscious of the shortened shelf life of hardcover books. Computers have brought many blessings to the bookselling industry, but booksellers are tempted to drop quickly what doesn't move. It has become extremely important to maximize sales in the first three, four weeks."[4]

Arlynn Greenbaum, marketing director of Little, Brown, says "For the most part, it's right out of the gate that a book gets some sort of push. After that, it's on its own."[5]

And so a publisher will spend $200,000 to promote an anticipated best-seller, with budgets rising with expectations. Warner Books, for example, invested $600,000 to promote *Scarlett*, and Viking Penguin was in the habit of spending over $750,000 to promote each new Stephen King. There are counter top displays and cardboard dump bins and buttons for store clerks; ads in newspapers and magazines and for buses and subways; billboards; commercials on television during soap operas and talk shows and some prime-time spots — anything and everything to get a buzz going in the industry and then to get consumers talking. As Samuel Butler knew — and it's just as true today — "getting talked about is what makes a book sell."[6]

Publishers have proved that they can carry out a promotion campaign as perfectly planned and executed as D-Day. Farrar, Straus & Giroux exploited each piece of good news about Scott Turow's first novel, *Presumed Innocent*, and used it to build excitement about the book — the record advance for that house, the fact that Turow turned down a higher advance from another house, the book club sales, the foreign sales, the film rights. Publicizing each success created a head of steam behind the book, pushing it on to huge success. Simon & Schuster teased the country, leaking information, withholding information, right until the last minute before publication of Kitty Kelley's biography of Nancy Reagan, just as years before Scribner's had kept every copy of Hemingway's *The Old Man and the Sea* under guard until the dawn of its own launch day.

The success of such campaigns, however, even if well executed, is not inevitable. An article in the *New York Times* of January 20, 1992, an off-the-book-page article — itself a sign that something unusual was afoot — described how author Eileen Goudge's publisher, Viking, was trying to mold her into the next Danielle Steel, and her latest book, *Such Devoted Sisters*, into a blockbuster novel. Ms. Goudge had done her homework and studied the women's novels on the best-seller lists. ("What I discovered about Danielle Steel is that she is unstinting in the shameless — and I don't mean for that to sound bad — way that she tugs at hearts and goes for the jugular; she has 16 horrible things happen to her character.") Two years before, Eileen Goudge's novel *Garden of Lies* had reached the number 8 spot on The List, and *Such Devoted Sisters* had just been named a main selection of the Literary Guild, so the ingredients were there to elevate the standing of the glamorous Ms. Goudge to the top of The List. It was a worthwhile endeavor, for once the author of this type of book reaches the head of The List, the success of every future book is assured.

Her publisher was behind her. It had paid her a $900,000 advance on a two-book deal, and had committed itself, according to its president Michael Jacobs, "to do whatever it takes to break this author out," including spending $200,000 on publicity and promotion. This meant such finishing touches (à la Jackie Susann) as sending out deluxe sets of galleys, each boxed with fancy chocolates (the gourmet chocolate business figured in her novel); hiring an outside public relations firm to complement the work of its publicity department; and sending Ms. Goudge out to meet the important booksellers during her publicity tour and book signings. The author took it upon herself to telephone or send notes to many bookstore owners, to print bookmarks with the book's cover on one side and her picture on the other, and to invite the managers and buyers from the key book chains to parties at her Manhattan townhouse, for which she baked the desserts. Her book popped onto the *New York Times* Best Sellers List on February 2, 1992, in spot 11; held steady in the same spot the next week; fell to the bottom of The List, spot 15, on February 16; and had slipped off altogether by the week of February 23, for a total of three weeks with a fingerhold on The List.

What's the lesson here, if there is one? Maybe it's that there can be only one Danielle Steel (especially when, as was the case with *Such Devoted Sisters*, a Danielle Steel novel is riding The List at the same time). Maybe there can be only one Stephen King, only one James Michener. Would a novel *Czechoslovakia*, like Michener's *Poland* in all respects except with another author's name on the cover, do as well as his *Poland*? Would a novel *California* do as well as his *Texas* or his *Alaska*? Most likely not. Maybe the reading public has its fill of Danielle Steel books with the books of Danielle Steel, of Michener novels with Michener's own output. Or maybe the lesson is that a book "in the style of" a blockbuster author may do alright — being

148

on The List for any weeks, after all, is not so bad — but that a rip-roaring best-seller can't be made; it happens. A new voice, an excit-ing voice, comes along to capture the public's interest and pocketbook. No way to predict it. No way to call it. Look at the two top nonfiction sellers of 1989, each of which sold over one million hardcover copies: *A Brief History of Time* by Stephen Hawking, which was a scientist's review of efforts to create a unified theory of the uni-verse, and Robert Fulghum's *All I Really Need to Know I Learned in Kindergarten,* which was a collection of inspirational essays. That's how it goes. Look at the first big book of Richard Simon and Lincoln Schuster, two young men who started a publishing house in 1924: a crossword puzzle volume. Their next big hit was Will Durant's *The Story of Philosophy.*

True, the Capote promotion principle doesn't always work. But as the best shot publishers and authors have at making something happen, by now it should be standard operating procedure. But not all publishers understand how to orchestrate (or even the need to orchestrate) the promotion of their books, and certainly not all pub-lishers are prepared to adequately promote all the books they pub-lish. Most authors should assume the worst right from the outset, and take steps themselves to plan and implement a campaign to supple-ment their publisher's primitive efforts. As Capote knew, "a boy has to peddle his book,"[7] because most of the time, no one else will.

Every once in a while, not very often, the personality of an author is so striking as to draw endless attention to his work: that cultural hero Mark Twain, who was the consummate performer; the extravagantly flamboyant Oscar Wilde, who lectured in hundreds of hamlets and cities in England, France, and the United States; Ernest Hemingway, whose public persona was so strong that it threatened to overshadow his work; the one and only Truman Capote ("I don't know anybody who gets as much publicity as I do for doing noth-ing"[8]); Norman Mailer with his advertisements for himself; the ele-gant Tom Wolfe with his handmade white suits. These are the sorts of authors who have garnered endless off-the-book-page publicity and large audiences for their books. And then there's the occasional personable, smooth-talking salesmen who are great hits on the tele-vision talk shows. Charles J. Givens appeared on *The Today Show,* and when the phones rang off the hook, he was summoned back the next day. He then returned several months later for an unprecedented three days in a row. And so his *Wealth Without Risk: How to Make a Personal Fortune Without Going Out on a Limb* hung on the best-seller lists for over one hundred weeks in the how-to category and sold over 1.4 million copies, and Simon & Schuster threw him a $3 million advance for a sequel.

But these are rare exceptions. Most authors do not have the necessary gregarious personality. Quite the contrary.

"Why," asked novelist Anne Tyler, "do people imagine that writers, having chosen the most private of professions, should be any good at performing in public, or should have the slightest desire to tell their secrets to interviewers from ladies' magazines?"[9]

"Why," wondered Eugene Ionesco, "do people always expect authors to answer questions? I am an author because I want to *ask* questions. If I had answers I'd be a politician."[10]

"Why," questioned John Steinbeck, "do they think a writer, just because he can write, will make a good after-dinner speaker? I'm so increasingly afraid in crowds," he confided, "that I do not talk comfortably to a pair of dice any more."[11]

Good questions all, yet questions that don't seem to trouble publishers one whit as they pack up their authors and send them on the talk show circuit to hawk their wares, willing to let the sales success of a book ride on the degree of personal charm its author can muster.

Author Michael Chabon and movie star Brad Pitt are probably about the same age. Why would anyone believe that Michael Chabon could go on television and entertain us, any more than Brad Pitt could sit down and write a short story that *The New Yorker* would publish? Indeed, Brad Pitt's chances of publishing a book (especially if he wrote his memoirs) are probably much greater than Michael Chabon's chances of landing a role in a movie or on television. Yet publishers fantasize that authors can be actors, a fantasy fueled when author Alexander King appeared on Jack Paar's *Tonight Show* in 1959 to plug his memoirs, *Mine Enemy Grows Older*, and so charmed the audience with his glib and irreverent banter that he was invited back to the Paar show again and again, and his book hit the top of the nonfiction best-seller lists. So good was King that he got his own show on public television and wrote more volumes of his memoirs: *May This House Be Safe from Tigers, I Should Have Kissed Her More,* and *Is There Life After Birth?*, each of which reached the best-seller lists. That was trouble: For Alexander King, it worked. As Russell Baker noted in writing about one of his own book tours, "Publishers ever since have operated on the theory that even their dullest hack may be the next Alexander King, which explains why a recent frigid dawn found a desperate NBC makeup artist plastering me in dense layers of rouge while urging me 'not to worry, I've seen worse.'"[12]

The other trouble is that it is dirt cheap for a publisher to send an author off to see the world, compared to the cost of advertising the book. It costs the television and radio shows nothing to land these author-guests (in Great Britain, in contrast, authors are paid a fee to appear on radio and television), and it costs the publisher nothing to garner this publicity, other than the expense of getting the author's body into the recording studio.

So off the publishers launch them, off into these United States, often without a moment's thought as to which television shows or which radio programs of the hundreds of possibilities would be the best for an author promoting a particular book. Just get them on. Not every author can visit Leno or Letterman, Oprah or Giraldo—let's face it, they're looking either for the Name or a freak—but considering the appetite of radio and television talk shows for an endless diet of guests, pretty much any author can get on some show, somewhere. For a publisher, the economics are too good to be true: For the cost of a full-page ad in the *New York Times Book Review*, an author may be sent on a ten-city national tour.

But is it worth it? How is it all that different from pulling a GM worker off the assembly lines and sending him on the talk show circuit to be a pitchman for the Buick LeSabres that he builds?

Now, you might think that a publisher might at least sit down with the author and tell him what to expect, what to do, and what to wear. You would think that publishers, at least sensing something of the difference between an actor and an author, would train their authors how to assume for a week or two the ego of a megalomaniac and the unmitigated gall of a carnival huckster, both of which will be necessary to go before an audience to peddle their product. After all, the better the author does, the more money the publisher is going to make. You might even think that the publisher would call the author in for a dress rehearsal or two, put a practice interview on videotape, offer suggestions.

But no. Having taken the author to lunch and ascertained that he can at least pass for a human being, the publisher sends him two days before departure a wad of tickets, an incomplete itinerary, and a threatening form letter, warning him to keep original invoices for every Coke he consumes if he ever wants to see a reimbursement check. And suddenly, there he sits, alone in a green room.

John Cheever recalled that when it was time to leave the green room for his appearance on *The Dave Garroway Show*, "it took two strong men pushing and pulling to get me into the studio…. I sat down at a baize-covered table and quivered like a bowlful of chicken fat for fifteen minutes…."[13] Margaret Mitchell, who hated public speaking, remembered an occasion when she was forced into it: "When I got to my feet and saw that enormous room jammed with something over two hundred people, I ardently wished I was dead for by that time I was incapable of connected thought as far as a speech was concerned. While the president was introducing me I sat like a newly gigged frog and tried to think of what I would say and I couldn't think of a thing."[14] At least, as Russell Baker has noted, "the typical TV interview, like a well-handled execution, is swiftly over."[15]

Stephen King knows the secret: "Talk shows, TV, and radio don't really want writers to discuss anything. They want you to entertain. You've got to get out there and tap dance your balls off."[16]

For those without the captivating personality or the ability to tap dance, anything goes. Author and publisher should be able to think of something. Publicity is cheaper than advertising. And the only bad publicity is no publicity.

When *This Side of Paradise* was not the subject of any coverage one week, young Scott Fitzgerald to get attention stood on his hands in the lobby of the Biltmore in New York City. And he and Zelda would travel to a party, one on the roof of the taxi, one clinging to the hood. William Nickerson, author of *How I Turned $1,000 Into a Million in Real Estate—In My Spare Time*, appeared on *The Dave Garroway Show* with one million dollars in cash and fifteen armed guards. The publisher of *Auntie Mame* sent prepublication notes to book-sellers on pink notepaper with the design of a jeweled hand holding a long cigarette holder. One such note read: "My scurrilous nephew has written a scandalous book about me.... If you dare to sell one copy of it, I will sue you, my nephew and the publisher!"[17] A New York bookstore was unable to unload a stack of dictionaries which forever had been sitting on its shelves until one day it hired an actor to stand in the window and juggle three dictionaries. Every one in the store sold. In the summer of 1992, the Brentano's on Fifth Avenue in New York City paid an actress, dressed in beach attire, to sit for a week in its front window reading *War and Peace* under a beach umbrella to attract attention to its sale of Penguin classics. Were Dylan Thomas's tours of American campuses in which he started fights, told dirty stories, urinated on the floor, a means of getting attention? The words "Sheila Levine is Dead and Living in New York" appeared on sidewalks all over Manhattan to publicize Gail Parent's novel by that name. Random House threw a book party at a topless bar for its mystery novel *Topless*, with performances by eight topless dancers. "It's a bit unusual, but unusual things cause unusual sales," said Alberto Vitale, the chairman of Random House. The president of Warner Books, Laurence Kirshbaum, agreed. "Sales are very tough these days," he said, "and I applaud any creative marketing. I'm just upset that I wasn't invited."[18]

With book sales declining, publishing houses have finally begun to get with it, having authors appear on cable television shopping channels to hawk their books in between "camcorders, ruby rings and facial-hair removers" as the *Wall Street Journal* put it,[19] with one channel claiming that when a best-selling novelist appears, the channel can sell 100 to 150 books a minute. Ken Follett agreed to participate in a contest used to promote his paperback, *Pillars of the Earth*, in bookstores across the country, with the winner getting a trip to England and a personal tour of Westminster Abbey conducted by the author.

Is it possible to be *too* aggressive in promoting a book? No! Impossible! The time is short, and people are in such a daze that the most aggressive tactics imaginable — let your imagination run wild — would hardly stir them. "Anything honorable that the young writer can do to gain the serious attention of readers is justifiable," James Michener once said. "If I were starting over with no track record and no reputation, I would be on the road three nights a week, and I would go wherever and do whatever my publisher's publicist advised."[20]

The results can be spectacular. It may take just one piece of media attention to get a book rolling. *Final Exit*, the how-to-commit-suicide manual by Derek Humphry, was in the bookstores but not moving. At all. Steven Schragis, the owner of Carol Publishing, had written personal letters to journalists and television studios trying to interest them in the book, saying that the publication of such a book was newsworthy, the fact that bookstores were carrying it was newsworthy, and the fact that some bookstores were refusing to carry it was newsworthy: Take your pick, media. The *Wall Street Journal* looked into the story and published an article on the first page of the second section. That opened the floodgates: Schragis was besieged by the media. "Because the *Wall Street Journal* thought it was newsworthy, it *was* newsworthy," he explained. "If Norman Pearlsteine [the Journal's executive editor] had been in a bad mood that day, or if it happened during [the overthrow of Russian president] Gorbachev, it's possible the story wouldn't have been written. Society can only get obsessed with one thing at a time."[21]

Every new book need not be, and cannot be, promoted as a potential blockbuster. Frightened though publishers may be of their authors' dreams, by and large most authors understand this about their own books. They're not saying, "Hey, give me the chance to joke with Jay on *The Tonight Show*, get me on *The Today Show*, book me on *Oprah*." Nor are they saying, "I want one of those Hollywood billboards like Joan Collins used to get." Or, "Go out and buy me a full page ad in the New York *Times*." They're not even saying, "Pretty please, make sure I get reviewed in *Time* and *Newsweek*." What they're saying is much more simple. It is, "You bought this book, publisher; when you laid down your money you must have had some idea of the market for the book. Any book that is published has some market. Now my book is on deck: Let's work together, let's pitch it to that market, however humble it might be. Let's make a good faith effort to reach the market for this book. Let's do some work and give the book a chance to prove itself."

And if that good faith effort truly is made, the results may be extraordinary — or the results may be pretty blah. But publisher and author can rest assured that they gave that book their best shot.

CHAPTER 14

With a Little Bit of Luck

Any successful writer who is honest with himself will admit that luck contributed to the success of his book. James Dickey once commented in an interview:

> The talent game is a tough game. Luck plays an enormous part in it.... You can write one good poem by luck or haz-ard that's going to make people want your work. Whether or not you can produce anything good later on is not the important thing. It's that you struck it right then. It's the same with a novel — I wrote *Deliverance.* The movies bought it; it was serialized, written into a dozen languages; it's the best novel I can write, but there's also an enormous element of luck in it. I wrote the right book at the right time.... My next novel could be a failure.[1]

Hemingway expressed it another way: "The blue-backed notebooks, the two pencils and the pencil sharpener (a pocket knife was too wasteful), the marble-topped tables, the smell of early morning, sweeping out and mopping, and luck were all you needed. For luck you carried a horse chestnut and a rabbit's foot in your right pocket. The fur had been worn off the rabbit's foot long ago and the bones and the sinews were polished by wear. The claws scratched in the lin-ing of your pocket and you knew your luck was still there."[2]

Many writers are conscious enough of the need for luck to take measures to create or safeguard their own through acts of propitia-tion. And so we see the young Hemingway feeling the rabbit's foot in his pocket, and Stephen King, who will "never stop work if the page number is 13 or a multiple of 13; I'll just keep on typing till I get to a safe number."[3]

Dig around in the story of any best-seller and you're bound to uncover a shining vein of luck. What if Harold Latham of Macmillan hadn't made his literary scouting trip in search of new authors, and what if he hadn't come across little Margaret Mitchell and her big manuscript? What if the Naval Institute Press had stuck to its policy of not publishing novels and turned down Tom Clancy's *The Hunt for Red October*? What if? What if? Let's look at a few case histories.

Throughout his long writing career, James Michener never failed to attribute his success to chance, to "an extremely lucky Pulitzer Prize."[4] His first novel, *Tales of the South Pacific*, published when he was forty, enjoyed what he called "a faltering life of about five weeks. It was published in silence, reviewed by only a few journals and sold to a small number of people."[5] In fact, eight of the nine major review publications made no mention of the book.

Before the dismal reception of *Tales of the South Pacific*, Michener's agent had had high hopes for the manuscript of his next novel, *The Fires of Spring*, and had planned to submit it to a contest offering a $10,000 prize for the best new novel of the year. As *Tales of the South Pacific* was disappearing from sight, the agent sent Michener a special delivery letter in which he stated the "regrettable conclusion that I had no future as a writer. Therefore he was terminating our contract and would be returning my manuscript under separate cover, for he doubted it would ever be publishable.... In short, he was dropping me because there was no chance of my ever attaining commercial success and that consequently I had no place in his stable." Michener later described this letter, which he immediately tore up, as "one of the most crushing letters I would ever receive."[6]

Later that same dismal Monday morning on which he received this letter, Michener was lambasted by his boss at Macmillan (where he was a textbook editor) "for a wide variety of offenses." It was one of those mornings—until, in the middle of the harangue, came a frantic knocking at his office door. One of Michener's colleagues burst in with the news he had just heard on the radio: "Jim, you've won the Pulitzer Prize!"

After a while, when the room had cleared of well-wishers, Michener's boss went right back to his carping. And a day or two later, Michener received a letter from his agent, congratulating him on the award, "but he did not indicate in any way that he had changed his earlier opinion that as a possible author I was a dead duck."

The award of the Pulitzer Prize did not accelerate hardcover sales of *Tales of the South Pacific,* for the book had just gone out of print in hardcover. The award did, however, bring his book to the attention of Richard Rodgers, Oscar Hammerstein II, and Josh Logan, whose smash musical *South Pacific* would assure that anything Michener wrote thereafter turned to gold. ("I have only one bit of advice to the beginning writer," Michener later would joke; "be sure your novel is read by Rodgers and Hammerstein."[7])

Even fifty years and thirty-four best-selling books later, Michener was still awed by what he considered his good luck. Because of the sale to *The Saturday Evening Post* of several stories from his about-to-be published first novel, the publication of *Tales of the South Pacific* had been postponed from 1946 until 1947. To this chance event, Michener attributed the winning of the Pulitzer Prize, believing there was less competition for the 1947 prize than the 1946 prize. Much later in his life, he learned that Alice Roosevelt Longworth, a friend of Arthur Krock of the *New York Times* who was serving as chairman of the Pulitzer Prize committee, convinced Krock to award the prize to Michener's book rather than another book upon which the committee already had decided. Without the fortuitous delay in the publication of his book and the behind-the-scenes work of this guardian angel, Michener said, the Pulitzer Prize would not have been his. Had the prize not descended upon him on that very morning when he received his agent's letter terminating their relationship, might Michener have thrown in the towel on any future books? Or if his next book had been published without the aura of a Pulitzer Prize behind it, would the disappointing reception of *The Fires of Spring,* generally conceded to be one of Michener's lesser works, have sealed his fate as a lifelong textbook editor?

Luck of a different sort was important to the success of Harper Lee's *To Kill a Mockingbird.* Three events converged for Miss Lee, any one of which would have been quite extraordinary, the three in combination all but miraculous.

The first was that her literary agent saw a novel in the draft of a short story she was working on, and encouraged her to expand it. The next was that her editor at Lippincott could see in her manuscript the exquisite novel that could emerge, and so encouraged Miss Lee to rework and rewrite her book. And the third was that, one

Christmas, a wonderful couple who saw in young Harper Lee the makings of an author hung on their Christmas tree an envelope addressed to her. Inside was a note: "You have one year off from your job to write whatever you please. Merry Christmas!"

There were no strings attached. The couple believed in her talent and wanted to give her time to develop her craft. It was that simple — and that miraculous.

Surprisingly, the reviews of *To Kill a Mockingbird* were not particularly generous. *Booklist* was concerned about its "melodramatic climax and traces of sermonizing."[9] The reviewer for the *Atlantic* found the book "frankly and completely impossible, being told in the first person by a six-year-old girl with the prose style of a well-educated adult," reaching a verdict that "a variety of adults, mostly eccentric in Scout's judgment, and a continual bubble of incident make *To Kill a Mockingbird* pleasant, undemanding reading."[10] The reviewer for the now defunct *New York Herald Tribune Book Review* concluded that Lee "fails to produce a novel of stature or even of original insight," though he admitted "it does provide an exercise in easy, graceful writing and some genuinely moving and mildly humorous excursions into the transient world of childhood...."[11]

The rather short review in the *New York Times Book Review* appeared on page five under the title "One-Taxi Town." The reviewer damned the novel with faint praise, noting that Harper Lee "writes with gentle affection, rich humor and deep understanding of small-town family life in Alabama"; then he qualified even that praise by noting that "oftentimes Scout's expository style has a processed, homogenized, impersonal flatness quite out of keeping with the narrator's gay, impulsive approach to life in youth. Also, some of the scenes suggest that Miss Lee is cocking at least one eye toward Hollywood,"[12] an assumption which today, knowing as much as we are ever going to know about Harper Lee, seems rather silly. What the reviewer was groping (unsuccessfully) to say was that here was a book of remarkably vivid imagery written for the mind's eye.

Lee's editor at Lippincott was not sure the book would sell 2,000 copies, but she didn't care; she liked it. Harper Lee did not expect her book to sell. "You see, I never expected any sort of success with *Mockingbird*.... I was hoping for a quick and merciful death at the hands of the reviewers, but at the same time I sort of hoped that maybe someone would like it enough to give me encouragement. Public encouragement. I hoped for a little, as I said, but I got rather a whole lot, and in some ways this was just about as frightening as the quick, merciful death I'd expected."[13]

Despite these modest expectations, everyone other than a handful of nearsighted reviewers loved the book. It became the first book to be a selection of four major book clubs — a selection of the Literary Guild, an alternate for the Book-of-the-Month Club, a selection of the British Book Society, and a Reader's Digest condensation. It sold 500,000 copies in the year it was published, staying near the top of the *New York Times* Best Sellers list for most of the year; was translated into ten languages; won the 1960 Pulitzer Prize for fiction as well as a host of other literary awards; and was turned into a movie that won an Academy Award.

To isolate Harper Lee's three initial strokes of luck is not in any way to diminish her remarkable creation or to suggest that today we would not have *To Kill a Mockingbird* had these three felicitous events not come to pass. (Then again, who knows?) Rather, it is to suggest that perhaps there are writers out there — good writers, even superb writers — who have not encountered such a string of luck, who have not encountered one miracle, let alone a run of three, and so today are unknown or even unpublished.

Some years ago, journalist Ted Morgan wrote a cover story for *The New York Times Magazine* analyzing just how Peter Benchley's *Jaws* became a best-seller.[14] Let's look at an instant replay of Benchley's touchdown pass, and freeze the frames at the critical moments.

In June of 1971, Tom Congdon, a senior editor at Doubleday, had a prospecting lunch with thirty-one-year-old Peter Benchley, the third generation of writing Benchleys, a young man whose literary output had been confined to some magazine pieces and reporting for the *Washington Post* and *Newsweek*. What are you working on? Congdon asked him. A book about pirates, Benchley responded. Ohhhh. What else? Any thoughts of writing fiction? Well, yes, as a matter of fact, Benchley said, he had been mulling over the story of a Long Island resort community terrorized by a great white shark. This sounded interesting to Congdon. Sharks were an "in" topic just then. Give me a one-page description, said Congdon, and I'll see if I can get you some money to work on it.

Congdon returned to Doubleday and started bouncing the proposal off his colleagues. Oh, come on, one of Doubleday's veteran fiction editors groaned; Benchley's been talking about this book forever and does nothing about it. But Congdon, hinting at best-seller material, persuaded Doubleday's publishing board, comprised of members of the business and advertising departments, to give it a try. Okay, okay, said the board; we'll throw him a thousand bucks. A conditional thousand bucks at that: $500 would have to be returned to Doubleday if the first four trial chapters were not up to snuff. This contractual provision calling for the return of the $500 if the draft manuscript was not acceptable turned out to be a sticking point in the negotiations, which dragged on for ten days. Finally Doubleday agreed; Benchley could keep the thousand if he wrote four chapters and submitted them by April of the next year.

A $1000 option. A squabble over $500. So far, this book was nowhere near the front of the pack of the seventy-five novels that Doubleday would bring out the same year Benchley's book would be published, and though the dream of a best-seller might have crossed Congdon's mind, it was, at that time, his dream alone. Congdon was fully aware of the odds stacked against him. "In fiction," he knew, "track record means everything. Bookstores are very conservative; they won't even stock a novel until they've heard of the author."[15] They had never heard of Peter Benchley. It was definitely a long shot.

Through the next nine months, Congdon sent Benchley periodic encouraging notes to spur him along. Benchley, as it happened, really needed the encouragement; he was working hard, but without too much confidence in the fruits of his labor, regarding the odds for the book's success as practically insurmountable. But he persevered, and delivered the first four chapters a little ahead of schedule, ten months after the Congdon-Benchley lunch. For all his encouraging words to Benchley, Congdon was (privately) discouraged by the results.

"There is no question but that Peter Benchley's material is conscientiously wrought," wrote Tom Congdon. "I'm not entirely sure, however, that it's successfully wrought."[16] That's editor talk for major disappointment. Congdon dared not show the chapters to anyone else at Doubleday. Please rewrite it, he pleaded with Benchley, who complied and returned the manuscript a month later, having tried to address Congdon's concerns about the corny jokes, the weak, uncertain pace of the narrative, the repetitious nature of the shark scenes, and other problems. Okay, it was at least getting better, though the story, in Congdon's opinion, still had too many predictable elements and not enough character to drive the plot. Doubleday would work with Benchley to improve it. Congdon approved a $7,500 advance for Benchley.

After several complete and several partial rewrites in which he followed all of the Doubleday recommendations, Benchley turned in the completed manuscript on January 2, 1973. The veteran editor who had pooh-poohed the idea of the initial proposal for the book was enchanted when Congdon showed him the manuscript. Congdon relayed his enthusiastic response back and forth around Doubleday, again drumming up support for the book. "That was my first piece of gold. I could spew that out all over the company. If I get praise here I take it there, back and forth, until everyone is behind the book." It was the beginning of what he termed his "psychological build-up."[17] He then set about to line up the support of Doubleday's fifty-three salespeople, sending each a copy of the first five pages of the book.

What is the sense of all this in-house politicking, of everyone telling everyone else how great a book is going to be? "As unlikely as it may sound," Barbara Grossman, publisher of Viking Books, has said, "You can make a book if you really get the whole house behind it early on." Agent Lynn Nesbit agrees: "Money doesn't necessarily matter. There has to be a buzz within the house, and of course, they might only get behind one book a season."[18] This is just what happened with *Jaws*: A strong nucleus of enthusiasm started shooting out sparks that ignited fires outside of the company. If Doubleday thinks it's good, it must be good, reasoned Bantam as it placed a floor bid of $200,000 for the reprint rights, a figure that stunned Doubleday. (If Bantam thinks it's that good, maybe this thing really is good!) That's an interesting offer, Doubleday casually replied, absolutely flabbergasted at such a high bid for a first novel. We'll get back to you. Quickly, Doubleday shopped the book around, submitting it to eight other paperback houses. This was still not in the bag: Two houses rejected it outright.

After the all-important in-house sales conference in which *Jaws* was billed as "one of the big books of 1974," the sales manager contemplated the number of copies that could be placed in stores by the October publication date. The figure was 25,000, with a promotion budget of $25,000. Certainly this was respectable, even a bit unusual in an industry where few of the novels published by Doubleday or any other major house sold more than several thousand copies; yet still there was no awareness of the blockbuster *Jaws* would become.

Not long after the sales conference, the Book-of-the-Month Club, Reader's Digest, and the Playboy Book Club all picked up the book for their lists, paying advances that totalled about $85,000. Thereafter, Bantam, which believed the book would make a tremendous movie (Benchley believed a movie was out of the question — how do you catch and train a great white shark?), came in with its winning bid of $575,000 for the paperback rights. "Good God, Thomas," was Benchley's response when his editor phoned with the news. Brown-Zanuck paid $150,000 for the screenplay, and foreign sales totalled another $100,000. Thus, before the first day of publication, *Jaws* had earned $1,000,000. Yet Doubleday was still conservative in its initial printing, raising it only to 35,000. Within a month of publication, the novel had sold 40,000 copies and was racing up the best-seller lists, eventually selling 200,000 hardcover copies in the 44 weeks it stayed on the *New York Times* Best Sellers list.

Without taking anything away from the extraordinarily compelling narrative Benchley spun in *Jaws*, there is ample evidence that senior editor Tom Congdon made the book a best-seller. Having Congdon on his team was Benchley's luck. It was Congdon the fortuneteller who saw the potential in Benchley's idea and encouraged him to write the book. It was Congdon the matchmaker who convinced Doubleday to enter into the option with Benchley. It was Professor Congdon who taught Benchley and worked with him in rewriting and revising until the gem he saw in Benchley's idea came shining through. It was Cheerleader Congdon who loudly rooted for the book in front of everyone at Doubleday. It was Boss Congdon who used the political skills of a Hague and Curley to pull all the pieces together for the book, struggling with the author to get just the right title, going back to the art director time and again to revise the book jacket, energizing the book salespeople, pushing the head of subsidiary rights, championing the book at the company's sales conference, overseeing the advertising and promotion of the book, orchestrating all the steps in just the right sequence and at just the right time to turn the public's vote into a landslide in Benchley's favor.

Editors with this ability to champion a book through the many months or years it takes to bring it to publication; to stand by it through the inevitable ups and downs, to ramrod it past the naysayers, the incompetent, the incapable, the indifferent, that may populate a publishing house; these are the editors who can make best-sellers. Max Perkins was one of those special editors. Phyllis Grann, who began her career as secretary to Nelson Doubleday, worked her way through editorial jobs at different publishing houses, and ended up president of the Putnam Publishing Group, is another, an editor and publisher personally overseeing the publication of a number of Putnam's books, and in the process, becoming recognized as the publisher with a sure touch for best-sellers that turned Putnam into one of the most profitable houses. Benchley had happened upon one of those golden editors.

Stephen King's luck was in stumbling across a particularly prescient publishing house. He had been caught in that claustrophobic Maine trailer where the "pressure to break through in my work was building into a kind of psychic crescendo, and when it appeared to be thwarted, I felt desperately depressed, cornered. I felt trapped in a suicidal rat race, with no way out of the maze." In the wee hours of the night, thinking of his sixty stories and four novels that had been rejected, he would pace the trailer's small living room, saying to himself, "Shit, King, face it; you're going to be teaching fuckin' high school kids for the rest of your life."[19]

In the midst of his despair, Doubleday purchased his novel *Carrie* in 1974, when he was twenty-six, for an advance against royalties of $2,500. But it was New American Library who saw something special in the book, took a giant leap of faith, and purchased the right to publish the paperback for $400,000, *before* the hardcover was published. King was freed from his trailer, and the brand name, Stephen King, was born. Without that purchase by New American Library, would King now be living out his nightmares as the faculty advisor to a Maine high school student newspaper?

It was a publishing house, Farrar, Straus & Giroux, that made

Scott Turow a best-selling author by purchasing his novel, *Presumed Innocent*, in 1986 for $200,000, the most money that house had ever paid for a first novel. The "most for a first paid by a quality publisher" buzz was enough to get the ball rolling. "There's a network of people who buzz around the Four Seasons grill," David Brown, the producer, said. "I heard the author had accepted a bid from Farrar, Straus for $200,000. And that wasn't even the top bid. So I pricked up my ears."[20] The film rights went for $1 million. Then the bids for the paperback reprint rights were set to begin at $670,000, and were purchased by Warner Books for $3 million, also a record for a first novel. And then the Literary Guild chose the book as a main selection, foreign sales to fourteen countries brought in $500,000, and the *New York Times Magazine* published a full-length article about Turow and his book a month before the publication date. Farrar pumped out a first printing of 135,000 copies; *Presumed Innocent* had pulled out in front of the pack.

These stories of how an author became a best-selling author could go on and on, each with its own special twist, but all with a common denominator. Luck comes in many guises, but beneath each of its costumes is a cheerleader. Every book needs a cheerleader. Every best-seller finds one. In each case of best-seller achievement, someone came along, deus ex machina, who expressed and held an unqualified faith in a book or its author: Alice Roosevelt Longworth, who convinced the Pulitzer Prize Committee to select James Michener's *Tales of the South Pacific*; Harper Lee's Christmas friends, who gave her the freedom to write a masterpiece; Peter Benchley's talented editor; the paperback purchaser of Stephen King's *Carrie*; Scott Turow's publisher, who ventured the highest bid for a first novel. Each of these authors, of course, had written a special book that could appeal to a large audience. But before such appeal can be recognized, there must be someone willing to stand up and cheer: "Rah! Rah! Look at this! This is great!" and not stop cheering until every spectator in the stadium has joined in.

CHAPTER 15

Hats Off to Jackie!

A uthors may keep a shiny horse chestnut and worn rabbit's foot in their pockets, and make sure they never stop writing on page thirteen, and see to it that all their pencils are pointing in the same direction when they begin writing each morning, but the luck necessary to turn a book into a best-selling book cannot be coaxed. It comes when it damn well pleases.

There's one author, though, who grabbed luck by the short hairs and pulled it out of hiding, and she, Jackie Susann, should be the patron saint of writers.

Jacqueline Susann? Yes. That tough broad who Truman Capote said looked "like a truck driver in drag"?[1] That's the one. The one about whom Gore Vidal quipped, "she doesn't write, she types"?[2] Right. The one who wrote all that dreck, those trashy novels about drugs and sex and scandal? Precisely. Jacqueline Susann? You bet.

That tough broad who, as it turned out, was of course not as tough as she pretended, suffered every defeat, every humiliation, every indignity the publishing world has to dish out, and then turned right around and kicked some publishing butt. She caught everyone's attention.

SCENE I
Jackie Bangs at the Locked Door of Publishing

What was Jackie's first book? No, not *Valley of the Dolls*. No, it wasn't *Every Night, Josephine*, the story about her French poodle. For a dozen years she had been trying her hand at plays and books, each of which was rejected. She was no young success who burst upon the scene. She had known all the anguish and frustration of trying to break into print. Her writing was going nowhere, and her dreams of an acting career, her years of bit parts (she was often cast as a murderess or murder victim) were pretty much over in 1962 when, at the age of forty-four, she was diagnosed as having breast cancer. She later revealed she bargained with God: Just give me ten more years, ten years to prove I'm the writer I think I am.

Scene II

Jackie Is Humiliated by the Publishing World

Jacqueline Susann signed a contract with Doubleday for the publication of *Every Night, Josephine.* (Can't you just hear her telephoning all her friends: I've written a book and it's being published. By Doubleday! Yes! Doubleday!) But to her disbelief, she discovered that the book contract had no fixed publication date and that Doubleday would not publish her book until another dog book that was under contract had been completed and published. Jackie's husband — television producer, agent, and hustler Irving Mansfield — was furious and pulled the book back from Doubleday. Jackie, according to Mansfield, "had a fit." "But I've told all my friends that Doubleday is publishing my book! What will I tell them now? They'll think I lied to them!"[3]

As always, Irving knew just what a book needed, and brought this one to Bernard Geis Associates, a new publishing house.

Bernard Geis had been the editor at Prentice Hall who worked on Art Linkletter's book, *Kids Say the Darndest Things,* which came out in 1957. Linkletter, who constantly promoted the book on his TV show, was so taken by its rise to the top of the nonfiction best-seller lists, where it lodged for a year, that he backed Geis in starting up his own publishing house. That house would devote itself exclusively to the publication of ten or twelve books each year, books that could be promoted on television, that is, books that had the potential to be promoted into best-sellers. As Geis explained it, his publishing house was founded on the premise "that books are underpromoted and undermerchandized — the distribution of trade books is moribund. I can take any book, Stendhal or Max Shulman, and double or triple its sale by exposing it to the mass media."[4] Added Geis's director of promotion: "Our authors can rest assured we'll do our part. Other publishers live in an ivory tower. They think mass communications are a nasty business. But the rest of the world is watching TV. It's not enough to seek the habitual book buyers, a few thousand urban sophisticates. We reach out to the people who read gossip columns and women's pages. We present the author as a celebrity in her own right."[5] Helen Gurley Brown's *Sex and the Single Girl* was one of Geis's best-sellers.

SCENE III

Jackie Sets Off on the Tour from Hell

Bernard Geis Associates might have been headed in an interesting direction, but it still had a lot to learn. Jackie's first publicity tour was a disaster. On the West Coast, only one television show had been booked, and that show wanted Jackie only if her dog was with her; Josephine was back home in New York. No Josephine, no Jackie. The Mansfields checked out the local bookstores and found not a single copy of *Every Night, Josephine*, nor a bookstore manager who had even heard of it. Mansfield concluded that the book business "must be a pretty funny business to mess up on getting books and announcements to bookstores."[6] In Chicago, Jackie had an interview on what her husband called a "five-watt radio station." "I think maybe four people heard the interview," Mansfield complained. "It cost us thirty dollars by taxi each way."[7] When, through her husband's own promotional efforts, carried out with his own cash, the book began to get some publicity and sneaked onto a regional best-seller list or two, Jackie happened to learn the good news not from her publisher, but while browsing through a magazine.

SCENE IV

Jackie Confronts the Opacity of the Publishing World

For her next book, *Valley of the Dolls*, Jackie received (now mind you, her previous book had indeed grazed some best-seller lists) the munificent stipend of $3,000. So much for the loyal support of a publisher. The first readers of *Valley of the Dolls* at Bernard Geis Associates pleaded with Bernie Geis to drop it and run. "You've already invested three thousand dollars in an advance on this book. Don't

167

throw good money after bad. It's literary trash." "*Valley of the Dolls* was hardly written in English," another of Geis's editors sighed. "She is a painfully dull, inept, clumsy, undisciplined, rambling and thoroughly amateurish writer whose every sentence, paragraph and scene cries for the hand of a pro.... I really don't think there is a page of this ms. that can stand in its present form."[8] So much for the perspicacity of the editors of the one publishing house in the United States devoted solely to making best-sellers.

When the bids for a paperback reprint of *Valley of the Dolls* were due (before the hardcover publication), there was a distressing, numbing silence. Not one had been submitted. At the last moment, at Bernard Geis's personal prodding, Bantam put in an insignificant bid that discouraged Susann and her publisher alike. Geis reported the bid to other paperback houses to see if some action could be stirred up, to no avail. Geis then went back to Bantam and implied that there were other bids and that to get the book it would have to raise its offer, which it did.

As it turned out, Bantam need not have been upset about being taken for a ride. That bid proved to be quite a bargain when *Valley of the Dolls* became the fastest paperback seller of all times, with eight million copies sold in seven months. But Bantam's bid had not been based on its insight into the potential of the book; Bantam's was a clouded vision shared by the professionals at the host of other paperback houses to which the book had been submitted. Not one book club bid on the book.

SCENE V

Jackie Is Panned by the Critics

To the extent she received reviews at all, Susann's novels were trashed. Gloria Steinem concluded that "for the reader who has put away comic books but isn't yet ready for editorials in the *Daily News*, V.O.T.D. may bridge an awkward gap."[9] Later, Christopher Lehmann-Haupt of the *New York Times* called her next novel, *The Love Machine*, "popcorn." "It goes down quickly and easily. It is the kernel of an idea, the seed of an inspiration, exploded into bite-sized nothingness."[10] "Once is more than enough, as this book, and all of Jacqueline Susann's books prove," the *New York Times* review of *Once Is Not*

Enough quite predictably began. *Time* dismissed it as "the dirty book of the month."[11]

SCENE VI
Who the Hell Cares?

Jackie and Irving were very quick studies; or maybe, knowing that Jackie's time was short, they were ready to work harder and faster and longer than anyone else. Whatever it was, neither their publisher's ineptitude, nor the discouraging reviews, nor the lack of interest of the paperback houses and book clubs and national television shows bothered them one bit. Takeoff time, T minus 1, was at hand.

Off went fifteen hundred free copies of *Valley of the Dolls*—at that time an extraordinary number—to anyone, anywhere, who might help publicize the book.

Off went Jackie and Irving, right behind them. Together, Jackie and Irving carefully plotted how to promote Jackie's new book. The staid world of book publishing was outdated, archaic, they concluded. "Usually all they ever do to help an author is give a little luncheon attended by two or three editors including one from The New York Times who perspires too much," Jackie remarked. "It seemed to me that if I'd spent eighteen months writing the book the least I could do was spend three months promoting it."[12]

Those three months turned into twelve as the Mansfields, at their own expense, traveled the country, back and forth, again and again, for Jackie to appear on national and local television shows, at the bookstores and for the newspaper and radio interviews that Irving had lined up. In each city, they hired a taxi and made the rounds of all the bookstores, talking to the manager and clerks, making sure *Valley of the Dolls* was prominently displayed. Because Jackie and Irving cared, the bookstores cared and helped promote the book. When Jackie found a bookstore clerk with the brass to admit he hadn't read her book, she bought him a copy, paid for it right then and there, and autographed it for him. "A clerk won't really push a book if he hasn't read it himself," she explained.[13] Each bookdealer was given an autographed photograph of himself with Jackie; another copy was sent to his local newspaper. She wrote personal notes to each bookstore owner, to everyone who had helped her or been nice to her on her tour, each with a personal anecdote. She kept a card file on book-store clerks and knew their first names, intentionally cultivating friendships with owners of bookstores across the country to the point where some of them indeed numbered among her closest friends.

The Mansfields visited the book distributors at four o'clock in the morning as the books were being loaded onto trucks, bringing them coffee and Danish, talking to the drivers, giving them auto-graphed copies of her book. What a great idea! What great copy! The newspapers ate it up as much as the truck drivers.

It was Irving Mansfield who thought of advertising *Valley of the Dolls* in the entertainment pages as well as in a newspapers' book review sections, a successful stratagem that had never before been tried or apparently even contemplated, a plan that helped the book reach a new group of readers.

Jackie recalled how, in the beginning, none of the television shows had wanted to have her; how her publicist had "threatened, cajoled and begged" to get her a spot on a late night radio show; how she had gotten on Merv Griffin's show only because he was a friend; and how what she accomplished had been done without the benefit of national television. "Almost every city has its own version of *Today*. At that time, there were Roger Grimsby and the late Gypsy Rose Lee in San Francisco, Regis Philbin in San Diego, Marie Torre in Pitts-burgh, Tom Snyder in Philadelphia, Irv Kupcinet in Chicago. If you were willing to travel, you got on. I traveled! I made the list without *Today*, without the *Tonight Show*. I kept 'touring.' I went to Detroit, Cincinnati, Dallas, Houston. I developed sciatica from sitting on planes."[14]

Although Jacqueline Susann once said that plugging books on the talk show circuit "ought to rate combat pay,"[15] it must be remem-bered that Jackie was not just any old writer appearing on television. In addition to a husband who had been a television producer and who had the industry contacts and the chutzpa to use them and then some, raven-haired Jackie, with her perfect tan and sparkling capped teeth, had great stage presence, and a sexy smoker's voice to boot. She had been an actress and now was relishing her leading role. She had the ability, the knack, the stamina, for giving six or more interviews a day, enthusiastically answering the same questions time and again, day after day, appearing on one hundred television shows and two hundred radio shows to promote *Valley of the Dolls* (Bernard Geis once commented that "someone said then the only thing you could turn on without getting Jacqueline Susann was the water faucet"[16]), adeptly returning any straying interviewer to the only important topic, her book. She was clever enough not to talk directly about the plot of *Valley of the Dolls*, but rather, for example, the abuse of pills by the rich and famous. As Geis noted, "She would *deny* that the characters were based on well-known real people. She would *deny* that one character was really modelled on Judy Garland. She would *deny* that it was really Ethel Merman she was portraying in the book."[17] With each denial, the resulting rumors and speculation flamed more interest in *Valley of the Dolls*.

Jackie was comfortable and relaxed enough before a camera to have some fun, which guaranteed return appearances. When her *The Love Machine* and Philip Roth's *Portnoy's Complaint* were vying for the top position on the fiction best-seller lists, she commented about Roth: "I like the book but I'd hate to shake his hand,"[18] adding in another interview that "Philip Roth's started a 'do-it-yourself club' and that it had taken him so long to write the novel because 'he could only type with one hand.'"[19]

On the David Frost show, critic John Simon asked her, "Do you think you are writing art or are you writing trash to make a lot of money?"

"Little man," she snapped, "I am telling a story. Now does that make you happy?"[20]

An interviewer asked her, "Don't you ever wake up in the middle of the night and realize you haven't done anything that is really artistic?"

"You're sick," Jackie shot back. "Do you wake up and think you're not Huntley-Brinkley?"[21]

When one interviewer asked, "What do you think is the reason for everybody reading your book, apart from the obvious?" Jackie responded with a question of her own: "What's the obvious reason?"

"Sex, pure and simple," answered the interviewer.

No, Jackie responded, it was not sex that sold her books. "I'm a today writer. The novel today has to compete with television and the movies. It has to come alive quickly and be easy to read. When people tell you they couldn't put the book down, that is good writing."[22]

Jackie's editor remarked once that "Jackie and Irving were the most phenomenal, tenacious, successful, innovative, and inventive book promoters who ever lived. With Jackie and Irving there was no limit. They called in every IOU they had and pulled every trick they knew."[23] These tricks included a book buying campaign described by Jackie's biographer, Barbara Seadman, in *Lovely Me*:

> Clearly *Valley's* momentum was largely due to the publicity. However, there was a second factor that inflated the early sales: a book-buying campaign apparently orchestrated by Irving and possibly financed in part by Bantam and Twentieth Century-Fox, both of which had much to gain if the book could be made a success.... Exactly how buyers in key cities were recruited and financed remains a secret. However, Letty Pogebrin [Geis's director of publicity] says that in those days the names of the specific bookstores reporting to the list were "common knowledge."[24]

It would not be surprising if Irving had indeed been able to shake down Bantam, which had bought the paperback rights, and Twentieth Century-Fox, which had bought the movie rights, to contribute funds to keep the book at the top of the lists for as long as possible. "If anyone tells you that publishing is a gentleman's profession," he once scoffed, "I suggest you just laugh."[25]

Jackie and Irving's relentless work got the momentum going, and going, and going, until sales of *Valley of the Dolls* jumped from a few hundred copies a week to over six thousand weekly, peaking at 8,500 a day. On the best-seller lists for sixty-two weeks, *Valley of the Dolls* eventually sold over 25 million copies in hardcover and paperback, was purchased by more people than any other American novel of the twentieth century, and according to the *Guinness Book of World Records*, is the best-selling novel of all time. "Money is applause," the actress turned novelist said.[26] The applause she had never known in her acting career was bringing down the house in her writing career. "The biggest thing of all," Jacqueline Susann believed, "is *being* Number One, being on top of that list that's in every bookstore." She went on:

> People just look at the list and buy the book. It's the in thing to do. And when a book hits a hundred thousand, it will do

two hundred thousand because now you're reaching people who rarely buy books. At ninety thousand you've hit all
the people who go to Brentano's and Doubleday; over that
you're getting people who buy in department stores and dis-
count houses. Men buy mostly nonfiction, history, biography. But if a book has that extra thing, if it's a real story, if
it's excitement, then men will buy it, if it's only to find out
why their wives sit up with it all night. And when that happens, the book will just sail, and nobody can stop it, critics, nobody.[27]

She would follow *Valley of the Dolls* with two more number one
best-selling novels, *The Love Machine* and *Once Is Not Enough*. "If I
knew what made a best-seller," Jacqueline Susann commented as *The
Love Machine* was just coming out with an advance sale of 200,000
(which quickly climbed to 300,000 copies in print a week later, and
which had just received a million dollar bid for the movie rights), "I
wouldn't sweat and stalk beaches, parks and the zoo when I get hung
up with my writing."[28] But she had a pretty good clue.

Jackie's editor of *The Love Machine* at Simon & Schuster, Michael
Korda, believed that Jackie's promotional skills were the key to her
success. Without them, he was convinced, the book would probably
have sold about 100,000 copies, "but it wouldn't have the great impact
it does. Jackie has succeeded where no one has before in tapping all
the modern means of communication in one great campaign —
movies, television, newspaper interviews, magazines, commercials,
all cleverly bound together."[29]

This was Simon & Schuster's first entry into the brave new world
of commercial fiction. "Just turn it into a book somehow, that's all I
ask" were the first instructions editor Michael Korda was given by
his boss when he reported that the manuscript was all but incoher-
ent. That proved to be the easiest part of the work. The publishing
house, accustomed to launching a big book with a sedate cocktail
party and a spot for the author on *The Today Show*, found itself
throwing lavish parties on both coasts, sending out thousands of gift
ankhs in presentation cases shaped like books, devising posters,
displays, cakes in the shape of a book: There was no end to Jackie's
ideas, her requests, her demands. Not satisfied with Simon & Schuster's performance, Jackie switched to William Morrow for her next
book. The head of Simon & Schuster sent her a single rose on the

publication date of *Once is Not Enough*, with a note: "For us, once *was* enough."[30]

It was only with the recurrence of cancer in 1972 that Jackie began cutting back her typical twenty-nine talk shows and newspaper interviews a week, a diminution of activity which worried her no end: "Even a good book can die on the vine if it's not promoted."[31]

Jackie's publishers hadn't learned all the lessons she had taught, though other authors had. Less than two years after Jackie's death in 1974, agent Morton Janklow brought to Simon & Schuster the first novel of one of his new authors, Judith Krantz. It was called *Scruples* and was about the sex and scandal of the super rich of Beverly Hills' Rodeo Drive. Simon & Schuster turned it down, as Judith Krantz remembered, "because they didn't like it."[32] Crown Publishers did like it and brought it out in March of 1978, at which time it soared to the top of the *New York Times* Best Sellers list and stayed on the list for about a year, selling over a million copies in hardcover.

Perhaps Simon & Schuster had not learned to recognize the winning formula of Jackie Susann that Judith Krantz applied to her book. Or perhaps the publishers did not recognize in Judith Krantz the same drive, the same marketability, that Jackie Susann had possessed. Off went Judith Krantz, crossing the country to appear on every television and radio show, at every bookstore and women's club that would have her, cultivating the booksellers, bubbling effervescently about her book. "I never realized before how much hustling was involved," she said after the completion of her hardcover tour and before she set off on her paperback tour. "Touring for a book — it's the literary equivalent of war."[33]

Harvey Mackay is another example of an author who followed in Jacqueline Susann's footsteps. The Minneapolis businessman was running an envelope company when he wrote *Swim with the Sharks Without Being Eaten Alive*, a title picked by a consulting firm which, for $5,000, tested it in the market against hundreds of others. That's indicative of how this businessman approached his first book. It wasn't just money he had to spend; it was also a lot of aggressiveness and a phenomenal sales technique.

Before he began writing his book, MacKay visited over one hundred bookstores across the country and talked with more than one hundred authors, reaching the conclusion that most books fail simply because they are not available in the stores. That would not happen to him. He persuaded his publisher, William Morrow & Company, to do an initial run of 100,000 copies by promising to pay the cost of a twenty-six city promotional tour. He persuaded forty-three Names, of the likes of Mario Cuomo, Gerald Ford, Ted Koppel and Robert Redford, to write blurbs for his book. At the Frankfurt Book Fair, which his publishers had discouraged him from attending, he sold the rights to his book to thirty foreign publishers. At each of the twenty-six cities he visited, he stopped in at dozens of bookstores, showing the owners how best to display his book. Need it be added that *Swim with the Sharks Without Being Eaten Alive* stayed on the best-seller lists for thirty-six weeks? It was Jackie's winning formula, carried out to perfection.

These stories of Jacqueline Susann and Judith Krantz and Harvey MacKay; of Thomas A. Harris, whose book, *I'm OK, You're OK*, had meager first year sales, but who didn't give up, giving talks to small audiences and stirring up enough sales that his publishers launched a first rate promotional campaign, resulting ultimately in sales of over one million copies; of Dr. Wayne W. Dyer, who packed 400 copies of his *Your Erroneous Zones* into the trunk of his car and set off, traveling around the country, talking with local newspapermen and on local radio stations, with his book thereafter making the best-seller lists: These stories of the triumph of authors over the system are heartwarming indeed. But beware their Circean seduction. It doesn't always work out that way. It's like what Annie Dillard said in *The Writing Life* about how long it takes to write a book: two to ten years for most authors, she posits, qualifying her statement by noting that "out of a human population on earth of four and a half billion, perhaps twenty people can write a book in a year. Some people lift cars, too. Some people enter week-long sled-dog races, go over Niagara Falls in barrels, fly planes through the Arc de Triomphe. Some people feel no pain in childbirth. Some people eat cars. There is no call to take human extremes as norms."[34] The Susanns and the Krantzes and the MacKays of the world are the car-eaters, those very exceptional individuals who can successfully promote a book themselves. It's not easy.

"Am damned tired just now," Ernest Hemingway wrote to Charles Scribner after the publication of *For Whom the Bell Tolls*, "and so do not want to be unjust but I sometimes wonder if you, Charley and company ever worked as hard selling the damned book as I worked writing it what the sales would be."[35] Interesting thought. What if publishers would work with their authors in selling their books? "No publisher is so happy as a publisher with an author across the sea," John Cheever joked,[36] but there was an element of truth in his joking. Even late in his career, Hemingway was begging his publishers just to communicate with him, just to let him know how his books were selling. "Where the hell you been, boy?" he wrote to Charles Scribner after the publication of *Across the River and Into the Trees*. "Did you read the Time review and take off for the wilds of Jersey to launch your counter-attack from there? Well everybody has their own way of doing things. But isn't it sort of customary to inform an author about how things go and what people say when a book comes out that he has bet his shirt on and worked his heart out on nor missed a deadline nor failed to keep a promise?"[37]

Publishers can make it hard for an author to do anything to help. "Unless forced to do so," Kenneth Roberts complained, "publishers will *not* let their authors — who, of course, are the persons most interested in their books' progress — discover anything whatever about that progress until the last possible moment."[38] This, of course, is ridiculous if the author is going to be a partner with the publisher in promoting a book. Jacqueline Susann switched from Simon & Schuster to William Morrow, she reported, because of her frustration at not being able to get the weekly sales reports that would have helped her fine-tune her promotional work. Her new publishers tried harder.

If that proverbial conundrum tree falls in the forest with no one there to hear it, was there any sound of its falling? If people have heard or seen nothing about an author's new book, has the author really written a book? Well, the answer to that one is easy: No, the author has not. He may pick up his book and fondle it, and read pages at random and be possessed by the wonder of it all, but it is no more real now than when he first conceived and contemplated and began working on it, and drafted chapters, and revised paragraphs, all the while imagining the book.

Blessed are those who believe without seeing. But for most people, seeing is believing. And to believe a book exists, they must have seen it, or read about it, or heard about it. No matter what or where, any publicity is good publicity.

And that is why an interview with a world famous author will appear, improbably, in the Anyplace-but-Here Gazette; and that is why Famous Author will patiently respond to the questions of the local women's sewing group as to the type of pencil he uses for each draft; and that is why he will sit at the shaky cardtable in the town bookstore to sign fourteen copies of his book. For even if he is among the handful of blockbuster authors, he will always welcome any publicity and criss-cross the country to get it and build an audience, reader by reader, for his next book. As Nan Talese, editor at Doubleday, has said, "Publishing literary novels is like sailing a small craft. Either you catch the wind or you have to paddle very hard."[39]

Jacqueline Susann: Patron Saint of Writers. Not because her novels were literary masterpieces. Not because *Valley of the Dolls* holds the record as the fastest paperback seller of all times or because it was purchased by more people than any other American novel of the twentieth century. Not because of her succession of number one hits. And not because Jackie established a road map for others to follow in promoting books; few authors have the special personality, the resources, the stamina to replicate what she accomplished. But what Jacqueline Susann showed is that the more attention and time an author and his publisher devote to the promotion of a book, the more likely it is that the book will achieve the sales it deserves. She showed that it is not enough just to toss a newly-published book out into the world to see what will happen, and then to sigh, "Those are the breaks," when the inevitable nothing happens. As Michael Korda has said, "Jackie and Irving taught me that books can be merchandised, just like anything else — something that a lot of publishers have yet to learn. Today, she is a prophet without honor, but John Grisham, Robert James Waller, Judith Krantz, Jackie Collins, Danielle Steel and the rest all owe her a debt."[40] Jacqueline Susann proved that the sales success of a book can be made. Hats off to Jackie!

CHAPTER 16

Apply It to
the Problem

O nce, when Andrew Carnegie was playing golf with Frank Nelson Doubleday, the great industrialist turned with a question
for the great publisher.

"How much money did you make in your book business last
month?" Carnegie asked Doubleday.

Doubleday admitted he didn't know; publishers, he explained,
had no way to determine their profits on a monthly basis.

"Do you know what I would do if I were in a business in which
I couldn't tell the amount of monthly profit?" the amazed Scotsman
asked. "I would get out of it."[1]

J. P. Morgan did just that at the turn of the century. He had taken
over Harper's, but he dropped it like a hot potato as soon as he realized that the business principles on which his empire had been built
seemed to have little relevance to publishing.

Ambling along through the twentieth century as a cottage industry, a refined gentleman's club, book publishing has quietly become
a multinational, twenty-six billion dollar a year industry.

Twenty-six billion dollars: That's big business indeed. And
fewer and fewer publishing houses are responsible for this volume of
business. Other corporations have sensed the presence of profits in
this slumbering giant and raided it, bringing about a fantastic transformation over the last decade or two. The wave of mergers, consol-
idations and acquisitions by foreign corporations has left the
publishing industry with just a handful of major houses that can grab
a seat at the table and bid on the megadeals that now dominate the
business.

The old line publishers — the Scribners, the Doubledays, the Knopfs — were proud of publishing books that they considered of literary value. Today, as Roger Straus, Jr., has said, "A lot of publishing houses are being run by accountants, businessmen and lawyers who have very little concern for the books. They could just as well be selling string or spaghetti."[2] For example, Peter Davis, the chief executive officer of Reed International, Britain's largest publishing company, who worked his way up through the ranks of General Foods and then England's largest supermarket chain, has applied techniques of selling groceries to selling books. And found that they work.

Is it all that bad to have books treated more like commodities than art? Maybe not. Certainly in terms of finding an audience for books — which is, after all, the purpose of publishing — it's downright good. The inefficiencies, the sluggishness, the inadequate financial controls that characterized the publishing industry are being corrected. Publishers are shortening the time between when a decision is made to take on a book and when the book hits the shelves; improving sales projections and production schedules; lowering composition costs; shipping books faster; billing faster. The result has been increased productivity and sales. Any system that helps do that is not only not all that bad; it's a godsend.

The problem is that with a sharpening focus on the bottom line, houses tend to concentrate on books they believe have a high likelihood of being commercially successful, thereby restricting the range of books that might reach market. "When I began to write," John Updike remembered, "publishers were gentlemen in tweed jackets puffing pipes. Now ... publishing houses are owned by oil companies ... and their interest is naturally in the big strike, the gusher.... I don't want to write a gusher.... I want to write books that unlock the traffic jam in everybody's head."[3] Focusing on profit also means cutting overhead, which often means cutting staff, cutting promotion budgets, and raising the price of books, all of which can lessen the quality of books and shrink their market. Change clearly can be a two-edged sword.

It's all well and good to talk about long range financial projections and profit goals, but how can sales be projected when the books on which the sales projections are based have not yet been written; when maybe their authors have not yet even been discovered; when the public's tastes are changing from year to year, even from season to season? "If somebody asks me for a five-year plan, I can't do it," Peter Mayer, the former chief executive of Penguin Books, has noted. "The books are not written yet. It would be a fraud." Yet the head of the British conglomerate that owns Penguin, as well as *The Financial Times* and Royal Doulton china, can't understand this. "Royal Doulton does it, why can't you?" Mr. Mayer is constantly asked.[4] As successful a businessman as S.I. Newhouse, Jr., overseer of that part of the Newhouse empire which once included Random House, Alfred A. Knopf, Crown Publishing, Pantheon Books, Schocken Books, Time Books, Villard Books, Vintage Books, Clarkson N. Potter, Harmony Books, Orion Books and Ballantine/del Rey/Fawcett/Ivy Books, has conceded that "this is not a high-profit business. You can't think of it on a year-to-year basis, or in terms of a traditional fiscal year. What time span is reasonable? I wish I knew. We just try to manage the business through the inconsistencies and vagaries."[5] As always, publishers need quixotic faith in what they are doing and a run of gambler's luck.

Change, innovations — progress, if you will — come very slowly to this industry. "If you would be thrilled by watching the galloping advance of a major glacier," John MacDonald once said, "you'd be ecstatic watching changes in publishing."[6] "Book people think well," Stephen King noted, "but are innovative as a last resort."[7] Once, speaking at a luncheon meeting of publishers, Barbara Tuchman chided the assembled guests when she suggested a modest reform in the industry: the discontinuance of "the invidious practice" of sending out for review uncorrected page proofs or bound galleys rather than the finished product. "Like all reforms, I know you will say [it] cannot be done.... You are in a business requiring intelligence — apply it to the problem, gentlemen, solve it and don't go on and on about how nothing can be changed."[8]

Industry inefficiencies that have festered for a long time have suddenly, with a drop in book sales, become inflamed. Hardcover sales peaked in 1994 at 513 million copies sold, and have been declining at the rate of about 5 percent a year, with no let-up in sight. "The returns problem in 1996 has proved so widespread and persistent," reported Jean Srnecz, a merchandising vice president at Baker & Taylor, one of the largest book distributors, "that the industry has had to admit there is an underlying, fundamental problem."[9] As Charles Scribner, Jr., makes clear in his memoir, *In the Company of Writers*, the ability of a publishing house to innovate has become the key to its success and endurance — indeed, to its survival. "If I were advising a young publisher today, I would tell him that what seems unthinkable should be thought about."[10] How times are changing! Time and again, not so long ago, Hemingway would throw his hands up in despair about how business was conducted at Scribner's. "I would never go with any other publishing house," he wrote to Charles Scribner, "but Jesus Christ I would like to put yours in order. Sometime, Charlie, you ought to hire me at a dollar a year to put your joint on a disciplined basis."[11]

What might Hemingway have done if Scribner had taken him up on his offer today? What can publishers do to catch and keep the attention of an increasingly distracted public?

Before any progress can be made, publishers must muster the courage to do the unthinkable: to look back each season to see what went right, and wrong, with their latest crop of books.

Some of the saddest reading is to thumb through a major publisher's book catalog from a year or two ago, and review their best offerings for that particular spring or fall season. These, the books that were winnowed out from the thousands of proposals submitted to them; these, the books lovingly nourished and nurtured and brought to production; these, the books which at one time meant so much, at least to their author, and maybe to their editor. Novels and nonfiction alike. These, almost all, books that now mean nothing to anybody. Skim their enthusiastic write-ups in the catalogs, write-ups that such a short time later seem so flat and lifeless, and you have to wonder: Why did the publishers ever care about this book? Why would anyone have thought it would have done well? Why did the author even bother?

Once a year, each spring — a good spring cleaning, if you will — *Publishers Weekly* runs a postmortem on the "big" books of the year that weren't. These were the books that despite much ballyhoo by their publishers, with announcements of first printings of 150,000 and promotional budgets of $125,000, ended up selling 33,487 copies. Books, in other words, that fell flat on their faces. What went wrong?

Publishers, if they respond at all to the *Publishers Weekly* inquiries (and a number flat-out refuse to participate in this masochistic ritual of spring), are inclined to give wishy-washy answers, like "The demand for the book was such that we saw no need actually to print 150,000 copies," or "We sold enough copies to earn out the author's advance," or "I think the book furthered Jonathan's career and that his next book will be more successful." Once in a while they'll fess up: "Hey, this was bad misjudgment."

The reactions of some key bookstore owners who also are interviewed for these annual mea culpas are usually a lot more penetrating. Something along these lines:

> This was a publisher trying to put out a mass market paperback in hardcover.
> This could have made a magazine article but not a book.
> The cover was really horrible.
> The title was nondescriptive.
> The title was impossible to pronounce.
> The book was too expensive.
> The typeset was user unfriendly.
> The author's hardcover market has definitely been shrinking.
> She has a small following and still has it. He's been writing for a long time and gets a little worse with each book.
> People for a long time have not been that interested in Vietnam.
> The story was too well known from all the media coverage.
> Who wants to read about Bob Hope anymore?

There are lessons to be learned from this Monday morning quarterbacking, painful yet important lessons for the editors and publishers who will take the time to stop and ask and listen, rather than just plowing ahead with the next book without learning anything from the last.

Long ago, Richard Simon of Simon & Schuster made a habit of haunting bookstores, talking with the managers and clerks, asking for their ideas and suggestions about Simon & Schuster books and what made them sell, and giving advice to the owners on how books might be better marketed through bookstores. Frightened by flagging sales, Bantam Doubleday Dell in July of 1990 sent off sixty of its top executives to spend a few days in bookstores around the country to try to gain some insight into what sells books. The president of Bantam Doubleday Dell stated that this program, which the *New York Times* hailed as a bold, revolutionary experiment, would be worthwhile if it caused his executives "to think about such things as why stores decide to order certain books and not others, how they display them, whether display makes a difference and what Bantam Doubleday Dell's competitors do differently and better."[12] Revolutionary or not, the executives returned to the home office with new insights, reporting such findings as the importance of book jackets in helping to sell a book.

Like Richard Simon, publishers should make such forays into the world a regular program to stay in touch with what makes their industry hum. What might they discover?

Take, for example, the critical step of putting a price on a book. Are book buyers price sensitive? That's an easy one. Are they ever!

The publication of books slipped precipitously during the Depression, from 214,334,000 copies of new books printed in 1929, down to the 1933 total of 11,790,000, thousands of which never left the warehouse. During the roaring 1980s, the market share shifted from paperbacks to hardcovers, with mass-market paperback sales growing at a rate of 6.5 percent a year from 1982 to 1989, compared to a 12.4 percent annual increase for adult hardcovers. In the leaner 1990s, these figures again reversed themselves, with mass paperback sales rising and hardcovers falling.

The price that publishers put on a new book will have a direct and significant impact on its sales. A little too low, and publishers cut into their profit margin. A little too high, and prices reach the limits of tolerance and books don't sell. Richard Simon understood the delicate sensitivity of pricing. It was he who first experimented with setting the price of books at the odd figure like $4.95 rather than $5.00, just as consumer products were marked down so that the purchaser felt he was getting something of a bargain. This quickly became standard practice.

When Sally Bedell Smith's book, *In All His Glory: The Life of William S. Paley: The Legendary Tycoon and His Brilliant Circle*, was published by Simon & Schuster in the fall of 1990, it had everything going for it. The reviewers loved it, it was critically acclaimed, its promotion was dazzling, and to top off all of that, Mr. Paley cooperated by passing away, and his death and a review of his life was front page news. But the book never touched The List. Could it be because the book was priced at $29.95, at a time when eleven of the fifteen nonfiction best-sellers were selling for under $20? As Richard Simon knew, even a good book priced above the market of the day has an awfully tall hurdle to clear.

Every time publishers have figured out how to lower the price of books, there has been an explosive growth in the sales of books.

Before the first Pocket (paperback) Books were published on June 19, 1939, the hardcover houses begged the company not to go ahead with this hare-brained scheme, but the books were snapped up and the paperback revolution had begun. Total sales of all paperbacks in 1939, at twenty-five cents each, were three million; sales reached 231 million by 1951 and into the billions by 1990. Let's look at the top ten best-selling books of the 1970s. *The Godfather* sold 292,765 copies in hardcover, 13,225,000 in paper; *The Exorcist* sold 205,265 in hard, 11,948,000 paper; *Jonathan Livingston Seagull*, 3,192,000 hard (remember, this thin book was an inexpensive hardcover), 7,250,000 paper; *Love Story*, 431,976 hard, 9,778,000 paper; *Jaws*, 204,281 hard, 9,210,000 paper. Sure looks like price makes a mighty big difference in sales.

Dropping the cost of books and facilitating their distribution — paperbacks are now sold at newsstands, supermarkets, department stores, airports, drug stores, bookstores, variety stores, through over 100,000 outlets nationwide, anywhere that magazines and newspapers are sold — proved a winning formula, just as it would in two other publishing revolutions, the bookclubs and the book chains. And so it will again, for the creative publisher who figures out a new twist to this old formula.

Publishers and bookstores are tinkering with the formula. Book superstores, those user friendly stores of 12,000 to 37,000 square feet, have been the latest progression beyond the chains. By 1997, Barnes & Noble owned 439 of these stores and was planning to open 70 more each year for the next three years. Borders Group Inc. has 165 superstores, and Books-a-Million, 93. These stores are able to offer economies of scale and large promotion budgets to promote the big best-sellers, and are attracting new legions of customers.

From the rapid pace of expansion, one has to assume that these stores are making economic sense. But why not cut entirely the expensive overhead of operating stores? Why not sell on cable television? In 1993, Random House arranged a QVC appearance for Julia Child who, in 35 minutes, sold 10,000 copies of her latest cookbook. Gerald Posner went on and sold 3,000 copies of his book about the Kennedy assassination. "We've sold a lot of books on QVC," said Alberto Vitale, then chairman of Random House, "and I don't think we've even scratched the surface yet."[13]

If television can be a successful medium to sell books, why not the Internet? Amazon.com, which sells books over the Internet and bills itself as the world's largest bookstore, had 1997 sales of $165 million, with over 1 million customer accounts. Barnes & Noble has joined the parade and quickly has built up a customer base of over 250,000. These Internet stores are not just sitting out there in cyberspace waiting for customers to come calling; they are taking steps to attract them. Amazon.com, for instance, ran a lottery with a short story started by John Updike; anyone could tap in and add a sentence to the story (and tap in they did, with 200,000 entries in the first two weeks). Every day for 45 days, a winning sentence was selected by a committee of judges headed by Mr. Updike and awarded $1,000, with a grand prize of $100,000 given to one of the contestants in a random drawing.

What else might publishers and editors discover as they roamed the bookstores of their communities? That it would make sense for them to devote a certain percentage of their revenues to promote reading? Expanding the market for books, getting more people interested in reading, is the only way to force those barbarians back out through the gates.

In the early 1920s, advertising expert Earnest Elmo Calkins advocated that the publishing houses advertise not specific books, but reading in general; that they band together, make contributions to a war chest, and for several years focus their advertising on the joys of reading. "Books cannot be advertised," he said, "but reading can be."[14]

Very interesting concept. And would that not, at least in the long run, accrue to the benefit of the contributing publishers? An expanding market? J. Richard Munro, the co-chairman and chief executive officer of Time-Warner, has stated that in "industries like mine ... a literate populace is imperative to our shareholders' success. We don't have an option but to get involved."[15] Indeed publishers don't; they should be losing sleep every night worrying about the sad state of literacy in the United States.

Why couldn't reading be made fashionable? Why shouldn't shoppers frequent bookstores as often as other stores at the mall? Why can't Calvin Klein's models grace ads about the pleasures of reading? Publishers should become actively involved in promoting reading, just as Apple went into the schools and colleges to set up programs to build a market for its personal computers, just as Texas Instruments ran ads for its calculators as "tools for learning."

Readers must be recruited and enlisted by the publishing houses. Publishers, the book chains, and the American Bookseller's Association are all donating money to help launch television shows about books, from a book shopping show on cable, to shows with a round-table discussion format, to programs patterned after *Entertainment Tonight*. "I don't know if this will succeed in helping to sell more books" says Charles Cumello, the chairman of Waldenbooks, "but I do know we've got to try something in this industry. Even the dairy business promotes itself better than we do."[16] Publishers are recognizing the power of book groups — small groups of friends who meet regularly to discuss the books they are reading — and are sending authors to meet with them at their private homes to talk about new books. "For the first time in publishing history," said Jane Friedman, publisher of Vintage Books, a division of Random House, "we've figured out how to reach the true book addicts. We'll use this to market new titles and backlist books, but especially hidden gems that we believe book addicts would love, if only they knew they existed."[17] Here, publishers are recognizing, is the perfect spot to trigger word-of-mouth chain reactions about a book, since these are exactly the types of people who will talk about what they have been reading. Some bookstores are even getting into the act and are hosting the book groups at their stores, with store owners suggesting titles they think the groups might enjoy.

Publishing houses and bookstores need to work together in other ways. Together, they must re-examine the policy of permitting bookstores to return books for full credit. In what other industry does a manufacturer offer its brand-new-this-year-hot-off-the-lines model at 40 percent off list price the very first day it is for sale? What other industry sells its products on consignment, letting the distributors return the unsold product for full credit? Gradually abolishing this fully returnable policy might not be a bad idea.

This policy of selling books on consignment was first established by young Richard Simon in the 1920s. Simon himself quickly regretted what he had done. Across his publishing house's financials for 1926 he scrawled, "Bookstore returns too high!"[18] They were 3 percent. But by then it was too late. With other houses following suit, there was no turning back, and the percentage of returns kept growing. "Gone today, here tomorrow," was Alfred A. Knopf's lament.[19] "Do you keep a copy of every book you print?" a lady asked British publisher Jonathan Cape at a London cocktail party. "Madam," he replied, "I keep thousands."[20] Today, a publisher is jubilant if its returns are 20 percent or less, with a 42 percent return being average for hardcover fiction today, a return rate of 60 percent for fiction by unknown authors, and a 40 to 50 percent return just about average for mass market titles. Twenty years ago, a return rate of 10 to 15 percent was standard.

The policy of fully returnable sales makes the retailer safe from loss. Why should he be? Why shouldn't some of the risk be on his shoulders, some of the impetus to get out and hustle books? Shouldn't it be the role of the bookstores to help pull in customers? In some sense, life is too easy for the bookstore owners; a popular book draws customers to their stores, regardless of what the store owners do or don't do. A book they have stocked that doesn't sell is no problem: All they have to do is pack it up and return it to the publisher for a refund. Isn't this sort of like heads I win, tails you lose?

Imagine what might happen if the bookstore owners got involved in helping to hustle books. Certainly the owner would be more thoughtful in evaluating what types of books his customers were interested in and would stock books accordingly, which would help publishers in setting more realistically sized printings. The owner would have an incentive to advertise to help move his books; the relatively inexpensive local ads he could run would certainly help the publisher and author in reaching readers. Richard Simon always advised the bookstore owners he visited to run ads continuously, cautioning that not all would pay off, but that the cumulative impact of establishing that bookstore as the place to buy books would well justify the expense. The bookstore owner as partner of the publisher might be more inclined to be creative in moving books, by having more author signings, by writing or sponsoring a book column for the local paper, by supplying review books for the book column, by spearheading a book segment on community cable television or the local radio station, by putting together a local best-sellers list — what is selling best in Beamer, Indiana? — by working with the schools to help introduce students to books, by dreaming up ways to capture the attention of the public, even if by no other means than those of the store owner who hired the juggler to juggle a stack of slow-selling dictionaries in his store window.

Suddenly, the store owner is a partner of author and publisher in helping to make the stock move, in helping to widen the audience for books. It can work. The feisty, literature-loving owner of the Stuart Brent Bookshop in Chicago once sold 2,400 copies of Saul Bellow's *Humboldt's Gift* when it first came out by going out of his store and stopping shoppers on the sidewalks to tell them about a wonderful new novel.

Review publications must also be enlisted into the publishers' campaign to publish well. The number of publications in which books are reviewed is abysmally low. Why is New York the only city in the nation with a Sunday book review as good as the *New York Times Book Review*? The *Boston Globe*, the leading paper of what arguably may be the most literate city in the United States, has an anemic Sunday book review section because, it says, it doesn't get enough book ads. If that's the problem, wouldn't it pay publishers to spread their advertising dollars around to other papers to help develop book review sections which should, in turn, expand the market for their books?

Every newspaper in the United States, every magazine, every journal, could have a book review column devoted to books that would interest their readers. Is there a hamlet so small or remote that it doesn't have at least one resident who would love the opportunity to read a book and write his opinions of it? The reviewers are happy, the publishers are happy, the authors are happy, the bookstores are happy, and perhaps the readers will be happy too, learning of books they otherwise would have known nothing about. So what if publishers wind up sending out thousands of review copies? Chances are, if those copies were shipped to bookstores, they would just be coming back to the publishers' warehouses anyway. Why not give each new book a chance to reach its full potential audience?

The handful of national publications that do review books, and whose reviews have a significant impact on the success of a book, have a serious obligation both in printing a considered review of a book and in selecting the books that will be reviewed. They have been known to waste valuable space in more ways than one. Consider:

• The *Wall Street Journal*'s September 13, 1990, review of Donald Trump's latest, *Surviving at the Top*, was entitled "Drivel from the Con Donald," and reported that "the book stinks.... You would think that we, as a nation, would have had enough of a man who induced a coast-to-coast upchuck for the better part of a year.... Most of his book is aimed at readers who are stupid."[21]

• *Time* in its October 29, 1990, issue devoted a page to a forthcoming novel by twenty-six-year-old author Bret Easton Ellis, *American Psycho*, under the title "A Revolting Development," describing it as a book containing "the most appalling acts of torture, murder and dismemberment ever described in a book targeted for the bestseller lists." The prepublication review concluded that "to write superficially about superficiality and disgustingly about the disgusting and call it, as Ellis does, a challenge to his readers' complacency does violence to his audience and to the fundamental nature of his craft. So when editor Asahina comes to his writer's defense by claiming that *American Psycho* 'succeeds in taking readers into the mind of a madman,' the obvious question is, How long do they have to stay there? Ten pages, 50 pages, 150 pages? Less than zero?"[22]

• *The New Yorker* of December 24, 1990, contained a review by Frances FitzGerald of President Reagan's autobiography *An American Life*, the first line of which said it all: "It is hard to imagine the person who would sit down and read Ronald Reagan's newly published autobiography"—and then ran on for over eight *New Yorker* pages to tell us why.[23]

That's prime reviewing space — a column in the *Wall Street Journal*, a page in *Time*, eight pages in *The New Yorker*—all to tell the world about three books the reviewers clearly felt were better forgotten.

Consider, too, this question: Why should the book review column in the daily *New York Times* devote itself to Stephen King's or John Grisham's latest, as it has done, when every reader and even every non-reader already is aware of their existence and the review won't influence consumers one bit? What a waste, what a misuse, of precious space. O guardians of the gates of which books we will or will not hear about of the 50,000 published each year: Tell us about the books we should know about.

And speaking of review copies, publishers must get over being so stingy with them.

It seems a basic proposition that the more review copies sent out, the greater the opportunities for a book receiving coverage, and hence the greater the possibilities of selling a book. And it seems a basic proposition that out of a publisher's print run of each book on its list, it expects a certain percentage of those books to be returned, to come flying back to its warehouses like homing pigeons.

Now let's mix those two propositions together. Rather than sitting around their offices waiting for the carton-loads of unsold copies to return, why don't publishers send them out as review copies when the book is first published? A publisher publishes 10,000 copies of a book; he expects to see at least (let's be conservative) 20 percent of them coming home with their tails between their legs sometime within the next twelve months. Why not send out 2,000 prepublication review copies and see if the notices, articles and reviews they garner can get the ball rolling so that not only is the run of 8,000 sold, but maybe the interest in the book will justify another printing? With a touch more investment in time and postage, those thousands of review copies could be spread across the land; and if they are sent out with just a bit of forethought on the part of the editor, author, publicist, and agent as to where and to whom they should go, both publisher and author can rest assured that a meaningful and significant effort has been made to plumb the market for the book.

Gone with the Wind was no sure hit when published. "I don't see how they expect to sell any copies," Margaret Mitchell fretted to her husband before its publication. "Don't worry about that," her husband assured her. "You and I have so many cousins, we'll sell at least five thousand copies in Georgia alone."[24] It was the author's hope that she might earn $5,000 for her years of labor. Nor was Macmillan very sure of what it was doing. It ran a first printing of 10,000 copies and hired a publicist to help promote the book. In setting up a book signing in a major department store in Atlanta, the publicist recommended "a small party in the book department, run a small ad in the newspaper and let her autograph her book if anyone comes."[25] Nor did the Book-of-the-Month Club have any idea that it had stumbled upon the great American novel. The judges debated the merits of the book before deciding to take it on. In June of 1936, it was the club's book of the month, but as the head of the club recalled, "Many subscribers, as they had a right to, chose another book."[26]

What Macmillan did, and did well, was to make a joyful noise unto the world. Margaret Mitchell's publisher sent out thousands of prepublication copies of *Gone with the Wind*, not just to the customary reviewers and critics and newspapers, but even to the smallest weeklies and periodicals across the country, and to the buyers and sales people at hundreds of bookstores. It proved to be an inexpensive and ingenious way of getting almost free publicity through the resulting reviews and mentions in the book pages. This same simple system worked equally well more recently for Scott Turow's first novel, *Presumed Innocent*, when its publisher seeded the market with a mailing of 5,000 prepublication copies. Two thousand advance copies of *The Thorn Birds* by an unknown Australian writer, Colleen McCullough, were the backbone of what *Publishers Weekly* called "the biggest publicity campaign of the year."[27] John Naisbitt's *Megatrends* arrived on the desks of the chief executive officers of the nation's five hundred largest companies: "We created a groundswell of acknowledgement for an unknown book," commented Howard Kaminsky, then Random House's editor-in-chief.[28] A mass mailing of advance reading copies is credited with the lift-off of the 1991 best-seller *The Firm* by the then unknown John Grisham.

A current, computerized list of publications to receive review copies should be a publisher's priceless possession, continually refined and revised and updated, and always adapted to each new book, with each new book always accompanied by an appropriate covering note explaining its special relevance to the publication. With the expenditure of just a little prepublication time and effort and a little postage, a couple thousand carefully aimed review copies can open the market waiting for any book.

What else might publishers be thinking when they tour their neighborhood bookstores and see the endless aisles of books? How can our books ever be found among this horde? There are today some 1.3 million books in print. Compare that overwhelming figure to the 85,000 in print in 1947. Does the world really need each of these books?

Each year approximately 50,000 new titles are published. That's a lot. If a publisher is not prepared to devote its best efforts to each book on its list, why not cut back its list? This is just what publishers have begun doing, following the lead of Phyllis Grann, president and chief executive of the Putnam-Berkley Group, who cut her list from the 225 hardcover titles when she arrived at the scene in 1976 to about 75 by the early eighties, a level she maintains today. Macmillan trimmed its list by 25 percent between 1988 and 1991, and Simon & Schuster announced in 1989 it would cut back new titles by 10 to 15 percent.

Rather than publishing a lot of books and not devoting the necessary time and resources to each, an emerging strategy in the industry is to make certain that each book is well published, meaning that it has been capably edited and attractively printed, that the salesmen have gotten the book into the bookstores, and that there has been a well-structured marketing campaign. The result may be that a house can actually sell more books by publishing fewer books.

The major publishers have been responding to the most recent crisis of flagging sales by again trimming their lists. Simon & Schuster brought out six hundred books in 1997, fifty less than in 1996, and it was front page news when HarperCollins announced in 1997 that it was cancelling over one hundred books, even eliminating manuscripts listed in its catalog for the next season. "It's a way of trying to make sense out of the business," Anthea Disney, chief executive officer of HarperCollins, explained. "In all honesty, I don't want to publish books that we won't get behind and publish well."[29] Insiders at HarperCollins reported that they were being encouraged to focus on name authors, celebrity authors, authors who for one reason or another could attract the publicity necessary to sell huge quantities of books. Warner Books' list dropped from eighty in 1991 to sixty-nine books in 1996; ten of those books published in 1996 were best-sellers. Warner, too, is concentrating its resources on megabooks.

Might some deserving books never be published as the majors slash their lists? "I really believe a book that is really good will be published," Phyllis Grann has said, "even if it's a print run of only 4,000 or if it ends up with a small house."[30] And that's not necessarily a bad thing, that small house, for it may be able to devote more attention to each of its books.

Is it fiscal irrationality for publishers to attempt to bring quality books to the marketplace? The goal of publishing each book well certainly makes sense, though the understandable attempt to concentrate on the hits—a natural result of the commercialization of the industry, of corporate demands for profits, of superstore demands for big name books—may prove to be as simplistic a response to an extraordinarily difficult problem as Simon & Schuster's decision to use less expensive paper and eliminate full cloth covers. Publishing houses may be able to get a quick financial fix from the ghostwritten novel of the supermodel of the month or the earnest autobiography of today's sport's hero, but for their bottom line, how much better to have published the next *The Great Gatsby*, which will sell hundreds of thousands of copies year after year for the next sixty years? That publishing houses believe they cannot afford the time and the risk involved in finding and nurturing the author of the next *The Great Gatsby* is the central conundrum of the new world of publishing.

Time may prove that a misplaced faith in the sales power of megabooks leads to the downfall of those houses that cling to the quick fix, and to the rise of others. The focus of the majors on big names and nonbooks opens up for some of the smaller publishers, and even for start-up houses, the opportunity to find and publish quality books. And in so doing, would it be surprising to see them rise as the next Knopf or the next Simon & Schuster?

An extraordinary amount of the finite resources of publishing houses—their money, time, and talent—is being expended on non-books. After the success of Bill Cosby's *Fatherhood*, which spent fifty-five weeks on The List and sold over 2.5 million hardcover copies, it seemed that every television comedian published his or her own comedy routines, from Tim Allen to Jerry Seinfeld to Ellen DeGeneres.

194

Each of these books made The List. The huge radio audiences of Rush Limbaugh and Howard Stern have made strong best-sellers of their books.

Also crowding publishers' lists are not only books about celebrities, but novels ghostwritten for celebrities, like those of Ivana Trump and Martina Navratilova. Supermodel Naomi Campbell was said to have been presented with a two-page summary of "her" novel to study so that she could talk about "her" book on the television circuit. Even Fabio has "written" a novel.

Sometimes these sure bets blow up right in the publisher's face. While Tim Allen's and Jerry Seinfeld's books hit the number one spot on The List, thousands of copies of Jay Leno's book were returned to the publisher. Random House gave actress Joan Collins the astronomical advance of $4,000,000 in 1990 to write two novels. She turned in her books, *A Ruling Passion* and *Hell Hath No Fury*, and Random House found the manuscripts "unsatisfactory" and sued her for the return of her advance, all but calling her manuscripts drivel. (A drivel manuscript had never stopped the publishers of Jackie Susann's novels: "Just turn it into a book somehow, that's all I ask," Michael Korda's boss ordered him when Jackie submitted her manuscript of *The Love Machine*.[31]) One suspects that perhaps the fact that *Dynasty* was off the air and Ms. Collins's character of Alexis was no longer in the public eye may have played some role in Random House's change of heart. In any event, Ms. Collins counter-sued for her full advance, claiming she had submitted the novels as required by her contract; and, besides, she told the court, she had already spent the advance. The jury held for the aggrieved author, and Random House learned a $4 million lesson.

Nonbook best-sellers can have a beneficial effect on publishing, for they may lure into bookstores new customers who have previously never darkened their doors, customers who, for the first time, are exposed to the endless variety of available books, some of which may catch their attention and their money. The trouble is that the nonbooks swallow up so much of the publisher's available promotion and advertising budget, so much of the time of the publisher's professionals, so much shelfspace, that better books suffer. Explained Laurence Kirshbaum, the president of Warner Books, which was the publisher of Madonna's best-seller *Sex*: "The problem with a big celebrity book like Madonna's, though it was great for us, is that it takes over your entire publishing program. It isn't just the money, but the lost-opportunity cost, as the entire company focuses on that. From the long-term standpoint, you're better off building a real, reputable author."[32]

Other publishers who have wrestled with the dilemma agree. As Charles Scribner, Jr., described it:

> The man who daily oversees the business side of publishing thinks editors are numbskulls who know nothing about money. The editors think the business manager is a yahoo who knows nothing about books. Probably every firm is plagued in the same way. The business mind never understands that literary judgment takes imagination and flair. Even more important, the business mind never learns that best-sellers are not predictable. The truth is that business risks taken on the basis of experienced intuition alone oftentimes pay off handsomely. That is one of the most interesting features of publishing.[33]

Maybe its time again to mine the slush piles in search of hidden gems. Doubleday in 1974 shut down its slush pile, returning unopened the manuscripts that arrived from unknowns, and most of the major houses now will review only manuscripts submitted by an agent. Jim Landis, then an editor at William Morrow, scoffed at the notion that publishers were eliminating their slush piles because of the expense involved in reviewing each year several thousand unsolicited manuscripts when, in a typical year, only a handful would be published. "Any publisher could tell you twenty better ways to save money. The excuse I'd like to hear is that they won't read the stuff because reading it is so goddamn painful!"[34] With authors finding it more difficult to find an agent to open the door to a publishing house, and with agents focusing more of their attention on commercial books, perhaps publishers should rethink their policy on unsolicited manuscripts and have a sharp-eyed reader pan the slush pile for gold.

Another facet of having a book well published is taking advantage of today's technology to make publishing more efficient and cost effective, from the use of desk top computers to give editors the capacity to eliminate galley proofs, to centralized computer systems for accounting and inventory control — integrated computer systems which, with the touch of a key, can spit out current information on sales, inventory, and royalties. If Frito-Lay, a subsidiary of PepsiCo, can use personal computers on the desk of its thirty-two division sales managers to track what happens to each of the company's snack lines on a daily basis, enabling the company to turn on a dime from a national marketing strategy to one based on local responses, this sort of micro-marketing could be employed by publishing houses to their advantage.

Think what such a system would mean for getting books exactly to where they are needed, knowing how and where to promote a book, knowing how a book was selling, when to initiate another printing, when and where to advertise, what books to display where. Agent Mort Janklow has complained that "too many decisions in publishing are just seat-of-the-pants decisions. Colgate, for Christ's sake, won't *think* of introducing a new toothpaste without finding out things like 'Do people like mint?' and 'Do they like green? Or is green an offputting color?'.... I go to a big book publisher and say, 'You've got millions. Do this kind of research.'"[35] Despite the industry's protestations that books are different, the technology for carrying out this type of research is available — for analyzing, for example, where the returns are coming from and how different books are selling in different types of markets, and what customers want. Suddenly the imponderables of the publishing industry are translated into facts, and the facts are known, *now*, and can be acted upon, now.

As publishers poke around bookstores and examine what makes their industry hum, they should carry with them a watch and a calendar. These should be required accessories for those publishers who can have such a different sense of time than their authors, those publishers who sometimes seem to have imbibed a sip or two of that strange drink the tiny Dutchmen shared with Rip Van Winkle years ago up in the Catskills. Unconscionable delays so characteristic of publishing as we know it — in responding to inquiries, in determining whether to accept or reject a manuscript, in editing it, in letting publication dates slip by, in organizing a timely promotion and publicity campaign — none of that should be a part of a multi-billion dollar industry.

Time and again, since time immemorial, publishers have laid gentle hands on their authors' anxious shoulders and said, "Patience!

This all takes time." But they blew their cover when they discovered that they could publish, successfully, instant books.

Instant paperbacks to capitalize on a current news headline have been around for some time now. These books are written and published and flood the market within a matter of weeks or days of the news. Over 500,000 copies of *The Report of the Warren Commission* were for sale as a Bantam paperback eighty hours after the government released the document. A book on the 1967 Arab-Israeli war was written and published in twenty days. Random House had a hardcover book on Desert Storm in the bookstores within two months after the war. With the grinding recession of the early 1990s, publishers began speeding up the publication process for hardcover books, trimming the standard one year from receipt of manuscript to publication date to three to four months, to sooner achieve a return on their capital. "That old business of nine months for a nonfiction schedule has become a myth," said Ann Godoff, editor-in-chief of the Atlantic Monthly Press. "Books that are tied to a news event, books that you need to give more prominence on a list, or books that you need to get out to beat a competing title are all being published in very short deadlines."[36] It obviously can be done. Why not keep streamlining this process? Time is money, both for the publisher and the author; the faster the publication process goes, the better for all.

Publishers, of course, don't have to tour bookstores to discover any of this — how every element in the publication of a book can be important to its sales, how nothing can be left to the inexperienced or to chance. None of these ideas of how to publish a book well are new. Every publisher has known some of them and some publishers have known a lot of them, but very few have tried consistently to apply all of them to each book they publish. It can be done. "You are in a business requiring intelligence," Barbara Tuchman exhorted her captive audience of assembled publishers; "apply it to the problem, gentlemen, solve it and don't go on and on about how nothing can be changed."

There will always be that element of mystery, of magic, to what makes a book sell, but the ingredients are not a secret. They are well known. And like medieval alchemists, publishers must tend their bubbling cauldron as it fizzes and splashes, steams and sputters, tinkering with these ingredients, selecting the right manuscripts, stirring in the best title and blurbs, adding the coloring for the jacket, toss-ing in the author's photograph, watching the timing of when the book may best be marketed, sniffing out the right price, adding a pinch of advertising, a dash of a promotion tour, a helping of press releases, a dollop of radio, mixing and seasoning the brew to try to discover, once again, the ever-changing formula for turning an author's vision to gold.

Chapter Notes

Preface

1. *New York Times*, January 10, 1987, p. 4.
2. Newquist, *Counterpoint*, p. 410.
3. Stephen King, *The New York Times Book Review*, June 6, 1993, p. 59.

Chapter 1. A Matter of Mystery

1. Mizener, *The Far Side of Paradise*, p. 78.
2. Wilson (ed.), *The Crack-Up*, p. 86.
3. Phillips (ed.), *F. Scott Fitzgerald on Writing*, p. 109.
4. Wilson (ed.), p. 85.
5. *Ibid.*
6. Fitzgerald, *Afternoon of an Author*, p. 85.
7. Turnbull, *Scott Fitzgerald*, p. 137.
8. Fitzgerald, p. 86.
9. *Ibid.*
10. Turnbull, p. 139.
11. Wheelock (ed.), *Editor to Author*, p. 17.
12. *Ibid.*, p. 15.
13. Mizener, p. 112.
14. Wilson (ed.), p. 86.
15. *Ibid.*, p. 88.
16. *Ibid.*
17. Turnbull, p. 139.
18. Fitzgerald, p. 85.
19. *Ibid.*, p. 86.
20. *Ibid.*
21. Burlingame, *Of Making Many Books*, p. 3.
22. Silverman (ed.), *The Book of the Month*, p. 74.
23. *Newsweek*, June 18, 1984, p. 93.
24. Mizener, p. 128.
25. Wilson (ed.), p. 90.

26. *New York Times*, April 15, 1981.
27. *People*, September 22, 1980, p. 57.
28. *New York Times Book Review*, June 22, 1980, p. 8.
29. *Newsweek*, May 26, 1980, p. 86.
30. *Horizon*, September 1980, p. 6.
31. *New York Times*, April 15, 1981.
32. *Horizon*, June 1981, p. 9.
33. *New York Times Book Review*, June 22, 1980, p. 8.
34. *Horizon*, September 1980, p. 6.
35. *New York Times*, April 15, 1981, p. 14.
36. Turnbull, p. 115.
37. Wilson (ed.), p. 86.
38. Turnbull (ed.), *The Letters of F. Scott Fitzgerald*, p. 357.
39. Wheelock (ed.), p. 230.
40. *Ibid.*, p. 385.
41. Turnbull (ed.), p. 404.
42. Wheelock (ed.), p. 405.
43. *Ibid.*, p. 384.
44. Bruccoli, *The Short Stories of F. Scott Fitzgerald*, p. ix.
45. Scribner, *In the Company of Writers*, p. 161.
46. Trollope, *An Autobiography*, p. 14.
47. Winokur (ed.), *Writers on Writing*, p. 134.
48. Baker (ed.), *Ernest Hemingway*, p. 119.
49. Plimpton (ed.), *Writers at Work*, Sixth Series, p. 84.
50. Plimpton (ed.), *Writers at Work*, Eighth Series, p. 307.
51. *Book-of-the-Month Club "Book News" Special Issue*, (October-November 1991), p. 2.
52. *New York Times*, January 13, 1993, p. C20.
53. Roberts, *I Wanted to Write*, pp. 255–256.
54. Hart, *The Popular Book*, p. 288.

Chapter 2. Winning the Genetic Sweepstakes

1. Charlton and Mark (eds.), *The Writer's Home Companion*, p. 108.
2. Benjamin Cheever (ed.), *The Letters of John Cheever*, p. 212.
3. Daigh, *Maybe You Should Write a Book*, pp. 137–138.
4. Plimpton (ed.), *Writers at Work*, Fourth Series, p. 406.
5. Updike, *Self-Consciousness*, p. 109.
6. Moyers, *A World of Ideas*, p. 94.
7. Plimpton (ed.), *Writers at Work*, Eighth Series, p. 11.
8. Winokur (ed.), *Writers on Writing*, p. 23.
9. *Ibid.*, p. 8.
10. Plimpton (ed.), *Writers at Work*, Fifth Series, pp. 278–279.
11. *New York Times*, April 7, 1992, p. B7.
12. Cowley (ed.), *Writers at Work*, First Series, pp. 106–107.

13. Vidal, *Matters of Fact and Fiction*, p. 34.
14. Grobel, *Conversations with Capote*, p. 47.
15. Clarke, *Capote*, p. 62.
16. Grobel, pp. 45–46, 52.
17. Vidal, *Matters of Fact and Fiction*, p. 139.
18. Baker (ed.), *Ernest Hemingway: Selected Letters*, p. 670.
19. Phillips (ed.), *Ernest Hemingway on Writing*, p. 19.
20. John Cheever, "Journals: From the Sixties — I," *The New Yorker*, January, 21, 1991, pp. 37, 35.
21. Vidal, *Matters of Fact and Fiction*, p. 34.
22. Auchincloss, *A Writer's Capital*, pp. 44, 45.
23. Plimpton (ed.), *Writers at Work*, Seventh Series, p. 281.
24. Trollope, *An Autobiography*, pp. 4, 9, 11, 16–17, 42.
25. Balfour, *The Life of Robert Louis Stevenson*, vol. 1, p. 39.
26. Welty, *One Writer's Beginnings*, p. 22.
27. Plimpton (ed.), *Writers at Work*, Sixth Series, p. 80.
28. Gilbar, *The Open Door*, p. 61.
29. *Ibid.*, pp. 31–32.
30. Plimpton (ed.), *Writers at Work*, Fourth Series, p. 435.
31. DeMott, *John Steinbeck Working Days*, p. 41.
32. *Ibid.*
33. Steinbeck, *Journal of a Novel*, p. 98.
34. Baker (ed.), p. 351.
35. *Ibid.*, pp. 730–731.
36. Epstein, *Partial Payments*, pp. 76–77.
37. Steinbeck, p. 8.
38. Dillard, *The Writing Life*, p. 68.
39. Cowley, p. 139.
40. Theroux, *My Secret History*, p. 469.
41. Hemingway, *A Moveable Feast*, pp. 202, 206.
42. Phillips (ed.), *Ernest Hemingway on Writing*, p. 4.
43. Mizener, *The Far Side of Paradise*, p. 75.
44. George Steiner, "Grandmaster," *The New Yorker*, December 10, 1990, p. 154.
45. Plimpton (ed.), *Writers at Work*, Fourth Series, p. 453.
46. Cousins, *Writing for Love or Money*, p. 78.
47. Baker, p. 837.

Chapter 3. Sing, O Muse

1. Scott Spencer, "The Old Man and the Novel," *The New York Times Magazine*, September 22, 1991, p. 47.
2. Ruas, *Conversations with American Writers*, p. 206.
3. Valerie Martin, "Waiting for the Story to Start," *New York Times Book Review*, February 7, 1988, p. 36.

4. Robert Louis Stevenson, *Kidnapped*, New York: Scribner (from jacket copy of Scribner's reissue), 1986.
5. Martin, p. 36.
6. Cowley (ed.), *Writers at Work*, pp. 16–17.
7. Plimpton (ed.), *Writers at Work*, Second Series, p. 171.
8. Cowley (ed.), p. 42.
9. Plimpton (ed.), *Writers at Work*, Sixth Series, p. 99.
10. Winokur (ed.), *Writers on Writing*, p. 84.
11. Plimpton (ed.), *Writers at Work*, Second Series, p. 223.
12. Phillips (ed.), *Ernest Hemingway on Writing*, p. 55.
13. Plimpton (ed.), *Writers at Work*, Fourth Series, p. 340.
14. *Ibid.*, p. 235.
15. Steinbeck, *Journal of a Novel*, p. 34.
16. Plimpton (ed.), *Writers at Work*, Seventh Series, p. 85.
17. Vidal, *At Home*, p. 54.
18. Cowley (ed.), p. 125.
19. *Ibid.*, p. 294.
20. Plimpton (ed.), *Writers at Work*, Fifth Series, p. 191.
21. Winokur (ed.), p. 86.
22. Plimpton (ed.), *Writers at Work*, Sixth Series, p. 99.
23. Plimpton (ed.), *Writers at Work*, Fifth Series, p. 164.
24. *Ibid.*, p. 208.
25. Gallup (ed.), *The Journals of Thornton Wilder*, p. 176.
26. Holmes, *Coleridge*, p. 162.
27. King, *None but a Blockhead*, p. 243.
28. Grobel, *Conversations with Capote*, p. 221.
29. Plimpton (ed.), *Writers at Work*, Eighth Series, p. 437.
30. Plimpton (ed.), *Writers at Work*, Eighth Series, p. 303.
31. Gallup (ed.), p. 45.
32. Cowley (ed.), p. 9.
33. Horgan, *Approaches to Writing*, p. 232.
34. Plimpton (ed.), *Writers at Work*, Fourth Series, p. 277.
35. Plimpton (ed.), *Writers at Work*, Sixth Series, pp. 187–188.
36. Steinbeck, *Journal of a Novel*, p. 11.
37. Charlton and Mark (ed.), *The Writer's Home Companion*, p. 109.
38. Plimpton (ed.), *Writers at Work*, Fourth Series, p. 452.
39. Ruas, p. 203.
40. Winokur, p. 88.
41. Plimpton (ed.), *Writers at Work*, Fifth Series, pp. 118–119.
42. Trollope, *An Autobiography*, p. 121.
43. Plimpton, *Writers at Work*, Fifth Series, pp. 364–365.
44. Cowley (ed.), p. 105.
45. Baker (ed.), *Ernest Hemingway*, pp. 800–801.
46. *New York Times Book Review*, January 25, 1987.
47. Cowley (ed.), p. 88.
48. Turnbull, *Scott Fitzgerald*, p. 131.
49. Cowley (ed.), p. 79.

50. Ruas, p. 156.
51. Plimpton (ed.), *Writers at Work*, Fifth Series, p. 241.
52. Plimpton (ed.), *Writers at Work*, Sixth Series, p. 403.

Chapter 4. The Writing Life

1. Updike, *Odd Jobs*, p. 85.
2. Steinbeck, *Journal of a Novel*, p. 139.
3. Plimpton (ed.), *Writers at Work*, Fifth Series, p. 311.
4. Horgan, *Approaches to Writing*, p. 10.
5. Plimpton (ed.), *Writers at Work*, Seventh Series, p. 70.
6. Steinbeck, p. 38; Steinbeck and Wallsten (eds.), *Steinbeck*, p. 859.
7. Daigh, *Maybe You Should Write a Book*, p. 148.
8. Plimpton (ed.), *Writers at Work*, Fourth Series, p. 203.
9. Michener, *A Michener Miscellany*, p. 368.
10. Oates, *First Person Singular*, p. 171.
11. Baker (ed.), *Ernest Hemingway*, p. 232.
12. Underwood and Miller, *Bare Bones*, p. 2.
13. Benjamin Cheever (ed.), *The Letters of John Cheever*, pp. 185–186.
14. Roberts, *I Wanted to Write*, pp. 255–256.
15. Benjamin Cheever (ed.), p. 29.
16. Plimpton (ed.), *Writers at Work*, Eighth Series, p. 320.
17. Charlton (ed.), *The Writer's Quotation Book*, p. 24.
18. Plimpton (ed.), *Writers at Work*, Fourth Series, p. 216.
19. Fraser, *The Brontës*, p. 287.
20. Lynn, *Hemingway*, pp. 357–358.
21. *Ibid.*, p. 476.
22. *Ibid.*, p. 563.
23. "The Blockbusters," *Newsweek*, June 6, 1966.
24. John Cheever, "Journals: From the Sixties—I," *The New Yorker*, January 21, 1991, p. 55.
25. Winokur (ed.), *Writers on Writing*, p. 129.
26. *New York Times Book Review*, March 26, 1989, p. 27.
27. Joyce Carol Oates, "The World's Worst Critics," *New York Times Book Review*, January 18, 1987.
28. Auchincloss, *A Writer's Capital*, p. 114.
29. Plimpton (ed.), *Writers at Work*, Sixth Series, p. 209.
30. Charlton (ed.), p. 53.
31. Plimpton (ed.), *Writers at Work*, Seventh Series, p. 81.
32. Hemingway, *A Moveable Feast*, p. 5.
33. Cowley (ed.), *Writers at Work*, First Series, pp. 134–135.
34. Trollope, *An Autobiography*, pp. 209–210.
35. Dillard, *The Writing Life*, p. 11.
36. Steinbeck, *Journal of a Novel*, p. 119.
37. Daigh, p. 129.

38. Bettmann, *The Delights of Reading*, p. 56.
39. Plimpton (ed.), *Writers at Work*, Third Series, pp. 169–170.
40. Ruas, *Conversations with American Writers*, p. 179.
41. Baker (ed.), p. 557.
42. Updike, p. 833.
43. Vidal, *At Home*, p. 56.
44. Vanderbilt, *John Cotton Dana*, p. 17.
45. Roberts, *I Wanted to Write*, p. 234.
46. Plimpton (ed.), *Writers at Work*, Sixth Series, p. 24.
47. Winokur (ed.), pp. 61, 62.
48. Grobel, *Conversations with Capote*, p. 84.
49. Tom Dunkel, "Pieces of McPhee," *New Jersey Monthly*, August 1986, pp. 47–48.
50. "Postwritum Depression, False Stagnancy and Other Ills Caused by Writing Books," *New York Times Book Review*, March 8, 1987, p. 3.
51. Cowley (ed.), p. 146.
52. Plimpton (ed.), *Writers at Work*, Fourth Series, p. 356.
53. Cowley (ed.), p. 271.
54. Plimpton (ed.), *Writers at Work*, Third Series, p. 33.
55. Updike, p. 835.
56. May Sarton, "Rewards of a Solitary Life," *New York Times*, April 8, 1974, Op. Ed.

Chapter 5. Your Stupid Book Stinks

1. Bernard (ed.), *Rotten Rejections*, p. 22.
2. *Ibid.*, p. 91.
3. White, *Rejection*, p. 2.
4. Roberts, *For Authors Only*, p. 183.
5. Charlton (ed.), *The Writer's Quotation Book*, p. 98.
6. Cousins, *Writing for Love or Money*, p. 73.
7. Bernard (ed.), p. 16.
8. Cerf, *At Random*, p. 237.
9. *Authors Guild Bulletin* (Fall 1984), p. 7.
10. Tebbel, *Between Covers*, p. 357.
11. Silverman (ed.), *The Book of the Month*, p. xviii.
12. Goldin and Sky, *The Business of Being a Writer*, p. 41.
13. *New York Times*, February 23, 1986, sec. 2, p. 1.
14. *Time*, February 23, 1987, p. 92.
15. Charlton (ed.), p. 78.
16. Beahm, *The Stephen King Companion*, p. 167.
17. Silverman (ed.), p. 26.
18. *Ibid.*
19. Epstein, *Partial Payments*, pp. 178–179.
20. *New York Times Book Review*, July 21, 1985, p. 29.

21. *Ibid.*
22. Benjamin Cheever (ed.), *The Letters of John Cheever*, p. 252.
23. *Ibid.*, p. 285.
24. Nabokov (ed.), *Vladimir Nabokov*, p. 86.
25. *Ibid.*, p. 117.
26. *Ibid.*, pp. 137–138.
27. *Publishers Weekly*, March 2, 1946.
28. Bernard (ed.), p. 28.
29. *Ibid.*, pp. 24–25.
30. Daigh, *Maybe You Should Write a Book*, p. 51.
31. Charlton (ed.), p. 98.
32. Bernard (ed.), p. 85.
33. *Ibid.*, p. 64.
34. *Ibid.*, pp. 70–71.
35. *The New York Times Book Review*, December 9, 1990, p. 39.
36. Charlton and Mark (eds.), *The Writer's Home Companion*, p. 41.
37. Hamilton, *In Search of J.D. Salinger*, p. 114.
38. Schwed, *Turning the Pages*, p. 240.
39. N.R. Kleinfield, "A Golden Touch for Best Sellers," *New York Times Magazine*, April 7, 1985, p. 34.
40. Hemingway, *A Moveable Feast*, p. 73.
41. Edward Weeks, *This Trade of Writing*, p. 19.
42. Baker (ed.), *Ernest Hemingway*, p. 200.
43. Edward Weeks, pp. 19–20.
44. *People*, March 16, 1992, p. 44.
45. *New York Times,* September 12, 1991, p. Cl.
46. Stevenson, *Treasure Island*, p. xxi.
47. *New York Times Sunday Book Review*, July 21, 1985, p. 30.
48. Bettmann, *The Delights of Reading*, p. 82.
49. Oates, *First Person Singular*, p. 46.
50. *New York Times Book Review*, July 21, 1985.
51. *Time*, November 13, 1972.
52. Kreyling, *Author and Agent*, p. 38.
53. *Ibid.*, p. 41.
54. *Ibid.*, p. 45.
55. *Ibid.*, p. 67.
56. *Ibid.*, p. 64.
57. Winokur (ed.), *Writers on Writing*, p. 114.
58. Plimpton (ed.), *Writers at Work*, Fourth Series, p. 430.
59. *New York Times Book Review*, July 21, 1985, p. 30.
60. Thoreau, *The Writings of Henry David Thoreau*, vol. 1, p. xliii.
61. Jeff Shear, "A Lawyer Courts Best Sellerdom," *New York Times Magazine*, June 7, 1987, pp. 57, 21.
62. Underwood and Miller, *Bare Bones*, p. 31.
63. *Ibid.*, p. 44.

Chapter 6. We're All Connected

1. Hemingway, *A Moveable Feast*, p. 14.
2. Baker (ed.), *Ernest Hemingway*, pp. 500–501.
3. Turnbull (ed.), *The Letters of F. Scott Fitzgerald*, p. 167.
4. Plimpton (ed.), *Writers at Work*, Seventh Series, pp. 12–13.
5. Roberts, *I Wanted to Write*, p. 320.
6. *New York Times Book Review*, January 20, 1991, p. 3.
7. Oates, *First Person Singular*, p. 21.
8. Winokur (ed.), *Writers on Writing*, p. 143.
9. *Ibid.*, p. 148.
10. Clarke, *Capote*, p. 375.
11. Grobel, *Conversations with Capote*, p. 139.
12. *Ibid.*, p. 140
13. *Ibid.*, pp. 178–179.
14. *Ibid.*, p. 141.
15. *Ibid.*, p. 140.
16. Clarke, p. 415.
17. Grobel, pp. 143–144.
18. Winokur (ed.), p. 139.
19. *Ibid.*, p. 141.
20. Charlton and Mark (eds.), *The Writer's Home Companion*, p. 118.
21. Winokur (ed.), p. 142.
22. *Ibid.*
23. *Ibid.*, p. 147.
24. *Ibid.*, p. 142.
25. King, *None But a Blockhead*, pp. 244–245.
26. Plimpton (ed.), *Writers at Work*, Fourth Series, p. 103.
27. Winokur (ed.), p. 146.
28. Baker (ed.), pp. 500–501.
29. Epstein, *Plausible Prejudices*, p. 291.
30. Baker (ed.), p. 721.
31. Seadman, *Lovely Me*, p. 391.
32. *The New York Times*, April 22, 1991, p. D10.
33. *Authors Guild Bulletin*, Fall 1984, p. 8.
34. *The New York Times*, April 13, 1991, p. 1.
35. Evan Thomas, "The Art of the Techno-Thriller," *Newsweek*, August 8, 1988, p. 60.
36. Patrick Anderson, "King of the 'Techno-Thriller' or: How Tom Clancy Quit Selling Insurance and Became a Very Rich Novelist," *The New York Times Magazine*, May 1, 1988, p. 54.
37. *Time*, March 4, 1985.
38. Anderson, p. 54.
39. "Inside Edition," NBC, March 7, 1990.
40. *Time*, September 11, 1989, p. 27.
41. Charlton (ed.), *The Writer's Quotation Book*, p. 115.
42. Stevenson, *Treasure Island*, p. xiv.

43. Phillips (ed.), *Ernest Hemingway on Writing*, pp. 9–10.
44. Hemingway, *Green Hills of Africa*, p. 21.
45. Plimpton (ed.), *Writers at Work*, Fifth Series, p. 300.
46. Phillips (ed.), *F. Scott Fitzgerald on Writing*, p. 27.
47. Hendrick (ed.), *To Reach Eternity*, p. 57.
48. Moyers, *A World of Ideas*, p. 95.
49. Plimpton (ed.), *Writers at Work*, Sixth Series, p. 86.
50. Hemingway, *A Moveable Feast*, p. 133.
51. Cowley (ed.), *Writers at Work*, First Series, pp. 136–137.
52. Hemingway, *Green Hills of Africa*, p. 22.
53. Plimpton (ed.), *Writers at Work*, Sixth Series, p. 12.
54. Ruas, *Conversations with American Writers*, p. 284.
55. John Cheever, "Journals: From the Sixties—I," *The New Yorker*, January 21, 1991, p. 34.
56. Plimpton (ed.), *Writers at Work*, Third Series, p. 137.
57. Horgan, *Approaches to Writing*, p. 157.

Chapter 7. Barbarians Through the Gate

1. Page, *A Publisher's Confession*, pp. 127–128.
2. Charlton (ed.), *The Writer's Quotation Book*, p. 13.
3. Epstein, *Partial Payments*, pp. 51–52.
4. Donaldson, *Books*, p. 104.
5. Mortimer B. Zuckerman, "The Illiteracy Epidemic," *U.S. News & World Report*, June 12, 1989, p. 72.
6. John Ensor Harr, "The Crusade Against Illiteracy," *The Saturday Evening Post*, December 1988, p. 43.
7. Ann M. Morrison, "Saving Our Schools," *Fortune*, Spring 1990, p. 8.
8. *Publishers Weekly*, August 25, 1989, p. 9.
9. Christopher Hitchens, "Why We Don't Know What We Don't Know," *New York Times Magazine*, May 13, 1990, p. 32.
10. Paul Horgan, "On the Climate of Books," Wesleyan University Sesquicentennial Paper Number Three, 1981, p. 17.
11. Michener, *The World Is My Home*, p. 278.
12. Bettmann, *The Delights of Reading*, p. 31.
13. Charlton (ed.), p. 10.
14. *Ibid.*, p. 12.
15. Charlton and Mark (eds.), *The Writer's Home Companion*, p. 117.
16. *Wall Street Journal*, August 28, 1990, p. B1.
17. *New York Times*, June 19, 1994, p. 10.
18. Plimpton (ed.), *Writers at Work*, Fifth Series, p. 293.
19. *New York Times*, January 2, 1989; *Time*, May 17, 1993, p. 71.
20. Charlton (ed.), p. 13.
21. Plimpton (ed.), *Writers at Work*, Seventh Series, p. 121.
22. *Time*, August 6, 1990, pp. 20–21.

23. Vidal, *At Home*, p. 183.
24. Moyers, *A World of Ideas*, p. 92.
25. *The New Yorker*, May 7, 1990, p. 60
26. Hendrick Hertzber, "Roboflop," *The New Republic*, October 31, 1988, p. 18.
27. *New York Times*, September 10, 1990, p. D9.
28. *Wall Street Journal*, July 7, 1993, p. B1.
29. Dillard, *The Writing Life*, pp. 52–53.
30. Oates, *First Person Singular*, pp. 16–17.
31. David Streitfeld, "Life at Random," *New York*, August 5, 1991, p. 39.
32. Bennett, *Portrait of a Publisher*, Volume 1, p. 262.

Chapter 8. Judging a Book by Its Cover

1. Whiteside, *The Blockbuster Complex*, p. 60.
2. Walter Goodman, "The Truth About the Best-Seller List," *McCalls*, November 1966, p. 66.
3. Shirley Warner, "A Book Traveler on the Road," *New York Times*, March 9, 1986, p. 23.
4. *Ibid.*
5. Atwan, Orton, and Vesterman, *American Mass Media*, p. 135.
6. *Ibid.*, p. 133.
7. Bennett (ed.), *Portrait of a Publisher*, Volume II, p. 60.
8. Whiteside, p. 156.
9. Joanne Kaufman, "The Face on the Back of the Book," *New York Times Book Review*, June 8, 1989, p. 35.
10. *Ibid.*
11. Fensch (ed.), *Conversations with John Steinbeck*, p. 33.
12. Updike, *Picked-up Pieces*, pp. 15, 400.
13. Michener, *The World Is My Home*, p. 397.
14. Winokur (ed.), *Writers on Writing*, p. 97.
15. Charlton and Mark (eds.), *The Writer's Home Companion*, p. 85.
16. Henderson (ed.), *The Art of Literary Publishing*, p. 151.
17. Michener, p. 397.
18. Turnbull, *Scott Fitzgerald*, p. 99.
19. Turnbull (ed.), *The Letters of F. Scott Fitzgerald*, p. 168.
20. *Ibid.*, p. 169.
21. *Ibid.*, p. 170.
22. *Ibid.*, p. 177.
23. Burlingame, *Of Making Many Books*, p. 102.
24. Phillips (ed.), *F. Scott Fitzgerald On Writing*, p. 100.
25. Grobel, *Conversations with Capote*, pp. 96–97.
26. Joanne Kaufman, "Books as Tough to Name as Babies," *The Wall Street Journal*, May 7, 1991, p. A20.
27. *Ibid.*

28. Roberts, *I Wanted to Write*, p. 283.
29. Atwan, Orton, and Vesterman, p. 127.
30. Baker (ed.), *Ernest Hemingway*, p. 504.
31. *Ibid.*, pp. 547-548.
32. Farr, *Margaret Mitchell of Atlanta*, p. 107.
33. Steinbeck, *Journal of a Novel*, p. 86.
34. DeMott, *John Steinbeck Working Days*, p. 65.
35. *Ibid.*, p. 161.
36. Steinbeck, pp. 81–82, 86, 90–91, 104.

Chapter 9. De Gustibus

1. Updike, *Picked-Up Pieces*, pp. 397, 398, 402.
2. Theroux, *Sunrise with Seamonsters*, p. 5.
3. Roberts, *I Wanted to Write*, p. 347.
4. Brian Boyd, "The Year of 'Lolita,'" *New York Times Book Review*, September 8, 1991, p. 1.
5. Atwan, Orton, and Vesterman, *American Mass Media*, p. 132.
6. Henderson (ed.), *Rotten Reviews*, p. 42.
7. *Ibid.*, p. 41.
8. *Ibid.*, p. 47.
9. Henderson (ed.), *Rotten Reviews II*, p. 29.
10. Bennett (ed.), *Portrait of a Publisher*, Volume I, p. 250.
11. Henderson (ed.), *The Art of Literary Publishing*, p. 241.
12. Plimpton (ed.), *Writers at Work*, Seventh Series, p. 16.
13. *New York Times Book Review*, October 27, 1991, p. 21.
14. *Wall Street Journal*, November 11, 1991, p. B1.
15. *New York Times Book Review*, July 9, 1989, p. 15.
16. *Time*, November 20, 1989.
17. Kingston, *The Wages of Writing*, p. 86.
18. John Cheever, *The Letters of John Cheever*, p. 268.
19. Vidal, *At Home*, p. 288.
20. Ruas, *Conversations with American Writers*, p. 64.
21. Vidal, p. 289.
22. *Ibid.*, p. 45.
23. *Wall Street Journal*, December 11, 1989, p. A4.
24. Winokur (ed.), *Writers on Writing*, p. 120.
25. *Ibid.*, p. 124.
26. Plimpton (ed.), *Writers at Work*, Second Series, p. 304.
27. Sarton, *Recovering*, p. 21.
28. Winokur (ed.), p. 114.
29. John Cheever, p. 277.
30. *Ibid.*, p. 197.
31. Plimpton (ed.), *Writers at Work*, Sixth Series, pp. 225–226.
32. Wheelock (ed.), *Editor to Author*, p. 69.

33. Baker (ed.), *Ernest Hemingway*, p. 394.
34. Henderson, *Rotten Reviews II*, p. 12.

Chapter 10. Non Est Disputandum

1. *New York Times Book Review*, November 17, 1991, p. 38.
2. Plimpton (ed.), *Writers at Work*, Third Series, p. 178.
3. Henderson (ed.), *Rotten Reviews*, p. 92.
4. *Entertainment Weekly*, April 1, 1994, p. 20; Cousins (ed.), *Writing for Love or Money*, p. 106.
5. Winokur (ed.), *Writers on Writing*, p. 118.
6. Charlton (ed.), *The Writer's Quotation Book*, p. 89.
7. Charlton and Mark (eds.), *The Writer's Home Companion*, p. 61.
8. Baker (ed.), *Ernest Hemingway*, p. 162.
9. Henderson (ed.), *Rotten Reviews*, p. 71.
10. Updike, *Picked-Up Pieces*, p. 165.
11. Updike, *Self-Consciousness*, p. 109.
12. Cowley (ed.), *Writers at Work*, p. 293.
13. Grobel, *Conversations with Capote*, p. 160.
14. Epstein, *Plausible Prejudices*, p. 390.
15. Ruas, *Conversations with American Writers*, p. 126.
16. Steinbeck, *Journal of a Novel*, p. 157.
17. DeMott, *John Steinbeck Working Days*, p. 90.
18. Plimpton (ed.), *Writers at Work*, Fifth Series, p. 207.
19. Bettmann, *The Delights of Reading*, p. 76.
20. Charlton and Mark (eds.), p. 120.
21. Plimpton (ed.), *Writers at Work*, Sixth Series, p. 25.
22. Ruas, p. 70.
23. Plimpton (ed.), *Writers at Work*, Second Series, p. 150.
24. *New York Times*, March 6, 1996, p. C4; Updike, *Picked-Up Pieces*, p. 15.
25. Cousins (ed.), *Writing for Love or Money*, p. 217.
26. Updike, *Picked-Up Pieces*, p. 15.
27. Henderson (ed.), *Rotten Reviews*, p. 91.
28. *New York Times Book Review*, May 7, 1989.
29. Plimpton (ed.), *Writers at Work*, Eighth Series, p. 420.
30. *New York Times Book Review*, November 22, 1992, p. 3.
31. *New York Times*, August 6, 1990, p. A13.
32. Winokur (ed.), p. 36.

Chapter 11. Make a Joyful Noise

1. Seadman, *Lovely Me*, p. 459.
2. Whiteside, *The Blockbuster Complex*, p. 179; Michael Korda, "Wasn't She Great?" *The New Yorker*, August 14, 1995, p. 67.

3. *Publishers Weekly*, March 11, 1988, p. 75.
4. Page, *A Publisher's Confession*, p. 115.
5. Wheelock (ed.), *Editor to Author*, p. 183.
6. Bennett (ed.), *Portrait of a Publisher*, p. 83.
7. Wheelock (ed.), p. 138.
8. Scribner, *In the Company of Writers*, p. 56.
9. *New York Times Book Review*, July 28, 1985, p. 23.
10. Tebbel, *Between Covers*, p. 158.
11. Cerf, *At Random*, p. 208.
12. *Ibid.*
13. Wheelock (ed.), p. 183.
14. Bettmann, *The Delights of Reading*, p. 98.
15. Gross, *Publishers on Publishing*, p. 385.
16. Turnbull (ed.), *The Letters of F. Scott Fitzgerald*, p. 147.
17. Baker (ed.), *Ernest Hemingway: Selected Letters*, p. 399.
18. Wheelock (ed.), p. 138.
19. Phillips (ed.), *F. Scott Fitzgerald on Writing*, p. 109.
20. Turnbull (ed.), pp. 146–147.
21. Cerf, p. 207.
22. *Ibid.*
23. *Ibid.*, pp. 207–208.
24. Baker (ed.), p. 278.
25. Turnbull (ed.), pp. 146–147.
26. Phillips (ed.), *F. Scott Fitzgerald*, p. 103.
27. Charlton (ed.), *The Writer's Quotation Book*, p. 104.
28. Atwan, Orton, and Vesterman, *American Mass Media*, p. 139.

Chapter 12. Making the List

1. Roberts, *I Wanted to Write*, p. 296.
2. Plimpton (ed.), *Writers at Work*, Fourth Series, p. 192.
3. *Time*, October 6, 1986, p. 80.
4. *People*, March 16, 1992, p. 44.
5. Charlton and Mark (eds.), *The Writer's Home Companion*, p. 46.
6. Plimpton (ed.), *Writers at Work*, Sixth Series, p. 407.
7. Bettmann, *The Delights of Reading*, p. 48.
8. Winokur (ed.), *Writers on Writing*, p. 28.
9. Updike, *Odd Jobs*, p. 88.
10. Charlton (ed.), *The Writer's Quotation Book*, p. 29.
11. *Ibid.*, p. 53.
12. Silverman (introduction), *The National Book Award: Writers on Their Craft and Their World*, p. 41.
13. King, *Danse Macabre*, p. 97.
14. Underwood and Miller, *Bare Bones*, p. 54.
15. Phillips (ed.), *F. Scott Fitzgerald on Writing*, p. 14.

16. Plimpton (ed.), *Writers at Work*, Seventh Series, p. 239.
17. Bennett (ed.), *Portrait of a Publisher* (Volume I), p. 66.
18. Henderson (ed.), *The Art of Literary Publishing*, p. 141.
19. Horgan, *Approaches to Writing*, p. 41.
20. Winokur (ed.), p. 132.
21. *New York Times*, September 7, 1990, p. C26.
22. David Blum, "The Tome Machine," *New York Magazine*, October 24, 1988, p. 39.
23. *Ibid.*, pp. 39–40.
24. *New York Times*, September 7, 1990, p. C26.
25. *New York Times*, May 20, 1990, p. 22.
26. *Ibid.*
27. *Ibid.*
28. *Ibid.*
29. *Wall Street Journal*, February 7, 1990, p. 1.
30. *New York Times*, September 17, 1986, p. B40.
31. *New York Times*, January 25, 1990, p. 26.
32. Trip Gabriel, "Call My Agent!" *The New York Times Magazine*, February 19, 1989, p. 80.
33. *New York Times*, September 3, 1991, p. 31.
34. Baker (ed.), *Ernest Hemingway*, p. 278.
35. Blum, p. 36.
36. Vidal, *Matters of Fact and Fiction*, p. 21.

Chapter 13. A Boy Has to Peddle His Book

1. "Literary World Is Debating How Much of a Huckster a Book Writer Should Be," *Wall Street Journal*, August 2, 1990, p. B1.
2. Atwan, Orton, and Vesterman, *American Mass Media*, p. 137.
3. John Knowles, "Musings on a Chameleon," *Esquire*, April 1988, p. 178.
4. Meg Cox, "To Make Their Big Books Even Bigger, Firms Are Spending the Biggest Bucks," *Wall Street Journal*, June 19, 1991, p. B1.
5. *New York Times*, September 3, 1991, p. 31.
6. Bennett (ed.), *Portrait of a Publisher* (Volume I), p. 48.
7. Winokur (ed.), *Writers on Writing*, p. 127.
8. Grobel, *Conversations with Capote*, p. 37.
9. Oates, *First Person Singular*, p. 174.
10. Charlton (ed.), *The Writer's Quotation Book*, p. 64.
11. Fensch (ed.), *Conversations with John Steinbeck*, p. 6, p. 39.
12. Baker, "A Writer's 'TV Block,'" *The New York Times Magazine*, January 11, 1987, p. 12.
13. Benjamin Cheever (ed.), *The Letters of John Cheever*, p. 211.
14. Pyron, *Southern Daughter*, p. 322.
15. Baker (ed.), p. 12.
16. Underwood and Miller, *Bare Bones*, p. 109.
17. Watson, "How a Best-Seller Happens," *Cosmopolitan*, August 1959,

p. 52.
  18. *Wall Street Journal*, August 12, 1991, p. B1.
  19. *Wall Street Journal*, August 2, 1990, p. B1.
  20. Michener, *The World Is My Home*, p. 275.
  21. Dinitia Smith, "The Happy Hawker: Tyrl Publisher Steven Schragis's Genius for Promoting Schlock," *New York*, January 6, 1992, p. 43.

Chapter 14. With a Little Bit of Luck

  1. Plimpton (ed.), *Writers at Works*, Fifth Series, p. 207.
  2. Hemingway, A *Moveable Feast*, p. 91.
  3. Beahm, *The Stephen King Companion*, p. 30.
  4. Michener, *The World Is My Home*, p. 363.
  5. *Ibid.*, p. 280.
  6. *Ibid.*, p. 284.
  7. *Ibid.*, pp. 285, 286, 289. Bear, *The #1 New York Times Best Seller*, p. 79.
  8. Harper Lee, "Christmas to Me," *McCalls*, December 1961, p. 63.
  9. *Booklist*, September 1, 1960, p. 23.
  10. *Atlantic*, August 1960, p. 98.
  11. *New York Herald Tribune Book Review*, July 10, 1960, p. 5.
  12. *New York Times Book Review*, July 10, 1960, p. 18.
  13. Newquist, *Counterpoint*, p. 405.
  14. *New York Times Magazine*, April 21, 1974.
  15. *Ibid.*, p. 11.
  16. *Ibid.*, p. 85.
  17. *Ibid.*
  18. *New York*, February 10, 1997, p. 29.
  19. Beahm, pp. 26–27.
  20. Aljean Harmetz, "What Makes Hollywood Bid Big for a Hot Novel," *New York Times*, October 18, 1987, p. 21.

Chapter 15. Hats Off to Jackie!

  1. Clarke, *Capote*, p. 415.
  2. Seadman, *Lovely Me*, p. 391.
  3. Mansfield, *Life with Jackie*, p. 129.
  4. Madison, *Book Publishing in America*, p. 544.
  5. Goodman, "The Truth About the Best-Seller List," *McCalls*, November 1966, p. 172.
  6. Mansfield, p. 131.
  7. *Ibid.*, p. 132.
  8. Seadman, pp. 284, 285, 286.
  9. Ken W. Purdy, "Valley of the Dollars," *Saturday Evening Post*, Febru-

ary 24, 1968, p. 76.

10. Petersen, *The Bantam Story*, p. 79.

11. *New York Times Book Review*, April 1, 1973.

12. *Newsweek*, February 5, 1968.

13. Purdy, p. 78.

14. Seadman, p. 429.

15. *Ibid.*

16. Whiteside, *The Blockbuster Complex*, pp. 25–26.

17. *Ibid.*, p. 35.

18. *Time*, June 20, 1969.

19. Seadman, p. 382.

20. Petersen, p. 80.

21. Sara Davidson, "Jacqueline Susann: The Writing Machine," *Harpers Magazine*, October 1969, p. 65.

22. *Ibid.*

23. Leonore Fleischer, "How Green Was Her Valley," *Publishers Weekly*, February 13, 1987, p. 89.

24. *Ibid.*

25. Mansfield, p. 174.

26. *Time*, June 20, 1969, p. 38.

27. Purdy, p. 78.

28. "More Guys and Dolls," *Newsweek*, June 2, 1969, p. 98.

29. Davidson, p. 66.

30. Michael Korda, "Wasn't She Great?" *The New Yorker*, August 14, 1995, p. 67.

31. Martin Kazindori, "Jackie Susann Picks up the Marbles," *New York Times Magazine*, August 12, 1973, p. 11.

32. Whiteside, p. 158.

33. *Ibid.*, pp. 162, 163.

34. *Ibid.*, p. 34.Dillard, *The Writing Life*, p. 14.

35. Baker (ed.), *Ernest Hemingway*, pp. 522–523.

36. Benjamin Cheever (ed.), *The Letters of John Cheever*, p. 191.

37. Baker (ed.), pp. 712–713.

38. Roberts, *I Wanted to Write*, pp. 304–305.

39. *New York Times Book Review*, January 30, 1994, p. 25.

40. Michael Korda, "Wasn't She Great?" *The New Yorker*, August 14, 1995, p. 67.

Chapter 16. Apply It to the Problem

1. Charlton and Mark (eds.), *The Writer's Home Companion*, pp. 13–14.

2. Henderson (ed.), *The Art of Literary Publishing*, p. 255.

3. Bettmann, *The Delights of Reading*, p. 86.

4. *New York Times*, October 1, 1990, p. D1.

5. *Ibid.*, p. D10.

6. Winokur (ed.), *Writers on Writing*, p. 115.
7. Beahm, *The Stephen King Companion*, p. 105.
8. "Publishers Club Luncheon Menu: Candid Comments a la Tuchman," *Authors Guild Bulletin*, Winter 1985, p. 7.
9. *New York Times*, July 7, 1997, p. D1.
10. Scribner, *In the Company of Writers*, p. 175.
11. Baker (ed.), *Ernest Hemingway*, pp. 705, 704.
12. *New York Times*, July 30, 1990, p. D1.
13. *Wall Street Journal*, October 21, 1993, p. B4.
14. Tebbel, *Between Covers*, p. 309.
15. *Publishers Weekly*, November 17, 1989, p. 10.
16. *Wall Street Journal*, July 7, 1993, p. B1.
17. *Wall Street Journal*, March 30, 1993, p. B1.
18. Schwed, *Turning the Pages*, p. 7.
19. Charlton (ed.), *The Writer's Quotation Book*, p. 101.
20. *Ibid.*
21. *Wall Street Journal*, September 13, 1990.
22. *Time*, October 29, 1990, p. 100.
23. *The New Yorker*, December 24, 1990, p. 91.
24. Farr, *Margaret Mitchell of Atlanta*, p. 96.
25. Charlton and Mark, pp. 42–43.
26. Silverman (ed.), *The Book of the Month*, p. 43.
27. *Publishers Weekly*, April 11, 1979.
28. Sandra Salmans, "Why Best Sellers Sell Best, and Other Publishing Secrets," *New York Times Book Review*, June 9, 1985, p. 3.
29. *New York Times*, June 27, 1997, p. 1.
30. *New York Times*, March 30, 1992, p. D8.
31. Michael Korda, "Wasn't She Great?" *The New Yorker*, August 14, 1995, p. 67.
32. *Wall Street Journal*, September 8, 1993, p. B6.
33. *New York Times Book Review*, December 9, 1990, p. 41.
34. *New York Times Book Review*, March 10, 1974, p. 37.
35. Whiteside, *The Blockbuster Complex*, p. 62.
36. *New York Times*, September 24, 1990, p. D12.

Bibliography

Ackroyd, Peter. *Dickens.* New York: HarperCollins, 1990.

Adler, Elmer (editor). *Breaking Into Print.* New York: Simon & Schuster, 1937.

Appelbaum, Judith. *How To Get Happily Published.* New York: Harper & Row, 1988.

Atlas, James. *Battle of the Books: The Curriculum Debate in America.* New York: Norton, 1992.

Atwan, Robert, Barry Orton, and William Vesterman. *American Mass Media: Industries and Issues.* New York: Random House, 1982.

Auchincloss, Louis. *A Writer's Capital.* Minneapolis: University of Minnesota Press, 1974.

Baker, Carlos. *Ernest Hemingway: A Life Story.* New York: Scribner, 1969.

_____. *Hemingway: The Writer as Artist.* Princeton: Princeton University Press, 1980.

_____ (editor). *Ernest Hemingway: Selected Letters.* New York: Scribner, 1981.

Balfour, Graham. *The Life of Robert Louis Stevenson.* New York: Scribner, 1901.

Balkin, Richard. *A Writer's Guide to Book Publishing.* New York: Hawthorn, 1977.

Beahm, George. *The Stephen King Companion.* Kansas City, Missouri: Andrews & McMeel, 1989.

Bear, John. *The #1 New York Times Best Seller.* Berkeley, California: Ten Speed, 1992.

Bennett, Arnold. *The Truth About an Author.* New York: Doran, 1911.

Bennett, Paul A. (editor). *Portrait of a Publisher: Reminiscences and Reflections by Alfred A. Knopf.* New York: The Typophiles, 1965.

_____ (introduction). *Portrait of a Publisher: Alfred A. Knopf and the Borzoi Imprint: Recollections and Appreciations.* New York: The Typophiles, 1965.

Berg, A. Scott. *Max Perkins: Editor of Genius.* New York: Dutton, 1978.

Bernard, Andre (editor). *Rotten Rejections: A Literary Companion.* Wainscott, New York: Pushcart, 1990.

Bettmann, Otto L. *The Delights of Reading.* Boston: Godine, 1987.

Boswell, John. *The Awful Truth About Publishing.* New York: Warner, 1986.

Bowen, Catherine Drinker. *Adventures of a Biographer.* Boston: Little, Brown, 1959.

_____. *Biography: The Craft and the Calling.* Boston: Little, Brown, 1969.

Brande, Dorothea. *Becoming a Writer.* New York: Harcourt, Brace, 1934.

Brooks, Paul. *Two Park Street: A Publishing Memoir*. Boston: Houghton Mifflin, 1986.
Bruccoli, Matthew J. *Ross MacDonald*. New York: Harcourt Brace Jovanovich, 1984.
_____ (editor). *The Short Stories of F. Scott Fitzgerald*. New York: Macmillan, 1989.
Burlingame, Roger. *Of Making Many Books: A Hundred Years of Reading, Writing and Publishing*. New York: Scribner, 1946.
Cerf, Bennett. *At Random: The Reminiscences of Bennett Cerf*. New York: Random House, 1977.
Charlton, James (editor). *The Writer's Quotation Book*. Stamford: Freiman, 1985.
Charlton, James, and Lisbeth Mark (editors). *The Writer's Home Companion*. New York: Penguin, 1987.
Cheever, John. *The Journals of John Cheever*. New York: Alfred A. Knopf, 1991.
Cheever, Benjamin (editor). *The Letters of John Cheever*. New York: Simon & Schuster, 1988.
Clarke, Gerald. *Capote: A Biography*. New York: Simon & Schuster, 1988.
Cousins, Norman (editor). *Writing for Love or Money*. New York: Longmans, Green, 1949.
Cowley, Malcolm. *Writers at Work: The* Paris Review *Inverviews*. First Series. New York: Penguin, 1958.
Curtis, Richard. *Beyond the Bestseller*. New York: New American Library, 1989.
_____. *How to Be Your Own Literary Agent*. Boston: Houghton Mifflin, 1984.
Daigh, Ralph. *Maybe You Should Write a Book*. Englewood Cliffs, New Jersey: Prentice Hall, 1977.
DeMott, Robert (editor). *John Steinbeck Working Days: The Journals of* The Grapes of Wrath *1938–1941*. New York: Viking, 1989.
Dillard, Annie. *Living By Fiction*. New York: Perennial Library, 1988.
_____. *The Writing Life*. New York: Harper & Row, 1989.
Donald, David Herbert. *Look Homeward: A Life of Thomas Wolfe*. Boston: Little, Brown, 1987.
Donaldson, Gerald. *Books*. New York: Van Nostrand Reinhold, 1981.
Edel, Leon. *Writing Lives: Principia Biographica*. New York: Norton, 1984.
Ellmann, Richard. *Along the Riverrun: Selected Essays*. New York: Alfred A. Knopf, 1989.
_____. *Oscar Wilde*. New York: Alfred A. Knopf, 1988.
Elson, Ruth Miller. *Myths and Mores in American Best Sellers: 1865–1965*. New York: Garland, 1985.
Epstein, Joseph. *Partial Payments: Essays on Writers and Their Lives*. New York: Norton, 1989.
_____. *Plausible Prejudices: Essays on American Writing*. New York: Norton, 1985.
Farr, Finis. *Margaret Mitchell of Atlanta: The Author of Gone with the Wind*. New York: Morrow, 1965.
Fensch, Thomas (editor). *Conversations with John Steinbeck*. Jackson: University Press of Mississippi, 1988.

Fenton, Charles A. *The Apprenticeship of Ernest Hemingway.* New York: New American Library, 1954.

Field, Andrew. *Nabokov.* Boston: Little, Brown, 1967.

Fitzgerald, F. Scott. *Afternoon of an Author.* New York: Scribner, 1957.

Fraser, Rebecca. *The Brontës: Charlotte Brontë and Her Family.* New York: Crown, 1988.

Fugate, Francis L., and Roberta B. Fugate. *Secrets of the World's Best-Selling Writer: The Storytelling Techniques of Erle Stanley Gardner.* New York: Morrow, 1980.

Fussell, Paul. *The Boy Scout Handbook and Other Observations.* New York: Oxford University Press, 1982.

Gallup, Donald (editor). *The Journals of Thornton Wilder, 1939–1961.* New Haven: Yale University Press, 1985.

Gardner, John. *The Art of Fiction.* New York: Alfred A. Knopf, 1984.

_____. *On Becoming a Novelist.* New York: Harper & Row, 1983.

Ghiselin, Brewster (editor). *The Creative Process.* New York: New American Library, 1952.

Gilbar, Steven. *The Open Door: When Writers First Learned to Read.* Boston: Godine, 1989.

Gill, Brendan. *Here at The New Yorker.* New York: Carroll & Graf, 1975.

Goldin, Stephen, and Kathleen Sky. *The Business of Being a Writer.* New York: Harper & Row, 1982.

Grannis, Chandler B. (editor). *What Happens in Book Publishing.* New York: Columbia University Press, 1967.

Grobel, Lawrence. *Conversations with Capote.* New York: New American Library, 1985.

Gross, Gerald (editor). *Publishers on Publishing.* New York: Grosset & Dunlap, 1961.

Hackett, Alice Payne. *70 Years of Best Sellers.* New York: Bowker, 1967.

Hamilton, Ian. *In Search of J. D. Salinger.* New York: Random House, 1988.

Hart, James D. *The Popular Book: A History of America's Literary Taste.* New York: Oxford University Press, 1950.

Hemingway, Ernest. *A Moveable Feast.* New York: Scribner, 1964.

Henderson, Bill (editor). *The Art of Literary Publishing: Editors on Their Craft.* Wainscott, New York: Pushcart, 1980.

_____. *Rotten Reviews: A Literary Companion.* Wainscott: Pushcart, 1986.

_____. *Rotten Reviews II: A Literary Companion.* Wainscott, New York: Pushcart, 1987.

Hendrick, George (editor). *To Reach Eternity: The Letters of James Jones.* New York: Random House, 1989.

Hinckley, Karen, and Barbara Hinckley. *American Best Sellers: A Reader's Guide to Popular Fiction.* Bloomington: Indiana University Press, 1989.

Holmes, Richard. *Coleridge: Early Visions.* New York: Viking, 1989.

Horgan, Paul. *Approaches to Writing.* New York: Farrar, Straus & Giroux, 1973.

Hughes, Dorothy B. *Erle Stanley Gardner: The Case of the Real Perry Mason.* New York: Morrow, 1978.

Jovanovich, William. *Now, Barabbas*. New York: Harper & Row, 1964.

Kaplan, Fred. *Dickens: A Biography*. New York: Morrow, 1988.

Kazan, Elia (editor). *Five O'Clock Angel: Letters of Tennessee Williams to Maria St. Just*. New York: Alfred A. Knopf, 1990.

Kelley, Karol L. *Models for the Multitudes: Social Values in the American Popular Novel 1850–1920*. Westport, Connecticut: Greenwood, 1987.

King, Larry L. *None But a Blockhead: On Being a Writer*. New York: Viking, 1986.

King, Stephen. *Danse Macabre*. New York: Everest House, 1981.

Kingston, Paul William, and Jonathan R. Cole. *The Wages of Writing: Per Word, Per Piece, or Perhaps*. New York: Columbia University Press, 1986.

Kreyling, Michael. *Author and Agent: Eudora Welty and Diarmuid Russell*. New York: Farrar, Straus & Giroux, 1991.

Lee, Charles. *The Hidden Public: The Story of the Book-of-the-Month Club*. Garden City, New York: Doubleday, 1958.

Leggett, John. *Ross and Tom: Two American Tragedies*. New York: Simon and Schuster, 1974.

Ludwig, Richard M., and Clifford A. Nault, Jr. *Annals of American Literature: 1602–1983*. New York: Oxford University Press, 1986.

Lynn, Kenneth S. *Hemingway*. New York: Simon & Schuster, 1987.

Madison, Charles A. *Book Publishing in America*. New York: McGraw-Hill, 1966.

Mansfield, Irving. *Life with Jackie*. New York: Bantam, 1983.

Martin, Jay. *Nathaniel West: The Art of His Life*. New York: Farrar, Straus & Giroux, 1970.

Meyers, Jeffrey. *Scott Fitzgerald*. New York, HarperCollins, 1994.

Michener, James A. *A Michener Miscellany: 1950–1970*. New York: Random House, 1973.

_____. *The Novel*. New York: Random House, 1991.

_____. *The World Is My Home*. New York: Random House, 1992.

Milford, Nancy. *Zelda: A Biography*. Garden City, New York: International Collectors Library, 1970.

Miller, Arthur. *Timebends*. New York: Harper & Row, 1987.

Mizener, Arthur. *The Far Side of Paradise: A Biography of F. Scott Fitzgerald*. Boston: Houghton Mifflin, 1965.

Mott, Frank Luther. *Golden Multitudes: The Story of Best Sellers in the United States*. New York: Macmillan, 1947.

Moyers, Bill. *A World of Ideas*. Garden City, New York: Doubleday, 1989.

Nabokov, Dmitir (editor). *Vladimir Nabokov: Selected Letters: 1940–1977*. New York: Harcourt Brace Jovanovich, 1989.

Newquist, Roy. *Counterpoint*. New York: Simon & Schuster, 1964.

Nowell, Elizabeth. *Thomas Wolfe: A Biography*. Garden City, New York: Doubleday, 1960.

Oates, Joyce Carol (editor). *First Person Singular: Writers on Their Craft*. Princeton, New Jersey: Ontario Review, 1985.

Page, Walter H. *A Publisher's Confession*. Garden City, New York: Doubleday, Page, 1923.

Petersen, Clarence. *The Bantam Story: Thirty Years of Paperback Publishing.* New York: Bantam, 1975.

Phillips, Larry W. (editor). *Ernest Hemingway on Writing.* New York: Scribner, 1984.

_____. *F. Scott Fitzgerald on Writing.* New York: Scribner, 1985.

Plimpton, George (editor). *The* Paris Review *Anthology.* New York: Norton, 1990.

_____ (editor). *Writers at Work: The* Paris Review *Interviews.* Second Series. New York: Penguin, 1963.

_____ (editor). *Writers at Work: The* Paris Review *Interviews.* Third Series. New York: Penguin, 1967.

_____ (editor). *Writers at Work: The* Paris Review *Interviews.* Fourth Series. New York: Penguin, 1976.

_____ (editor). *Writers at Work: The* Paris Review *Interviews.* Fifth Series. New York: Penguin, 1981.

_____ (editor). *Writers at Work: The* Paris Review *Interviews.* Sixth Series. New York: Penguin, 1985.

_____ (editor). *Writers at Work: The* Paris Review *Interviews.* Seventh Series. New York: Penguin, 1986.

_____ (editor). *Writers at Work: The Paris Review Interviews.* Eighth Series. New York: Penguin, 1988.

Pyron, Darden Asbury. *Southern Daughter: The Life of Margaret Mitchell.* New York: Oxford University Press, 1991.

Ring, Frances Kroll. *Against the Current: As I Remember F. Scott Fitzgerald.* Berkeley, California: Ellis, 1985.

Roberts, Kenneth. *For Authors Only: And Other Gloomy Essays.* Garden City, New York: Doubleday, Doran, 1935.

_____. *I Wanted to Write.* Camden, Maine: Down East, 1977.

Ruas, Charles. *Conversations with American Writers.* New York: Alfred A. Knopf, 1985.

Sarton, May. *Recovering: A Journal.* New York: Norton, 1980.

_____. *Writings on Writing.* Orono, Maine: Puckerbrush, 1980.

Schwed, Peter. *Turning the Pages: An Insider's Story of Simon & Schuster, 1924–1984.* New York: Macmillan, 1984.

Scribner, Charles, Jr. *In the Company of Writers: A Life in Publishing.* New York: Scribner, 1990.

Seadman, Barbara. *Lovely Me: The Life of Jacqueline Susann.* New York: Morrow, 1987.

Silverman, Al (editor). *The Book of the Month: Sixty Years of Books in American Life.* Boston: Little, Brown, 1986.

Silverman, Al (introduction). *The National Book Award: Writers on Their Craft and Their World.* New York: Book-of-the-Month Club, 1990.

Spark, Muriel. *Curriculum Vitae.* Boston: Houghton Mifflin, 1993.

Spiller, Robert E., et al (editors). *Literary History of the United States.* New York: Macmillan, 1975.

Steinbeck, Elain, and Robert Wallsten (editors). *Steinbeck: A Life in Letters.* New York: Penguin, 1975.

Steinbeck, John. *Journal of a Novel: The* East of Eden *Letters.* New York: Viking, 1969.

Sternburg, Janet. *The Writer on Her Work.* New York: Norton, 1980 (Volume II, 1991).

Stevens, George. *Lincoln's Doctor's Dog and Other Famous Best Sellers.* Philadelphia: Lippincott, 1939.

Stevens, George, and Stanley Unwin. *Best-Sellers: Are They Born or Made?* London: George Allen & Unwin, 1939.

Stevenson, Anne. *Bitter Fame: A Life of Sylvia Plath.* Boston: Houghton Mifflin, 1989.

Stevenson, Robert Louis. *Treasure Island.* New York: Scribner, 1902.

Stuckey, W. J. *The Pulitzer Prize Novels: A Critical Backward Look.* Norman: University of Oklahoma Press, 1966.

Sutherland, John. *Bestsellers: Popular Fiction of the 1970's.* London: Routledge & Kegan Paul, 1981.

Tebbel, John. *Between Covers: The Rise and Transformation of Book Publishing in America.* New York: Oxford University Press, 1987.

Theroux, Paul. *Sunrise with Seamonsters.* Boston: Houghton Mifflin, 1985.

Trollope, Anthony. *An Autobiography.* Edited by Michael Sadleir and Frederick Page. New York: Oxford University Press, 1980.

Turnbull, Andrew. *Scott Fitzgerald.* New York: Scribner, 1962.

_____ (editor). *The Letters of F. Scott Fitzgerald.* New York: Scribner, 1963.

Underwood, Tim, and Chuck Miller (editors). *Bare Bones: Conversations on Terror with Stephen King.* New York: McGraw-Hill, 1988.

Updike, John. *Hugging the Shore.* New York: Vintage, 1984.

_____. *Odd Jobs: Essays and Criticism.* New York: Alfred A. Knopf, 1991.

_____. *Picked-Up Pieces.* New York: Fawcett Crest, 1975.

_____. *Self-Consciousness.* New York: Alfred A. Knopf, 1989.

Vanderbilt, Arthur T. *John Cotton Dana: The Centennial Convention.* New Brunswick, New Jersey: Rutgers University Press, 1957.

Vidal, Gore. *At Home. Essays 1982–1988.* New York: Random House, 1988.

_____. *Matters of Fact and Fiction.* New York: Random House, 1977.

Weeks, Edward. *This Trade of Writing.* Boston: Little, Brown, 1936.

Weeks, Robert P. (editor). *Hemingway: A Collection of Critical Essays.* Englewood Cliffs, New Jersey: Prentice Hall, 1962.

Welty, Eudora. *One Writer's Beginnings.* New York: Warner, 1984.

Wheelock, John Hall (editor). *Editor to Author: The Letters of Maxwell E. Perkins.* New York: Scribner, 1987.

White, John. *Rejection.* Reading, Massachusetts: Addison-Wesley, 1982.

Whiteside, Thomas. *The Blockbuster Complex: Conglomerates, Show Business, and Book Publishing.* Middletown, Connecticut: Wesleyan University Press, 1981.

Williams, Tennessee. *Memoirs.* Garden City, New York: Anchor/Doubleday, 1983.

Wilson, Edmund. *Letters on Literature and Politics: 1912–1972.* New York: Farrar, Straus & Giroux, 1977.

_____ (editor). *The Crack-Up: F. Scott Fitzgerald.* New York: New Directions, 1956.

Winokur, Jon (editor). *Writers on Writing.* Philadelphia: Running, 1986.

Wolff, Cynthia Griffin. *Emily Dickinson.* New York: Alfred A. Knopf, 1987.

Woolf, Leonard (editor). *A Writer's Diary.* New York: Harvest/HBJ, 1982.

Zinsser, William. *A Family of Readers: An Informal Portrait of the Book-of-the-Month Club and Its Members on the Occasion of Its 60th Anniversary.* New York: Book-of-the-Month Club, 1986.

_____ (editor). *Extraordinary Lives: The Art and Craft of American Biography.* New York: American Heritage, 1986.

_____ (editor). *Inventing the Truth: The Art and Craft of Memoir.* Boston: Houghton Mifflin, 1987.

Index